BAKU: CONGRESS OF THE PEOPLES OF THE EAST

Congress of the Peoples of the East

BAKU, SEPTEMBER 1920

STENOGRAPHIC REPORT

Translated and annotated by
Brian Pearce

NEW PARK PUBLICATIONS

Published by New Park Publications Ltd.,
21b Old Town, Clapham, London SW4 0JT

First English edition

First published in Russian by the
Publishing House of the Communist International,
Petrograd, 1920

Set up, Printed and Bound
by Trade Union Labour

Distributed in the United States by:
Labor Publications Inc.,
540 West 29th Street, New York
New York 10011

ISBN 0 902030 90 6

Printed in Great Britain by
Astmoor Litho Ltd. (TU),
21-22 Arkwright Road, Astmoor, Runcorn, Cheshire

Contents

CONTENTS

Foreword

The Congress of the Peoples of the East held in Baku in September, 1920 holds a special place in the history of the Communist movement. It was the first attempt to appeal to the exploited and oppressed peoples in the colonial and semi-colonial countries to carry forward their revolutionary struggles under the banner of Marxism and with the support of the workers in Russia and the advanced countries of the world. That is why today, as the development of the capitalist crisis brings the workers of America, Europe and Japan into revolutionary struggles alongside the colonial peoples, its lessons assume a new importance for the building of the world party.

The summons to Baku was issued by the Second Congress of the Communist International, which met in July and August in Moscow. In making this call, the Second Congress made a conscious break with the neglect of the national and colonial question by the Second International, based as it was almost exclusively on European parties. It recognised both that it was a prime duty of working class revolutionaries to support the struggle of their colonial brothers and that the colonial revolution could be a valuable ally in the overthrow of imperialism in its strongholds. Further, in 1920 the whole colonial and semi-colonial world was aflame, especially in the countries bordering the Soviet republic, so that these movements could be of direct assistance in warding off the offensive of the imperialists, notably the British, with the aim of establishing their power on the ruins of the Ottoman Empire. This was the atmosphere in which the Congress met.

Its delegates came from former Tsarist colonies now fighting to become Soviet republics, from Turkey and Persia, then in revolutionary ferment, and even from China, India and Japan. For some of them the journey was hazardous. The Russian historian Sorkin describes how the British imperialists tried to prevent delegates from Turkey and Persia from getting to the Congress. British naval vessels based on Constantinople patrolled the Black Sea coast, and only when stormy weather caused them to put back into port did the Turkish delegates succeed, at great risk, in getting across to Tuapse, from where they proceeded to Baku. In the Caspian British aircraft

— presumably based in Persia — bombed the ship in which Persian delegates were crossing to Baku: two were killed and several wounded.

Although of the almost 1,900 delegates who flocked to Baku some 1,200 were recorded as Communists, few of them had much experience in the Marxist movement. There was a leaven of seasoned revolutionaries, including some who had been members of the Bolshevik Party in Azerbaidzhan, Armenia and Kazakhstan since well before the 1917 revolution.

Baku, the great oil capital of Russia, had been a stronghold of the party, with its large and cosmopolitan proletarian population drawn by the prospect of jobs in the petroleum industry. After joining the Revolution, the city had been temporarily lost and had only recently again been brought under Bolshevik rule when the Congress opened. It was, however, a most appropriate place in which to hold such a gathering, by virtue of its revolutionary traditions and the successful struggle to hold it for the revolution so recently concluded. Moreover, it was familiar to Turks and Persians as well as the former subject peoples of the Tsarist Empire as a great industrial and cultural centre, and, for many, as a place of work.

In his concluding speech, Zinoviev spoke of the Congress as 'a great historical event'. He pointed out that people the bourgeoisie had looked upon as draught animals were now rising in revolt and that nationalities separated by language and historic enmities were now coming to recognise their common interests in a struggle against imperialism. 'Our congress has been heterogeneous, motley, in its composition,' he pointed out, but it had been united on all fundamental questions. There is little doubt, unfortunately, that Zinoviev's optimism was premature. The follow-up to the Congress did not fulfil its promise, nor was it possible to resolve the difficulties and differences resulting from the national and colonial question with speeches alone.

This does not mean that the documents of the Congress are not worth studying. If its lessons have been neglected, that must be laid at the door of the Stalinists who, in the 1920s, threw the weight of the Communist Parties behind bourgeois nationalist movements like the Kuomintang and condemned them to disaster. It is due to Stalinism that the Baku Congress has usually been passed over with a few 'safe' references and no attempt has been made to reprint its proceedings or discuss its lessons. In fact this is the first time the minutes have been made available in an English translation, as part of the necessary education of the revolutionary movement about its past.

There are of course other reasons why the Stalinists and their apologists do not encourage study of the Baku Congress. Its leading figures, entrusted by the Communist International with the important work of encouraging the building of sections in the underdeveloped areas and among the national minorities in the Soviet Union, Zinoviev, Radek and Béla Kun, were to be murdered by Stalin in the 1930s. But the same fate was to await countless delegates to the Baku Congress. Of those who made speeches printed in this volume, Ryskulov and Narimanov are known to have perished in Stalin's purges after having become leading figures in the Communist Party. Also victims were two of those nominated to the Council for Action and Propaganda — Avis (A.S. Nuridzhanian) from Armenia, Guseinov from Azer-baidzhan, as well as Kareyev and perhaps others. The purges struck deep into the republics of the nationalities, reflecting no doubt Stalin's own past record of contempt for the peoples of these regions of which the Baku Congress was a living condemnation.

At the time when the Congress was held, it should be remembered, Communist Parties properly speaking had not been established in most of the colonial and semi-colonial countries. These countries remained extremely backward; it might be said that in many respects they continued to live under medieval conditions and some of the speakers describe the extent of feudal oppression and exploitation which still remained. In most of them, too, the native bourgeoisie was extremely weak and the nationalist movement was still at its beginnings. There was, therefore, a great opportunity for Communists to place themselves at the head of the mass movement by establishing the connection between the struggle against imperialism and the need for social revolution and particularly the agrarian revolution in these lands. These principles were expressed by the speakers and in the documents approved by the Congress. The question was to carry them out in practice in the building of revolutionary parties.

This was, perhaps, the greatest weakness of the Congress. Zinoviev, who dominated it, counted too much upon the Soviet example generating spon-taneous support from the oppressed masses as though a few rousing speeches would be enough. He never understood or supported the theory of the permanent revolution and thus the connection between the tasks of the Communist International, and the colonial revolution. It was not enough to call for a holy war against imperialism: this would remain rhetoric if it was not followed up by the training of cadres and consistent work among the masses. It was not enough to point to the fact that members of hostile nationalities were able to work together in the enthusiasm of a great Congress, it was necessary also to combat all the sources of division and enmity. Particularly careful attention had to be given to the hold of Islam in many of the countries to which the Congress was directed and the best way to prise the masses away from their traditional alleginaces without antagonising them.

The very heterogeneity of the Congress caused problems, as the reader will observe. Some of them resulted from difficulties in translation into the many languages represented, a process which consumed time and led to some impatience on the part of delegates. The present translation has been made from the official Russian report, published in 1920. Brian Pearce, the trans-lator, points out that this report contains many misprints, and there is evidence that the stenographer misheard some of what was said, not surpris-ingly since there was a background of noise and movement on the part of delegates, many of whom spoke in unfamiliar accents. A good deal of the material in the Congress proceedings was translated into Russian on the spot, perhaps by interpreters whose knowledge of one, or both, languages involved was far from perfect. There was little constructive editing and it may be that some of the speeches were considerably abridged in the official report. Some writers who refer to the Congress claim that some Muslim representatives protested against alleged massacres of their co-religionists by pro-Bolshevik forces, including many Armenians, during the Civil War. Whatever the truth of the matter, there is no doubt that there was high-handedness and disregard for national rights and susceptibilities on the part of some Soviet officials, an issue which contributed to the break between Lenin and Stalin. At the same time it should be remembered that opposition to the Bolsheviks came from reactionary Muslim feudalists and semi-bandit movements like the Basmachi, themselves given to looting and massacre. The situation had been made still more complex by the ebb and flow of battle and the changes in political control in former Tsarist territory since the Revolution. Some of the delegates worked with or may have been sympathisers of the bourgeois-democratic Musavat movement which had held power in Baku and Azerbaidzhan for a time. Some nationalists may have seen in the Congress a way of enlisting support for their cause without sharing the social revolutionary aims of the Bolsheviks. This was evidently the case with many of the Turks and Persians, including the notorious Enver Pasha who obviously tried to use the Congress for his own ends (see note p.195). At the same time agents of imperialism were active in these circles and a report of the Congress reached the British authorities through an Indian agent (p. 194). The imperialists obviously had an interest in stirring up national and religious differences and then blaming the friction onto the Soviet regime. Most accounts of the Congress by bourgeois historians, it may be added, are strongly biased by anti-Sovietism and Cold War feeling, at once identifying Zinoviev's call for a 'holy war' as being an appeal to the Muslims and accusing him of neglecting religious susceptibilities. In short, they are still fighting the wars of intervention and trying to defend the policies of the imperialist countries.

The question of who would win was decided in the former Tsarist colonies by the victory of the Red Army in the Civil War, to which the sympathy of the masses for the aims of the Bolsheviks and their actions against the landlords and capitalists made a decisive contribution. But the political questions still remained in suspense as the subsequent history of the nationalities in the Soviet Union was to show. On the one hand there was the 'Great Russian chauvinism' expressed by Stalin and displayed in the policy of the bureaucracy, on the other the 'nationalist deviations', real or imputed, of which some of those who took part in the Baku Congress were later to be accused. In fact, despite its boasts, the bureaucracy has not solved the nationalities question in the Soviet Union to this day.

The other question was the help which the Soviet state and the Communist movement should render to nationalist movements in the colonial and semi-colonial countries. This gave rise to important discussions at the Second Congress of the Communist International at which theses embodying a principled position were passed. Even in the early 1920s the attitude towards particular movements, for example that in Turkey, was influenced by the exigencies of Soviet foreign policy and the fear that adjacent countries could become springboards for further wars of intervention. Also, as Trotsky was aware, involvement in these countries could give rise to difficulties just at the time when the Soviet state needed a breathing space for internal consolidation.

There is a difference between such strategic and diplomatic considerations which the Soviet government had to contend with and the opportunism in relation to the national bourgeoisie as manifested in China in the mid-1920s with disastrous results. It is perfectly clear from the speeches made at Baku that the appeal to the peoples of the East was based upon the destruction of class as well as national oppression. The principal enemy at that time was British imperialism, with its stranglehold over India and now extending its tentacles all over the Middle East, though already frustrated in its attempt to move into the former Tsarist colonies. But the Congress, in issuing its call for a 'holy war' against British imperialism, also called on the masses to rise against their internal enemies, and to establish Soviet power against local oppressors as well as foreign capitalists. In predominantly agrarian countries successful revolution meant the seizure of the land and thus the elimination of landlordism. Everywhere the native bourgeoisie was closely allied with the landlords, or would become so, in defence of private property; this was to be demonstrated within a few years in China. Today, in countries like India where the national bourgeoisie is in power, it has steadfastly opposed an agrarian revolution and rules in alliance with the landlords and rural capitalists while using all the forces of the state to crush the revolutionary struggles of the peasantry.

Central to the decision to hold the Congress was the need for solidarity between the working class of the advanced countries and the oppressed peoples of the colonies and semi-colonies. This was not only stressed in the speeches by the representatives of the Communist International, but also by the presence at the Congress of leading figures from the Communist Parties of the metropolitan countries: Tom Quelch from Britain, Alfred Rosmer from France, Steinhardt from Austria and John Reed from the United States. This was intended to be more than a symbolic gesture: all of them came straight from the Second Congress of the Communist International, where the fight had been waged for these parties to break with the bad traditions of the Second International and become active campaigners against their 'own' imperialism and for the freeing of the colonies unconditionally.

There are many lessons for today in studying the proceedings of the Baku Congress. It was an historic Congress quite different from anything previously held in the working class movement and not at all like the peace fronts and international conferences sponsored by the Stalinist bureaucracy today at which representatives of the national bourgeoisie, butchers of the workers and peasants in their own countries, in many cases, are honoured guests. This was a Congress of fighters, enthusiastic and in some ways bewildering even to its sponsors. It was also a young Congress, of delegates in their twenties or thirties, most often lacking in political knowledge or experience. It met under very difficult conditions and it had to combat religious and other prejudices in its own ranks. It was significant that although many of the delegates were

Muslims, women were invited and spoke and a resolution was passed for the liberation of women from traditional bonds.

Above all, whatever its shortcomings, the keynote of the Congress was its internationalism. This was before Stalinism, with its 'theory' of 'socialism in one country', had trampled underfoot the principles fought for by the Communist International under the leadership of Lenin and Trotsky. It was understood that the revolutionary struggles in the different parts of the world were integrally related and that the fate of the Soviet Union itself hinged upon the spread of the revolution worldwide.

It is fitting that the publication of the Congress proceedings is undertaken today by the Trotskyist movement. It could not be otherwise. The determination, expressed at Baku, to fight for the proletarian revolution world-wide, stands in total opposition to the 'peaceful road' peddled by modern-day Stalinism. The victory of the Vietnamese revolution, the bitter struggle of the Palestinian liberation movement, and the explosive development of the revolution in Southern Africa, have already, as Europe and America stand on the brink of revolutionary class confrontations, dealt the heaviest blows to the Stalinist policy of peaceful coexistence. It is only Trotskyism, in the form of the International Committee of the Fourth International, which is able now to come forward to forge the alliance between the colonial peoples and the working class of the advanced capitalist countries, which was foreshadowed at the Baku Congress. The publication of these minutes is a contribution towards taking up its unfinished work.

T.K.
February 1977

Bibliographical Notes

Books which discuss the Congress include notably: E.H. Carr, *The Bolshevik Revolution*, Volume III; Stuart R. Schram and Hélène Carrère d'Encausse, *Marxism and Asia*; Nasrollah Saifpour Fatemi, *Diplomatic History of Iran, 1917-1923*, for reports from Persian papers, containing material not included in the official Congress report.

The Congress is also discussed, sometimes with substantial sections of the discussion paraphrased, in H.G. Wells, *Russia in the Shadows*; L. Pasvolsky, *Russia in the Far East*; H. Kohn, *History of Nationalism in the East*; Eudin and North, *Soviet Russia and the East*; Louis Fischer, *The Soviets in World Affairs*; I Spector, *The Soviet Union and the Modern World*; and Lenczowski, *Russia and the West in Iran*. Special aspects are touched on in M.N. Roy's *Memoirs* and George S. Harris, *The Origins of Communism in Turkey*; also in the various writings of Walter Laqueur. Alfred Rosmer, a participant, deals with it in Chapter XVI of *Lenin's Moscow*.

For a recent discussion of the Baku Congress, see Stephen White's article in *Slavic Review*, September 1974.

Other works to be noted include: D. Boersner, *The Bolsheviks and the National Question*; D.N. Druhe, *Soviet Russia and Indian Communism*; Muzaffar Ahmad, *Myself and the Indian Communist Party*; Shankar Usmani, *From Peshawar to Moscow* and *I Met Stalin Twice*; Sepehr Zabih, *The Communist Movement in Iran*; Lazitch and Drashkovitch, *Lenin and the Comintern*, Volume I; Alfred L.P. Dennis, *The Foreign Policies of Soviet Russia* (1924).

Summons to the Congress

To the Enslaved Popular Masses of Persia, Armenia and Turkey[1]

The Executive Committee of the Communist International is convening on August 15 [*sic*], 1920, in Baku, a congress of the workers and peasants of Persia, Armenia and Turkey.

What is the Communist International? It is the organization of the revolutionary working masses of Russia, Poland, Germany, France, Britain and America, who, awakened by the thunder of the world war and driven by hunger, have risen in order that they may no longer work for the rich, but for themselves, and in order that they may never again take up arms against their own suffering and deprived brothers, but instead bear arms to defend themselves against the exploiters. These working masses have understood that their only strength lies in unity and organization, that these alone can guarantee their victory, and last year they formed a mighty organization in the shape of the Third International. Despite all persecutions by capitalist governments, this International has in its eighteen months of existence become the moving spirit of all the revolutionary workers and peasants striving for liberation throughout the world.

Why is the Communist International convening at this time a congress of Persian, Armenian and Turkish workers and peasants? What has it to offer them? What does it want from them? The workers and peasants in Europe and America, fighting against capital, are turning to you because you, like them, suffer under the yoke of world capitalism and, like them, are obliged to fight against the world's exploiters: because if you join with the workers and peasants of Europe and America, this will hasten the downfall of world capitalism and ensure the liberation of the workers and peasants throughout the world.

Peasants and workers of Persia! The government of the Kajars[2] in

1

Teheran, and its underlings the provincial Khans, have robbed and exploited you for centuries. The land which according to the *shariat* was common property has been seized for themselves by the lackeys of the Teheran government. They deal as they will with this land and impose taxes and dues upon you as they see fit. After sucking all the juices out of the country and reducing it to poverty and ruin, they sold Persia last year to the British capitalists for £2 million, with which an army is to be formed in Persia which will oppress you even more than before. So that this army may squeeze taxes and tribute out of you for the khans and the Teheran government, they have sold to Britain the rich oilfields of Southern Persia, thereby co-operating in the plundering of your country.

Peasants of Mesopotamia! The British proclaimed the independence of your country, but 80,000 British soldiers stand upon your soil, robbing and killing you and violating your women.

Peasants of Anatolia! The British, Italian and French governments hold Constantinople under the muzzles of their guns: they have made the Sultan prisoner and forced him to agree to the partition of purely Turkish territory and to the placing of Turkey's finances at the disposal of foreign financiers, so as more easily to plunder the Turkisn people who have already been impoverished by six years of war. They have taken the coal mines of Heraclea [Eregli][3] and your seaports, sent their troops into your country, trampling your fields, they dictate their alien laws to the peaceful Turkish peasant, they want to make you their beasts of burden, on to whose backs they put whatever loads they choose. Some of your beys and effendis have sold out to the foreign capitalists, while others summon you to arms to fight against the foreign invader — but without allowing you to take power for yourselves in your own country and take over the lands and fields which the Sultan presented to various parasites, so that you may sow these fields for yourselves. And tomorrow, if the foreign capitalists should come to an agreement with your oppressors on less severe peace terms, your present leaders will use this opportunity to lay new chains upon you, just as this is being done by the landlords and former officials in the regions permanently occupied by the foreign armies.

Peasants and workers of Armenia! For years you have been the victims of foreign capital, which has talked at length about the massacres of the Armenians by the Kurds, has stirred you up to fight against the Sultan and has continually gained new advantages from your fight against him. During the war the foreign capitalists not only promised you independence but also incited your teachers, priests and merchants to lay claim to the land of Turkish peasants, so that unending war might rage between the Turkish and Armenian peoples, from which they might extract unending profit, since so long as this discord persists between you the foreign capitalists will profit by it, through frightening Turkey with the threat of an Armenian rising and frightening the Armenians with the threat of pogroms by the Kurds.

Peasants of Syria and Arabia! The British and French promised you independence, but today their armies have occupied your country, they are dictating their laws to you, and you, after liberation from the Turkish Sultan and his government, have now been made slaves of the governments of Paris and London, which differ from the Sultan's only in that they hold you down more firmly and plunder you more severely.

You understand all this very well. The Persian peasants and workers have risen against the treacherous government of Teheran. The peasants of Mesopotamia have rebelled against the British occupation forces and the British press writes about the losses suffered by the British army in fighting with the rebels near Baghdad.

Peasants of Anatolia! You are being urgently summoned to rally under the flag of Kemal Pasha, to fight against the foreign invaders, but at the same time we know that you are trying to form your own people's party, your own peasants' party, which will be able to carry forward the fight in the event that the pashas make peace with the predators of the Entente.

It has not been possible to establish peace in Syria, and you, peasants of Armenia, whom the Entente, despite all its promises, are allowing to starve, so as the better to keep control of you — you are coming to understand more and more clearly that hope of salvation through help from the capitalists of the Entente is utterly senseless. Even your bourgeois government of the Dashnaktsutyun party, those lackeys of the Entente, have been forced to turn to the workers' and peasants' government of Russia with a request for a peace treaty and for assistance. Now we see that you yourselves are beginning to understand your own needs, and so we address ourselves to you, in our capacity as representatives of the European proletariat, possessing great experience accumulated in our struggle, in order to help you achieve your emancipation. We say to you: the time when the European and American capitalists could suppress you by means of their own forces has passed, never to return. Everywhere in Europe and America the workers have risen in arms against the capitalists and are waging bloody war against them.

While we have not yet vanquished world capitalism, the capitalists are already no longer able to dispose of their people's blood at their own discretion. For two and a half years the Russian revolution has been struggling against the whole world. The French, British and American capitalists have tried by every means — armed force, famine — to conquer the Russian workers and peasants, to tighten a noose round their necks, and make them their slaves. They have not succeeded. The Russian workers and peasants have staunchly defended their government and formed an army of their own which has utterly smashed the reactionary forces supported by the capitalists of the Entente.

Workers and peasants of the Near East! If you organize yourselves and set up your own workers' and peasants' government, if you arm yourselves, uniting with the Russian workers' and peasants' army, you will beat the British, French and American capitalists, get rid of your oppressors and find freedom, you will be able to create a free world republic of the working people, and then use the riches of your native land in your own interests and those of the rest of working mankind, which will be glad to take them in exchange for the products you need, and will joyfully come to your aid. We want to talk about all this with you at your congress.

The Executive Committee of the Communist International, as the representative of the British, French, American, German and Italian workers, are coming to Baku in order to discuss with you the question of how to unite the efforts of the European proletariat with yours for struggle against the common enemy.

Spare no effort to ensure that as many as possible may be present on September 1 [*sic*] in Baku. Formerly you travelled across deserts to reach the holy places — now make your way over mountains and rivers, through forests and deserts,[4] to meet each other and discuss how to free yourselves from the chains of servitude, so as to unite in fraternal alliance, so as to live a life based on equality, freedom and brotherhood.

We appeal first and foremost to the workers and peasants of the Near East, but we shall be glad to see among the delegates also representatives of the popular masses who live much farther off — representatives of India — as well as representatives of the Moslem people who are developing freely in association with Soviet Russia.

On September 2 [*sic*] there must peacefully come together in Baku, for the liberation of the Near East, thousands of Turkish, Armenian and Persian workers and peasants.

May the congress proclaim to your enemies in Europe and America and in your own countries that the age of slavery is past, that you are rising in revolt and that you will be victorious.

May this congress proclaim to the workers of the whole world that you are defending your rights, that you are uniting with the mighty revolutionary army which is now fighting against all injustice and exploitation.

May your congress bring strength and faith to millions and millions of the enslaved throughout the world, may it instil into them confidence in their own power, may it bring nearer the day of final triumph and liberation.

The Executive Committee of the Communist International

Chairman: *G. Zinoviev*
Secretary: *K. Radek*

For the British Socialist Party: *W. McLaine, Tom Quelch*
For the British Shop Stewards Committee: *J. Tanner, J.T. Murphy*
For the French delegation to the Congress of the
Communist International: *A. Rosmer, Deslinières, J. Sadoul*
For the Italian delegation to the Congress of the
Communist International: *Bombacci, A. Graziadei*
For the Communist Party of the USA: *L. Fraina, A. Stocklitski*
For the Communist Labour Party of the USA: *A. Bilan*
For the Spanish Federation of Labour: *Angel Pestaña*
For the Central Committee of the Russian Communist Party:
N. Bukharin, V. Vorovsky, A. Balabanova, G. Klinger
For the All-Russian Central Council of the
Trades Unions: *S.A. Lozovsky*
For the Communist Party of Poland: *J. Marchlewski (Karski)*
For the Communist Party of Bulgaria and the
Balkan Communist Federation: *N. Shablin*
For the Communist Party of Austria: *Reussler*
For the Communist Party of Hungary: *Rakosi, Rudnyanszky*
For the Communist Party of Holland: *D. Wijnkoop*[5]

(*Kommunistichesky Internatsional*, no. 12, July 20, 1920)

Ceremonial joint meeting

of the Baku Soviet and the Azerbaidzhan
Trade Union Congress[6]
August 31

The meeting opened at 1.25 a.m., the members of the Congress of the Peoples of the East being present.

Chairman: Comrades, let us now proceed with our meeting. I call the assembly to order.

Allow me, comrades, to address in your name a warm fraternal greeting to our dear guests. [*Applause.*]

The enlarged Soviet of Workers', Red Army Men's and Sailors' Deputies of Baku, together with the district Soviets and the entire Trades Union Congress of Azerbaidzhan, are glad to see at this their ceremonial meeting representatives and leaders of world Communism [*Applause*], as well as representatives of the Baku proletariat and of the working masses of Azerbaidzhan. Those who are present here hope and believe that, under the experienced leadership of the comrades who have come to visit us, at this time when we have begun to forge a mighty weapon for the struggle against world imperialism, we shall fulfil with honour the task which has fallen to our lot. [*Applause.*]

We hope, comrades, that their brief visit will help us to unite our scattered forces, and rapidly to find the ways and means to achieve as soon as possible the victory we desire: under their leadership we shall perhaps enter sooner than we expect into the realm of Communism. Long live our leader who has come to visit us here, Comrade Zinoviev [*Applause*], leader of world Communism! [*Ovation: the band plays the 'Internationale'.*] Long live Comrade Radek, leader of the international proletariat! [*Ovation: the band plays the 'Internationale'.*]

Comrades, together with Comrades Zinoviev and Radek, we have among our visitors the leader of the Communist Party, of the Communist Revolution in Hungary, which has suffered so much under the

7

yoke of the White-Guard tyrants, a comrade who is known to you, Comrade Béla Kun. [*Ovation: the band plays the 'Internationale'.*]

Comrades, present here besides our own delegates are representatives of the Communist Parties of Britain, Germany, France, Italy and other countries of Western Europe and America. [*Applause: the band plays the 'Internationale'.*]

Comrades, present at our ceremonial meeting today along with the representatives of the proletariat of the West are delegates, assembled in congress, from the oppressed masses of the East. This alliance is for us a symbol of our fraternal unity and a pledge of lasting victory, the basis for which we are laying here today. Long live the representatives of the proletariat of the West and the representatives of the working masses of the East. [*Applause: the band plays the 'Internationale'.*]

Comrades, let us shout together a greeting to all present and to all our visitors. Hurrah! [*A loud* 'Hurrah'*: the band plays the 'Internationale'.*] I call upon Comrade Karayev to translate my remarks into Turkic.[7]

[*Karayev translates into Turkic. The 'Internationale'.*]

Chairman: Comrade Narimanov has the floor, to bring greetings from the Azerbaidzhan Revolutionary Committee. [*The 'Internationale'.*]

Narimanov: Dear comrades, I am happy to greet you in the name of the Workers' and Peasants' Government of Red Azerbaidzhan and of the Central Committee. [*Applause.*]

Dear guests, this significant moment shows that we are close to our aim, to the triumph of the Third International. [*Applause.*]

Victory to the Third International! [*Tumultuous applause. The 'Internationale'.*]

Chairman: Comrade Kasumov will give the Turkic translation.

[*Kasumov translates into Turkic. The 'Internationale'.*]

Chairman: The next speaker will be the Chairman of the Executive Committee of the Communist International, Comrade Zinoviev. [*Tumultuous applause, growing into an ovation. The 'Internationale'.*]

Zinoviev: Comrades! It is not without emotion that I address this gathering of ours today.

Comrades, we who are no newcomers to the revolutionary movement naturally recall those first years of the struggle which united the workers of all the peoples of Russia in close, unbreakable fraternity with the sections of the working people who live and fight in Baku. I greet you not only in the name of the Executive Committee of the Communist International and not only in the name of the Central Executive Committee of our Soviet Republic, but also on behalf of the workers of one of the cities of the Soviet Republic who cherish an especially warm feeling of fraternal friendship for you — the workers of the city of Petrograd. [*Tumultuous applause. The 'Internationale'.*]

Comrades, in those dark years, now so far-off and yet at the same time so near to us, when we were all held in the iron grip of Tsardom, and when all the peoples of Russia lived in our country as though in a big prison, in those years, among the first proletarian centres to come forth against Tsardom, the city of Baku was far from being the least outstanding.

Every old revolutionary knows that, after Petrograd and Moscow, in our strikes, demonstrations and risings, in the revolutionary struggle, we usually named, following those two cities: Baku, Warsaw and Riga. Everyone remembers how, on the eve of 1905 and during the bourgeois revolution of 1917, and at the beginning of the October events, the detachment of our workers living and fighting in the smoke-blackened city of Baku faithfully carried out its proletarian duty to the revolution, to the working class of Russia and to the working class of the whole world.

This day we remember tens and hundreds of our best friends who came from the ranks of the Baku workers, who worked in a number of other cities, took on responsible posts in the revolution and sometimes brought back life to our all-Russia organizations when the heavy paw of the Tsarist gendarmerie lay too weightily upon us.

We remember our best friends and brothers: Shaumyan and Dzhaparidze, with whom many of us were connected for years in common revolutionary work, in common fraternal friendship, and who, as you all know, were torn from our ranks by the violent hands of hangmen and traitors to the working class.[8] The names of such fighters of yours as Shaumyan and Dzhaparidze are on the lips of all the workers of Petrograd and Moscow, and of all Russia. The chidren in Soviet schools are taught to hold in respect those men who, standing at a post of glory at a hard moment of betrayal and perfidy, bravely defended the Red flag. And in those months, comrades, difficult both for you and for us, when you were cut off from your fraternal family of the working peoples inhabiting Russia, in that period the workers of Petrograd, the workers of Moscow and the workers of all Russia were sure, although they received no news from you, although the British

Press lied about you, although you were slandered by the traitor press of the Mensheviks, the SRs and all the other Judases who have betrayed the workers' cause — we knew very well that this slander was not true of you: we knew very well that here the workers of Baku were not surrendering but were awaiting the moment when they could get their own back and stretch out once more a fraternal hand to the workers of all Russia and the whole world. And, comrades, we were not deceived. We know that in the few short months and weeks that have passed since you were liberated you have again taken your place in the ranks, again assumed your rightful place, one of the most honourable, among the world's proletarians, among the peoples of Russia! [*Applause.*]

I mentioned Warsaw. Comrades, at the present time the White Guard flag still flies over Warsaw. Many of us, like the workers of other peoples, were worried at the setbacks our Red Army suffered before the walls of Warsaw.

You know that our army swept forward almost to those very walls, but that Polish capitalism, helped by the British, whom you know well, helped by French officers, whom you also know, helped by the bourgeoisie of the whole world, whom we all hate, dealt a blow to our Red Army and forced it briefly to retreat.[9] But, comrades, our forces have again gathered strength, and, if all the signs are not deceptive, and if it is possible to speak on the basis of previous experience, we can say: not months but only weeks will have to pass before our Red Army stretches out its red hand once more towards Warsaw. [*Tumultuous applause. The 'Internationale'.*]

Comrades, the war against White Poland is being waged, formally speaking, by the Russian Soviet Federal Republic, but in reality it is not merely a war between the Russian Socialist Republic and the White Polish Republic, but a war of labour against capital.

The Second World Congress of the Communist International, which recently ended its sessions in Moscow, and at which 37 countries were represented, declared to the whole world: the war of the Russian Soviet Republic against White Poland is our war, is the war of the Communist International against the bourgeoisie, against the imperialists of the whole world.

And I, comrades, am profoundly convinced that our congress of the working masses of the Eastern peoples will support this call and say: Yes, the war of the Russian Soviet Republic against White Poland is not only the war of the proletarians of the West but also the war of the working masses of the peoples of the East against our common oppressors! [*Tumultuous applause. The 'Internationale'.*]

Comrades, the Communist International was founded only a year and a half ago. At the First Congress we were still a propaganda society, we were only a group of people who were beginning to make propaganda for our ideas — in a variety of countries there were already Communist trends, but there were as yet no strong Communist Parties.

After a mere year and a half, at the Second Congress of the Communist International in Moscow, as I have already told you, we had representatives of organized Communist Parties and groups from 37 countries in Europe and America. We have with us all those who are honest and steeled in battle, all who are strong and ready to come to grips with the bourgeoisie throughout Europe and America.

And now, here in Baku, we are taking a second step forward. We do not want to become like the heroes of the Second International — traitors who sold the flag to the enemy. We are mindful that in the world there are living not only people with white skins, not only the Europeans whom the Second International took particularly into account; in addition, there are also in the world hundreds of millions of people who live in Asia and Africa. We want to put an end to the rule of capital everywhere in the world. And this will become possible only when we have lit the fire of revolution not merely in Europe and America but throughout the world, and when behind us march all the working people of Asia and Africa.

The Communist International wants to unite under its banners speakers of all the languages of the world. The Communist International is sure that under its flag will rally not only the proletarians of Europe but also the mighty mass of our reserves, our infantry — the hundreds of millions of peasants who live in Asia, our Near and Far East.

To your city has fallen the great honour of serving as the gate through which the Western proletariat is passing in order to extend its hand to the peasantry of the East. Your city is now the scene of new events, previously unknown in the history of mankind: representatives have assembled here from the hundreds of millions of peasants of the East who have learnt the lessons of the war and have understood that it is necessary to seize capital by the throat and kneel on its chest! We must put an end, once for all, to the shame of capitalism.

We are sure that those peasants who today are still illiterate and do not yet know our programme, but know very well that they have been slaughtered for hundreds of years to the greater glory of capital — that those tens and hundreds of millions of peasants of Asia will now take up the call that has reached them from the organized vanguard of the West European and American proletariat. The peoples of the East will come together in fraternal unity and forget everything that formerly divided them. They will forget the hatred that was artificially sustained among them by the capitalists, and will remember that we need a single union of the working people not only of Asia and Europe but of the whole world, so as to put an end to capitalism and begin to build a new and better life.

At the present time the Communist International could not choose a more appropriate place than Baku for the embattled people of the West to meet the awakening peoples of the East.

The Baku Soviet is certainly well aware of the historic importance of this moment and is doing everything in its power to create the atmosphere of unanimity and brotherhood in which a fraternal union of the proletarians of Europe with the peoples of the East will come into being.

I am sure that the workers of Baku, who have made so many sacrifices, will be glad that the Congress of the Peoples of the East is being held in their city, in Baku. They are thereby rewarded for the many trials they have suffered, over and above those that have been the lot of the workers of other cities.

The Second Congress of the Communist International made no mistake when it appointed the holding of this congress in Baku. Its voice will be heard in London, in Paris, in Constantinople and in New York. At first, perhaps, the imperialist gentlemen, who habitually stop their ears, will try to hush it up, but the East will know how to speak out so loudly that all the cotton wool will fall out of the diplomatic ears of the British and French imperialists. They will have to learn that the East wants no longer to serve as a field for exploitation by the world's beasts of prey, that historically decisive days have arrived.

Comrades, you are honoured to be living through a moment when millions of workers and peasants from all the Western countries are uniting with the hundreds of millions who make up the peoples of the East. Upon this moment depends the destiny of the world in the years that lie ahead. Let us give all that we can for the success of this alliance!

Let us get down to the work of organizing this congress. May the Eastern peoples realize that a new era has dawned, that a new page has been turned in the history of mankind, that the sun of Communism shines not only for the proletarians of the West but also for the working peasants of the whole world!

Long live the fraternal union of the peoples of the East!

Long live the unity of the hundreds of millions of peasants of the East with the millions of proletarians of the West!

May this alliance prove unbreakable. May the rule of capital perish forever. And may that order soon prevail, the bearer of which is the Communist International, created by the working people of the whole world! [*Tumultuous applause.*]

Chairman: Comrade Radek will deliver a speech of welcome.

Radek: The Congress of the Peoples of the East has been convened at an historical moment of exceptional gravity. The duel between the workers and peasants of Russia and the capitalist world — first and foremost with British capital — has passed through many stages, depending on the degree of strength possessed by Soviet Russia. British capitalism thought it could crush us either by armed force or by diplomatic negotiations. During the past year we experienced a tremendous wave of intervention by the Entente. Paid by the British capitalists, the armies of Denikin, Yudenich and Kolchak tried to throw down Soviet Russia. But the consciousness of Soviet Russia's working-class masses and of her advanced peasants wrested victory, by the hand of the Red Army, from the world's lord, Capital, which thought this victory was within its grasp. Then they began to talk with us, to conduct peaceful negotiations, but at the same time they unleashed against Soviet Russia a new bloodhound — White Poland. When the Red Army began to force White Poland to retreat, peace with Soviet Russia seemed to draw near once more, but since our first setbacks we have seen that British imperialism is again trying to terrorize us.

Warsaw seemed to be the nodal point of the struggle between Moscow and London. But at the very moment when the Red Army is preparing for a fresh offensive, which will show British imperialism that it still exists, that Soviet Russia is still strong, and stronger than ever — at that very moment we are showing here, at the Congress of the Peoples of the East, here in Baku, that Soviet Russia, that is, the world proletariat, whose representative Soviet Russia is, possesses a second sword as well — the revolt of the peoples who lived under the tyranny of world capitalism, and of British capitalism first and foremost. Soviet Russia approaches these peoples with fraternal words, it approaches them as brothers, as comrades in struggle.[10] The voice of the representatives assembled here, of the Red working masses of the whole East will tell British capitalism, will tell world capital, that the proletariat in revolt will strike at it not only in the streets of Europe's metropolitan cities but also in the villages and towns of Asia.

These millions in chains, whom they looked upon as slaves who were to be denied human rights, see that we, comrades, approach them in a different way from the way the bourgeoisie once approached them. You know that after the Great French Revolution, when Napoleon's France went to war against Britain, when young French imperialism approached the peoples of the East, approached Persia and India, it made contact only with the governments of those countries, which exploited the masses of the people. When, later on in the nineteenth century, the governments of Britain or Germany, in the course of the struggle between them, turned their eyes towards the East, they had one guiding idea: to strengthen their forces for this struggle. And the peoples of the East shed their blood; but they shed it not for themselves but so that one of the imperialist scoundrels might be victorious over the other. We approach these peoples not in order to use their strength for our struggle against capitalism, but in order to help them to escape not only from the yoke of capital but also from medieval relations, from the yoke of feudalism and ignorance, and to give them the opportunity to begin living as human beings. We approach them knowing that the young Communist world which is being born amid unheard-of suffering cannot yet bring them the wealth of the West, that this has still to be created, but we approach them so as to free them from the yoke of capital, to help them build a new, free life in whatever way they will consider corresponds to the interests of their working masses.

The city of Baku was not designated by accident when we planned the Congress of the Peoples of the East. Here in Baku, where for many years Persians, Turks and Tatars have worked, here in Baku where capitalism bullied and exploited these workers, socialist ideas also came to them at the same time, and found a common response in their hearts.

We know how the socialist revolution was born here in Baku, how the idea of struggle against Russian Tsardom spread from here, and how workers returning to Persia took with them this idea of struggle not only against Tsardom but against capitalism too, for the emancipation of all peoples from every kind of yoke. We are certain that this workers' city, which saw, on the one hand, unprecedented luxury on the part of the bourgeoisie, and, on the other, the most miserable conditions of existence for the workers and the whole people, that this city will be an arena of international revolution, that from here will flow an electric current of political awareness, that here will be set up the banner of struggle for the liberation of the East which the Communist International has entrusted to the Baku proletariat, that experienced fighter for the liberation of the working people.

Long live the Baku proletariat! Long live these front-rank fighters for the liberation of the peoples of the East! [*Applause*].

Chairman: Comrade Karayev will give the Turkic translation.

[*Karayev translates into Turkic. Applause.*]

Chairman: I call upon the leader of Soviet Hungary, which was born amid the fires of the terrible world war, Comrade Béla Kun. [*Applause: the band plays the 'Internationale'.*]

A voice: Long live Soviet Hungary! Hurrah! [*The band plays the 'Internationale'.*]

A voice: Vivat! Hurrah! [*Applause.*]

Béla Kun: Comrades, though I speak Russian very badly, please allow me to greet you in the language of the international revolution — in the Russian language. [*Applause.*]

Comrades, I greet you in the name of the most oppressed of proletarians, those of White Hungary. When Soviet power began in Hungary you, very probably, knew little about us. Few people in the East knew about those who were occupying the advanced positions of the international revolution, for during the period of Soviet power in Hungary you were being oppressed by Denikin, by the British and French imperialists and their hirelings — our enemies, your oppressors. You did not know all that was happening. If, comrades, you remember what was done in Baku by Denikin's men and by the British generals and officers who ruled in this place at that time and are now in prison here, then you will know what our Denikinites did, under the leadership of the American [*sic*] Horthy[11] and of British and French generals and officers. Just as happened here, comrades, so in

Hungary thousands and thousands of workers were slaughtered; just as here, our proletarians and peasants were crushed; and just as, during the White Terror in Azerbaidzhan, you looked forward to receiving help, so did our workers and peasants look forward to receiving help from the international proletariat, to liberation by them.

Comrades, in White Hungary the revolution will rise again, the proletarian revolution will live again, and we, the Hungarian proletarians, hope that this congress in Baku will secure the rear of the international revolution in the West, and that the fraternal alliance of the proletarians and peasants of the East and of the West — this Red Army of the East — will also go forward along with us against all the imperialists and capitalists, against the hirelings of imperialism and capitalism.

Long live this fraternal alliance of the peoples of East and West! Long live the Communist International! Long live Red Azerbaidzhan! [*Ovation; applause; the band plays the 'Internationale'.*]

Chairman: Comrade Sultanov will translate.

[*Sultanov translates into Turkic.*]

Chairman: I call upon the representative of the Communist Party of Great Britain, Comrade Quelch. [*Applause: the band plays the 'Internationale'.*]

[*Quelch speaks in English. Tumultuous applause. The 'Internationale'.*]

Chairman: Comrade Petrov will translate into Russian.[12]

Petrov: Comrade Quelch expresses his gratitude for the reception you have given him as the representative of the British Communist Party, and, for his part, greets you on behalf of the British Communists and of the British working class. [*Tumultuous applause.*]

The British working class, says Comrade Quelch, is very slow to get going, but when once it starts to move there is no force in the world capable of stopping it. [*Tumultuous applause.*]

At a certain moment, says Comrade Quelch, the British capitalists, the British Government threatened Soviet Russia with war. And what happened? A Council of Action of the British working class was formed, and we have heard no more of that threat from the British Government. The British working class is against war, the British working class is on the side of Soviet Russia. It knows very well that the British capitalists, the British imperialists have oppressed and are now oppressing Ireland, Egypt and a number of other countries. But the struggle of the British working class, which is advancing hand in hand with the working class of Russia and other countries, portends the downfall of British imperialism in the near future. [*Tumultuous applause.*]

The social revolution in Britain is near at hand. The congress of representatives of the Eastern people in Baku gives a fresh spur to it, and he hopes that the movement of the Eastern peoples will also contribute to sweeping away the British imperialists. [*Tumultuous applause.*]

He concludes his speech with: 'Long live Soviet Russia! Long live the world revolution!' [*Tumultuous applause. The 'Internationale'.*]

Chairman: Comrade Karayev will translate into Turkic.

[*Karayev gives the Turkic translation.*]

Chairman: I call upon the representative of the Balkan Communist Federation, Comrade Shablin. [*Tumultuous applause. The 'Internationale'*]

[*Shablin speaks in Bulgarian. Tumultuous applause. The 'Internationale'.*]

Chairman: I think everyone understood, and so no translation is required. Comrade Karayev will translate into Turkic.

[*Karayev gives the Turkic translation.*]

Chairman: I call upon the representative of the French Communist Party, Comrade Rosmer. [*Tumultuous applause. The 'Internationale'.*]

[*Rosmer speaks in French.*]

Pavlovich: [13] Comrade Rosmer says: The cordial greeting you have given me will touch the hearts of the proletarians of France.

Hitherto you have known and felt the consequences of one alliance, that between the French bourgeoisie and the Russian counter-revolution. But now the French proletariat has begun to rouse itself. It is groaning beneath the oppression of the bourgeoisie, which is striving to prevent it from allying with the Russian proletariat.

Comrade Rosmer refers to the example of the French sailors who were sent to bombard the maritime cities of Soviet Russia. They refused to carry out this order, and for that 46 of them were shot, while 340 are still languishing in the casemates of France's convict prisons.

The news of the heroic exploit of these sailors rang like a tocsin all through France, arousing vigour and revolutionary initiative in tens of thousands of workers, and finding a passionate response in the towns and in the villages.

The workers of France know and feel that Soviet Russia is the friend and ally of the world proletariat. And today Soviet Russia is the country the French proletariat love best. When the French rail-waymen went on strike recently,[14] they said: 'We want to leave capitalist France; we ask to be sent to Soviet Russia; we shall starve, be tormented and suffer there along with the Russian proletarians, but we shall at least know that we are suffering so that Soviet Russia may flourish.'

Capitalist France, ruined by the war and on the brink of economic bankruptcy, nevertheless dreams of strengthening its position by an alliance with the counter-revolutionary clique of agents of the Entente, Wrangel and others, but this alliance has been smashed, the link has been broken, and in place of this alliance a new alliance is developing — between the proletariat of Russia and that of France and all countries.

Long live the international proletariat!

Long live the Communist International!

[*Loud shouts of 'Hurrah' and applause.*]

Chairman: I call upon the representative of America, John Reed.[15] [*Applause*]

[*John Reed speaks in English, but ending in Russian with:* 'Long live the international Red Army!' *Applause.*]

Chairman: Comrade Petrov will translate.

Petrov: Comrade Reed begins his speech with these words: What does 'Baku' mean? Baku means oil, and American capitalism is striving to establish a world monopoly of oil. On account of oil, blood is flowing. A struggle is being waged for oil, and the American bankers and the American capitalists are everywhere trying to conquer the places and enslave the peoples wherever oil is to be found. Comrade Radek says that he would have liked to see Mexico represented as well at this congress in Baku — that Mexico which is now almost entirely in the grip of American capitalism, which has seized Mexican oil. But Comrade John Reed says: in Baku there are no more capitalists and this oil no longer belongs to the capitalists. If this can be done, he exclaims, in Baku, in Russia, why can such a social order not be achieved in America and throughout the world? [*Applause.*] The East, he says, will help us overthrow capitalism in Western Europe and America, the foundations of which lie in the exploitation of the East. As soon as the Eastern peoples rise in revolt, the last foundations of capitalism will collapse, and then the peoples will endeavour to create a social order in which not only oil but everything produced by human hands will belong to the working masses. [*Applause.*]

Chairman: The translation into Turkic will be made by Comrade Sultan-Zade.

[*Sultan-Zade translates into Turkic. Applause.*]

Chairman: I call upon the representative of the Communist Party of Austria, Comrade Steinhardt.[16]

[*Steinhardt speaks in German.*]

Chairman: Comrade Steinhardt greets you in the name of the Austrian workers. He says that the working class in Austria, as also in Germany, has had great opportunities for using cultural knowledge for the benefit of the working class. The working class has been in a very much better position there. But neither in Germany nor in Austria have they yet achieved what the Russian workers have achieved in the Soviet Republic. The bourgeoisie in Germany and also in Austria is better organized, it is stronger, and so the struggle of the working class is much more difficult there. The working class of Austria has fought resolutely and is still fighting, it has shed an enormous amount of blood — but it has not yet won victory over the bourgeoisie.

Just recently, in Moscow, from where Comrade Steinhardt came to Baku, world events of the greatest importance took place. The Second Congress of the Communist International was held there. At that congress the basis was laid for an international army of the proletarian revolution.

The world revolution and the working class march under the banner of the teaching of Karl Marx. The leader of a detachment of the armed forces of this army is Comrade Trotsky.[17] Incidentally, I forgot to say that Comrade Steinhardt spoke of the general staff of this world proletarian army, the chairman of which you comrades in Baku have the pleasure of seeing in the person of Comrade Zinoviev.

Today, says Comrade Steinhardt, the congress of peoples of the

East is a new form of this world struggle of the oppressed against capitalism. It is a blow struck directly at the British and French imperialists, who are the particular oppressors of the Eastern peoples. In the East, says Comrade Steinhardt, the sun of freedom has risen and is casting its beams westward. In the East decisions of the common, international congress of the Communist International will be realized. Comrade Steinhardt concludes his speech with: Long live the world Soviet Republic! Long live Red Azerbaidzhan!

Chairman [*sic*]: Comrades, the list of the speakers is concluded. We are rather tired. Our dear guests are also tired from their journey. I think we can close the meeting.

Comrades, allow me to thank on your behalf our comrades who have arrived among us here after long and hard travelling, in order to pour new strength into our veins and to help us, when we have absorbed this new strength, to carry on still further with our gigantic, stubborn and difficult struggle.

I greet you, comrades, in Red, revolutionary Baku, which is now lighting up the paths of revolution for the entire East — you, the incendiaries of Communist revolution and its leaders, our comrades Zinoviev, Radek, Béla Kun and the rest who are present here. [*Applause: The band plays the 'Internationale'*]

Comrades, let us break up to the sound of our anthem, the '*Internationale*'! [*They sing the 'Internationale'.*]

The meeting ended at 3.30 a.m.

First Session

September 1

The meeting opened at 9.40 p.m.

Narimanov: In the name of the Central Committee [*sic*] of the Communist International I declare the First Congress of the Peoples of the East open. [*Tumultuous applause. The Internationale.*]

Comrades, it is today my happy lot to open a congress which is the first of its kind, something unprecedented and unheard-of in the world — the Congress of the Peoples of the East.

The grey-headed East, which gave us our first notion of morality and culture, will today shed tears, telling of the sorrow, of the grievous wounds inflicted upon her by the capital of the bourgeois countries.

These peoples of the East, each living its own distinct life, could not be unaware of the terrible, oppressive effects of this capital.

But today, here, when we learn about each other's situations, the whole picture will unfold before us, and then only will all these peoples of the East realize all the terrible, oppressive effects of this capital. And the knowledge will impel all these peoples to unite, and they will come to one conclusion: to use their united strength to throw off and smash the chains of this capital.

The speeches we heard yesterday enable me, however, to stress another significant aspect of this first congress. It seems to me that two worlds are meeting here today: the world of the oppressed and the world of the oppressors. We can be sure that if the representatives of the world of the oppressors were delegates of the bourgeois class, the tears of the grey-headed East would have perhaps no influence at all. But it is our good fortune that the delegates who are here represent the

21

working class of the bourgeois countries; they will understand what these tears mean, and they will hasten the development of events, making it possible for us to announce triumphantly, in the near future, the reign of the Third International. [*Tumultuous applause. Translation into Turkic.*]

Narimanov: The Communist fraction at the Congress and the fraction of non-Party delegates are represented on the Presidium of the Congress of Peoples of the East by the following persons:

From the Communist fraction:

Ryskulov, Abdurashidov and Kariyev,[18] from Turkestan.

Mustafa Sup'hi, from Turkey.[19]

Wang, from China.

Acharya, from India.[20]

Mullavekdzhan-Rakhmanov, from Khiva.

Mukhamedov, from Bukhara.

Korkmasov, from Daghestan.

Digurov, from the Terek Region.

Aliyev, from Northern Caucasia.

Kastonyan, from Armenia.

Narimanov, from Azerbaidzhan.

Yenikeyev, from the Tatar Republic.

Amur Sanan, from the Kalmuck Republic.

Filipp Makharadze, from Georgia.

Haidar Khan, from Persia.[21]

Agazade, from Afghanistan.

From the non-Party fraction:

Narbutabekov, from Tashkent.

Makhmudov, from Ferghana.

Takhsim Baari, from Anatolia.

Haavis Mahomed, from Anatolia.

Wang, from Chinese Turkestan.

Kubeyev, from Mangyshlak District.

Niyas-Kuli, from Turkmenia.

Kara Tadzhi, from Samarkand.

Naazir Sedyki, from India.

Sidadzheddin Kardash Ogly, from Daghestan.

Yelchiev, from Azerbaidzhan.

Musayev, from Azerbaidzhan.

Azim, from Afghanistan.

Abdulayev, from Khiva.

Secretaries

From the Communist fraction: Ostrovsky (in Russian).

From the non-Party fractions: Abdul Hamid Yumusov (for the Moslems); Melikov (in Russian); Makhmud Khan and Akhmed Khan (for the Moslems).

All [*sic*] fractions at the Congress have proposed Comrade Zinoviev as chairman of the Congress of Eastern Peoples. [*Prolonged applause and shouts of 'Hurrah'.*] The Communist and non-Party fractions have proposed that the following comrades be elected as Honorary Chairmen of the Congress: Lenin [*applause: the band plays the 'Internationale'*], Zinoviev [*applause: the 'Internationale'*] and Trotsky [*applause: the 'Internationale'.*]

As honorary members of the Presidium the following dear guests have been nominated: Comrades Quelch (Britain), Rosmer (France), Shablin (Bulgaria), Jansen (Holland),[22] Reed (USA), Béla Kun (Hungary) [*Applause: the band plays the 'Internationale'*], Radek [*Applause*], Hodo-Yoshiharo (Japan),[23] Steinhardt (Austria), and also dear Comrade Stalin, whom we all know.

Let us now take the vote. [*A voice:* 'Translation.']

Do you think it necessary to translate the list of comrades who have been nominated? [*A voice:* 'Only into Turkic'.]

[*An interpreter translates into Turkic.*]

Chairman: Those in favour of the list proposed, please raise your hands. Anyone against? Almost unanimously in favour.

I call on Comrade Zinoviev. [*Tumultuous applause. All rise and greet Zinoviev.*] Please resume your seats.

Zinoviev: Comrades, my task is to explain to you how the Communist International sees the aims and tasks of this congress of the peoples of the East.

The idea of holding this congress was conceived when the Second World Congress of the Communist International was being prepared, at the time when some of the delegates of the present congress came to Moscow. Together with the Executive Committee of the Communist International they issued an appeal, in the name of a number of countries, to you, to the peoples of the East, proposing that preparations be undertaken for holding at Baku this congress at which we have today the pleasure of being present.

The Second World Congress of the Communist International was attended by representatives of the Communist workers and peasants of 37 countries in Europe and America. There were also present a few representatives of the East. Today, however, we have succeeded in assembling a fuller, mass representation of the working people of the entire East, and we consider that the Baku Congress will enter into the history of the struggle for freedom as the complement, the second part, the second half of the work of the Congress which recently finished its work in Moscow.

We feel very great pride in the fact that the Communist International has succeeded, for the first time in the history of mankind, in bringing together today under one roof representatives of more than one-fifth of the peoples of the East, some of whom have hitherto lived in mutual enmity, and some of whom knew little about each other — and, in any case, never had the chance to sit down together to discuss all those burning questions which confront us.

We regard this congress as a major historical event because it shows that now it is not only the advanced workers and working peasants of Europe and America who are awakening, but, at last, we have all lived to see the day of the awakening not just of individuals but of tens and hundreds of thousands, millions of the working elements of the peoples of the East — the peoples who make up the majority of the population of the entire globe and who therefore are alone in a position finally to settle the dispute between labour and capital.

Comrades, today's congress was convened, as you know, by the Communist International, by the Party organization. We have here with us today, however, not only Communists but also hundreds of delegates who do not yet belong to the Communist Party, who regard themselves as non-Party people, and also groups which belong, it may be, to other parties.

At first sight this may seem contradictory. How, indeed, can the Party organization have convened a congress made up not strictly and solely of Party members but containing, perhaps, a majority of non-Party people?

But this contradiction is only of a formal character. Actually, it is in complete conformity with the policy, aspirations, ideals and strivings of the Communist International. The latter has convened the peoples of the East without asking each of the representatives: 'Do you, at this moment, belong to the Communist International, to a Communist Party, or do you not?' We did not ask you: 'What party do you belong to?' We asked each one: 'Are you a man who lives by his labour? Do you belong to the working masses? Do you want to put a stop to the strife between the peoples? Do you want to organize a struggle against the oppressors? That is enough. Nothing more is required, you will not be asked for any Party card. Let us gather together in order to discuss the questions that today confront the whole world.'

Comrades, the dispute between the Second International, which has died, and the Third International, which is now growing stronger with each day, is not a narrow inter-party dispute, not a question of interest only to those who already belong to a particular party. No, it is a dispute between labour and capital, a dispute which concerns everyone who lives by his labour. In Russia, where there are also very many illiterate, ignorant, half-crushed peasants who are only now awakening to political life — in Russia today there is already not a single village, certainly not a single rural district, where the peasants have not heard that the Third International exists and that it is working to free the working people from the yoke of the rich. And we are sure that, in the East, too, the time will soon come when it will be impossible to find a single county, or a single large capital city [*sic*], or a single large settlement, where the best and most conscious peasants do not know that the Third International exists and that it is working to free the peoples of the East. For, comrades, life has now raised sharply the question of the emancipation of labour, and life is compelling every peasant to take stock of this question.

I can give you a graphic example. If you want to know what the Second International is, look at Georgia, which you all know well enough. There you have the embodiment of the Second International! In Georgia power is held by a government of Mensheviks, who belong to the Second International. The leaders of present-day Georgia are important representatives of this Second International. And every peasant in Georgia now knows from his own hard experience what it means when a party belonging to the Second International is in power. It means that the peasants do not get the land. It means there is freedom of the press only for the bourgeoisie, that this freedom does not exist for the workers and peasants. It means that the best leaders of the working-class masses are under arrest. It means that power belongs to a gang who defend, like house-dogs, the rule of the rich. It means that Georgia is governed by men who are ready at any moment to offer the sweat and blood of the proletariat on a plate to British capitalism. [*Applause.*] It means that Georgia is governed by men who are ready at any moment to crawl on their bellies before any British, French or Italian general, if it seems to them that this general is powerful. It means that power is in the hands of men who are always ready to wink, if only with one eye, at the Tsarist General Denikin when he seems to be the stronger and when it seems to them that Soviet power is going to perish in Russia. In Germany the most prominent representative of the Second International is Noske, the executioner who has shot down thousands of German workers. In Georgia the most prominent representatives of the Second International are Mr Noi Zhordania and his associates, who are also executioners of the people, ready to cut thongs from the peasants' skins. [*Tumultuous applause.*]

Naturally, Zhordania's policy is always presented to the Georgian peasants in the name of the independence of 'Georgia' and the defence of that country's 'national' interests. But comrades, what sense does it make to a Georgian peasant if Mr Gegechkori and other such gentlemen sing like nightingales about the 'independence' of Georgia, when the land remains as before the property of the old landowners, when the same old oppression continues, and when at any moment some British general can trample with his jackboots on the throat and on the chest of the Georgian peasant and worker?

That, comrades, is what is meant by the dispute between the Second and Third Internationals. It is no dispute of bookmen or scholars, it is a question of life and death for the workers and peasants.[24]

Even in its best days the Second International took the view that 'civilized' Europe can and must act as tutor to 'barbarous' Asia.

Already in 1907, at the international congress held in Stuttgart, the majority of the official Social-Democrats (Mensheviks) expressed themselves in favour of the need for a so-called 'progressive' colonial policy. In words, the Social-Democrats declared that this would be a human colonial policy — humane, mild and civilized. In fact, however, what they had in mind was support for the capitalists in their robber colonial policy, in the policy which conferred upon the colonies syphilis, opium and a debauched caste of officers, the policy which turned these countries into the bourgeoisie's rubbish dump, and which plundered them relentlessly, right and left.

And when the war of 1914 came, this Second International, rotten through and through, which already in 1907 had declared for helping the bourgeoisie with white skins to oppress the peoples with black and yellow skins — this Second International naturally sold itself to the bourgeoisie; but then at once collapsed like a house of cards.

From the first day of its existence the Communist International said: In Asia live four times as many people as in Europe, there are 800 million people in Asia, and we want to free all the peoples, all the working people of the world, regardless of the colour of their skins, regardless of whether they are white, black or yellow.

We want to do away with every kind of exploitation of man by man. We do not consider as a socialist anyone who does not understand this. We fight against those who help the bourgeoisie or who stand aside when the task is to help the oppressed peoples. We are for organizing the Negroes and all other men who live by their labour, for organizing all the working people and all suffering and weary humanity, for struggle against the capitalists, the world's oppressors.

This was why, when we concluded our work at the Second Congress of the Communist International, we swore an oath and issued a manifesto in the names of the Communists of 37 countries. In this manifesto, addressed to the workers and peasants of the whole world, we wrote these words: 'The socialist who aids directly or indirectly in perpetuating the privileged position of one nation at the expense of another, who accommodates himself to colonial slavery, who draws a line of distinction between races and colours in the matter of human rights, who helps the bourgeoisie of the metropolis to maintain its rule over the colonies instead of aiding the armed uprising of the colonies — for example, the British socialist who fails to support by all possible means the uprisings in Ireland, Egypt and India against the London plutocracy — such a "socialist" deserves, if not to be shot, then to be branded with infamy, but in no case merits either a mandate or the confidence of the proletariat.'

This was our declaration, this was the solemn oath which we took before the workers of Europe and America and which we solemnly repeat in Baku, before the representatives of the labouring masses of the entire East assembled here.

We shall fight to the death against those who forget, even for one moment, their duty to the oppressed nations, to the labouring masses of those countries which are being plundered and exploited by capital.

Comrades, I told you that the Communist International wants a bond of brotherhood with all the peoples of the East, with all the oppressed masses. I think that you, comrades, want this alliance too, and cannot but want it. The European proletariat sees now, at every step, that the course of history has united the working people of the East with the workers of Europe. Together they can conquer, or

together perish. At every step the workers of Germany and other
countries see how the bourgeoisie, when it finds itself in special
difficulties, brings in coloured troops for use against the European
workers. The bourgeoisie has brought black troops into Germany and
into other countries as well.[25]

The Italian bourgeoisie is now threatening its workers that, if they
should revolt, Italian capital will move coloured troops against them.
The workers of Europe are today learning by harsh experience what
they did not understand in the days when they trusted the Second
International. The workers are learning that they must, at any cost,
form a close alliance with the working masses of the entire East, of the
entire world. But it is now necessary that this be understood also by
the many-millioned masses of the entire East. Your first task when
you return home must be to explain to every peasant and every
peasant woman, to every shepherd, to everyone who lives by his
labour, to explain to everyone who will listen to you that today we
cannot take a single step without each other, that the proletarian
forces of the West must now be united with the working masses of the
entire East, of the entire world, so as, together, to defeat and finally to
smash our terrible foe, who is still quite powerful even today.

The first task of our congress is to rouse the millions of peasants, to
explain to them that it is necessary to plough the land more deeply, to
raise up fresh peasant forces and explain to them that unless a brotherly, friendly alliance is forged with the whole organized working class
of the world there is no way out, that if this is not done only ruin faces
them, but that, given such an alliance the complete victory of labour,
complete victory over the plunderers and oppressors of the world —
over the British and French who have oppressed you for decades —
such complete victory will be assured.

Comrades, in its very first statements the Third International
pointed out that today the world is divided into nations with power
and nations without power, into oppressed and oppressor nations.

The Second International avoided saying this. It spoke about equality, in a general way, without explaining precisely what the actual
situation is. At the Second Congress of the Communist International,
held in Moscow, we pointed out once again that the world is divided
into powerful nations and oppressed nations.

Comrades, as early as at the beginning of the war, and during the
war, we had occasion to point this out. In one of our writings (those
interested can read it in my book *The War and the Crisis of Socialism*)

we showed, with figures to support the statement, that before the war the world was divided up like this: six so-called Great Powers, with a population of 437 millions, oppressed all the other countries and states, the population of which amounted to 1,220 millions. That was the situation down to the end of the war. Now, the situation has changed for the worse. Now, as you know, some of the so-called Great Powers have lost their former status. There are now a smaller number of Great Powers, a smaller number of plunderers. America, Britain, France and Japan, these four big robbers, according to the calculation made by Comrade Lenin at our congress, with a total population of barely a quarter of a milliard, oppress a milliard and a quarter people in the dependent nations. In the book I mentioned I worked out that five per cent of the British people are large-scale property-owners in Britain, and these five men out of every hundred oppress not only the rest of the British but also 890 members of various other peoples: Indians, Persians, Chinese and so on. Each British capitalist forces to work for his benefit nearly a hundred British workers and several hundred working people who live in the colonies and oppressed countries. That's how it was before the war, and that's how it is today. The task before this congress is above all to take account of this fact and explain it to every toiler. Grasp this: every large-scale British capitalist forces to work for him not only tens and hundreds of British workers but also hundreds and thousands of peasants in Persia, Turkey, India and many other countries which are subject to British capital. From this the conclusion needs to be drawn that these one-and-a-half milliard oppressed people must, above all, unite, and then there will be no power in the world capable of compelling you to submit to these robbers, the British capitalists. And the representatives of the worker-Communists of the whole world appeal to you and stretch out to you the hand of fraternal aid in this hard but necessary struggle. We are passionately convinced that this hand extended to you by the worker of Europe and America, you will grasp honestly and respond with a handshake of friendship. [Applause.]

We know that the working masses of the East are in some places, through no fault of their own, very backward: illiterate, ignorant, they are sunk in superstition and believe in spirits, they are unable to read newspapers, they do not know what is going on in the world at large, they do not understand the most elementary principles of hygiene. Only the lackeys of imperialism can mock them for all this. The unfortunate Turkish and Persian toilers are not to blame for being illiterate. That is their misfortune. The 'civilized' bourgeoisie sitting in Paris and London have devised all sorts of methods for keeping the Indian peasants, the Persian and Turkish toilers, in a state of ignorance.

The task of the more civilized, more literate, more organized workers of Europe and America is to help the backward toilers of the East. Not to mock them, not to put on airs, not to swank about their superiority over the backward Eastern peasants, but to be concerned about the ignorance and backwardness of the latter, to extend the hand of aid to them, and to help them in the only way they can: by teaching them to master weapons and to direct these against the white, civilized beasts of prey who sit in the counting-houses and banks of London and Paris — so as to help the peasant of the East to take the land for himself, to help him carry further that great revolution which the Russian peasants have started, after such heavy labours.

We know that in some countries the clergy and feudal lords of the East know how to play tricks on the peasant, raising false hopes, so that he thinks he has obtained land when in fact he has not; they are able to set up legal traps to catch the backward, ignorant peasant. We must expose this deception and raise up the peoples of the East to carry out an agrarian revolution like that effected by the peasants of Russia, those Russian peasants who only half a century ago were still serfs and who are still largely illiterate. Why should the peasants of Turkey, Persia, India, China, Armenia and so on not do what has been done by the Russian peasants who so recently were serfs? We are sure that the peasants of the whole East, under the wise leadership of the organized workers of the West, will now be able to rise up in their hundreds of millions in order to carry out a real, thoroughgoing agrarian revolution, to clear the soil so that no large landowners are left, so that no debt-slavery, no taxes, dues or any other variety of the devices used by the rich are left, so that the land passes into the hands of the labouring masses. This is what the Communist International brings to you.

The proletariat wants to help you to take the land and to create a free union of all the peoples of the world. This is the simple, straightforward programme which is written in the heart of every honest worker in Europe and which must now be adopted by you representatives of the toilers of the East.

Comrades, our congress in Moscow discussed the question whether the socialist revolution could take place in the countries of the Far

East before these countries has passed through the stage of capitalism. You know that for a long time the view existed that, first of all, each country must pass through the capitalist stage, creating big factories and large-scale property-owners; it was indispensable for the workers to be massed together in cities, and only then could there be any question of socialism. We now think that this is not so. From the moment that even just one country has broken away from the chain of capitalism, as Russia has done, from the moment that the workers have put the question of the proletarian revolution on the agenda, from that moment we can say that in China, India, Turkey, Persia and Armenia it is possible and necessary to begin fighting directly for a Soviet system. The workers of Europe will use their power, of course, not in order to plunder Turkey, Persia and other countries, but to help them. Since this is so, such countries can and must prepare now for a Soviet revolution, can and must prepare to put an end within their boundaries to the division between rich and poor, so as to create a state of the working people and conclude a close alliance with the organized workers of the whole world.

In this connection we put the question to you: what will be the form of the state, of the organization of the East? We have come to the conclusion that it is necessary to set up Soviets even where there are no urban workers. In such cases we can create a state of Soviets of the working peasants. Not toy 'Soviets' such as they now sometimes palm off on you in Turkey, but real ones, for which every working peasant has the right to vote. I read in the journal *Krasny Daghestan* that in Daghestan they are now establishing the law governing elections to Soviets, and that the right to elect to the peasants' soviets is to be reserved to honest working peasants possessing no more than a certain number of animals. I will not undertake to decide whether or not the figures are what they should be, but the approach is right. Whoever possesses cattle, horned or otherwise, in greater numbers than are needed to work his holding and keep his family in comfort, and who profits by others' need, must be denied access to our peasant soviets. They must be truly Soviets of the working people, organized by men who live by their labour and who are concerned not with profit-making and speculation but with the common good. We must organize Soviets that will be genuine transmitters of the will of the working masses.

We address our appeal not only to those who take the standpoint of Communism but also to the non-Party people. We have two streams.

One is very fast, impetuous and strong — the stream of the workers' proletarian Communist struggle in Russia, Germany, France and Italy, which is everywhere spreading wider. But there is also another stream, which is as yet not strong enough, which in some places takes a zigzag course — this is the movement of the oppressed nationalities which have not yet chosen the road they will follow, do not yet know exactly what they want, but which feel that a strap is chafing their backs, that French and British capitalism are sitting astride their necks.

We want these two streams to draw closer and closer together, so that the second stream may be cleansed of national prejudices, so that they may be merged in one single tumultuous, powerful stream which, like the sea, will sweep all obstacles from its path and clear the land of all the evil from which we have suffered so long.

And so I say: we patiently support those groups which are not yet with us and even on some questions, are against us. For example, in Turkey, comrades, you know that the Soviet Government supports Kemal. We do not for one moment forget that the movement headed by Kemal is not a Communist movement. We know this. I have before me some extracts from the stenographic report of the first meeting of the Turkish people's government in Ankara. Kemal himself says that 'the person of the Caliph and Sultan is sacred and inviolable.'[26]

The movement which is headed by Kemal wants to rescue the 'sacred' person of the Caliph from enemy hands — this is the viewpoint of that party. Is it a Communist viewpoint? No, it is not. We respect the religious feelings of the masses and we know how to re-educate the masses. This requires many years' work. We approach with caution the religious beliefs of the working masses of the East and of other countries. However, it is our duty to tell this congress: what Kemal's government is now doing in Turkey, supporting the power of the Sultans, you ought not to do, even if this line be dictated by religious considerations. You must go forward and not let yourselves be dragged back. We think that the day of the Sultans is over, that you should not put up with autocracy. You should dispel and destroy faith in the Sultan, and establish genuine Soviets. The Russian peasants also had great faith in the Tsar. When, however, a real people's revolution flared up, hardly a trace of this faith in the Tsar was left. It will be the same in Turkey and in the whole East when a real earthy peasants' revolution flares up. Then the people will very quickly get rid of their faith in the Sultan and in their masters. Consequently, we repeat: the policy which is being pursued by the present people's government in Turkey is not the policy of the Communist International, it is not our policy. And at the same time we say that we are ready to help any revolutionary struggle against the British Government. Today the scales of the balance in Turkey are still tipped in favour of the richer people, but the time will come when matters are otherwise.

In Turkey, in Persia, everywhere that peasants are to be found, they are beginning to understand what Bolshevism means.

Recently I asked a prominent Turkish public man of the liberal tendency what the Turkish peasant understood by the word 'Bolshevik'. This prominent public man answered: 'In our country people usually understand by this a man who wants to fight against Britain and who wants to help us to do this.' I asked a second question: 'And what does the ordinary peasant in Turkey think about the fact that the Bolshevik is not only against Britain but against the rich in general, including both Russian and Turkish?' This the public man did not answer, and he was inclined to think that the peasant in question did not understand this point. I, however, have grounds for knowing, I think, that the word 'Bolshevik' does not need to be translated anywhere in the world, either into Persian or into any other language. [*Applause.*] I am convinced that the working masses will have need of this word in the struggle not only against Britain but against the rich generally. Yes, we are moving against bourgeois Britain, 'to take the British imperialists by the throat and set our knee on their chest.' The most powerful blow, at the very heart, has to be dealt against British capitalism. That is true. But at the same time we must educate the working masses of the East to hate and to want to fight against the rich in general — Russian, Jewish,[27] German, French. The great importance of the revolution that is beginning in the East lies not in requesting the British imperialist gentlemen to take their feet off the table, and then permitting the Turkish rich to put *their* feet on the table with the utmost convenience. No, we want to ask *all* the rich, ever so politely, to take their dirty feet off the table, so that there may reign among us not luxury, not charlatanry, not mockery of the people, and not idleness, but that the world may be ruled by the working man with toil-hardened hands. [*Tumultuous applause.*]

Accordingly, we say, directly and definitely to the non-Party delegates here: Pan-Islamism, Musavatism,[28] all these trends are not ours.

We have a different policy. We can support a democratic policy such as has now taken shape in Turkey and such as will perhaps tomorrow make its appearance in other countries. We support and will support national movements like those in Turkey, Persia, India and China not out of any mercenary calculation but because the conscious worker will say to himself: the Turks who have today not yet understood where all their interests lie will understand this tomorrow. We must support this Turk and help him, and wait for a real people's revolution to arise in Turkey, when veneration for Sultans and other survivals will all at once depart from his mind. I must, as the elder brother, hasten this movement, says the advanced worker. I will support the present national-democratic movement of the Turks, says the Communist worker, and at the same time I consider it my sacred duty to call upon the Turkish peasants, the Persian peasants, and downtrodden, oppressed working peasants of the entire East, to hate all the rich, all the oppressors, to teach them the simple truth that we need real economic equality between all men and real brotherly unity between all who live by their labour.

There, comrades, is our frank statement. We think that none of us is obliged to address the Congress of the Peoples of the East in the style of a diplomat. We must put aside every sort of despicable diplomacy at this time when we have brought together those peoples who have been oppressed more than any others, and who number hundreds of millions — the peoples upon whom, in the last analysis, the future of all mankind depends. Comrades, when the East really gets moving, then not only Russia but all of Europe will seem only a small corner of this vast scene. The real revolution will flare up only when we are joined by the 800,000,000 people who live in Asia, when the African continent joins us, when we see hundreds of millions of people in the movement. At this historic gathering nobody need hide behind diplomacy and reticence. Let all present open their hearts, so that they may hear from each other words of real and pure truth, so that we may choose the real path to victory. We hide nothing from you, we speak plainly to you about what separates us from the representatives of the current national movement and about what we have in common with them. We say to you: the task of this movement is to help the East free itself from British imperialism. But we have a task of our own to carry out, no less great — to help the toilers of the East in their struggle against the rich, and here and now to help them build their own Communist organizations, to explain to them what Communism means, to prepare them for a real labour revolution, for real equality, for the emancipation of mankind from every form of oppression.

Comrades, I think that the fact that I told you frankly what we think about these difficult matters and our differences in relation to them, has brought us closer to those whose views differ from ours, because it is better frankly to conclude definite agreements than to approach each other with hostility hidden in our hearts.

I say that we are now faced with the task of kindling a real holy war against the British and French capitalists. Comrades, remember what is being done, northward from here, by these bandits even at this moment. I will not speak about those peoples who are particularly well represented here. You yourselves know the situation that British and French capital has created in Turkey, the situation British capital has created in Persia, the situation of Armenia, which yesterday all the governments of the Entente wanted to defend and whom nobody is now defending.

I will say a little more only about those countries which are poorly represented here — about India and China.

Comrades, you know how many hundreds of millions of people live in India, which is being so ruthlessly pillaged by British capital. You have perhaps heard about the latest events there. Quite recently there was another case in India of Indians being fired on for only a feeble attempt at resistance — what has become known as the Dyer affair. An unarmed crowd was lured to within range of machine-guns and mown down.[29]

And when a Parliamentary inquiry into this affair was made, newspapers published in London had to write about this scene, immortalized by photography, showing how the British enjoyed themselves when order had been restored: armed British soldiers forcing Indians to crawl on their bellies through the streets of a city. This is the method used by the civilized British imperialists and their sons who have attended several universities. They send out their officers in order that by putting a rifle-muzzle to the ear of an Indian and making him crawl on his belly they may gladden the eyes of a British officer.

And the correspondent of an Italian newspaper has sent similar pictures from China, with the caption: 'A matinée in South China.'

Comrades, these little pictures which are to be seen in considerable numbers in any issue of a foreign newspaper, depict for us the unheard-of horrors that are being suffered by the peoples of India and China. Comrades, do not forget that the white British capitalist beasts

of prey who so shamefully oppress the Indian people have also cont-
rived to enlist tens of thousands of Indian soldiers, whom they send to
suppress the proletarian movement. Indian soldiers are at the present
time fighting on no less than seven fronts, under the conductor's
baton of British generals. Indian soldiers are in action in the Constantinople theatre of war, in Arabia, in Mesopotamia, in Egypt, in
Palestine, in North-Eastern Persia and in North-Western Persia.
There, comrades, you see the accursed situation of our oppressed
class: they seize Indians by the throat and force them to crawl on their
bellies in order to amuse a British officer, and at the same time our
brothers, the oppressed peasants of India, are so ignorant that the
same British can enlist Indians in their army, provide a few hundred
officers drawn from the landed gentry to command them, and send
them off to suppress the national revolutionary movement in Egypt or
Persia — that, comrades, is what is horrible about the position we are
in! We are helping our executioners with our own hands, helping the
British and French capitalists. This is what we must put an end to!

We must at last slam shut this book of the accursed past, so that it
may never return, and must open a new page of history, when the
oppressed peoples of the East will no longer be slaves, when they will
not allow British officers shamelessly to plunder the Indians and the
Persians, killing, insulting and mocking at everyone.

Comrades! Much has been said about 'holy war' in recent years.
The capitalists, when they were waging their accursed imperialist
war, tried to present that slaughter as a holy war, and made many
people believe this. When in 1914-1918 they spoke of a 'holy war',
that was a monstrous deception. But now, Comrades, you who have
for the first time assembled in a congress of peoples of the East, must
here proclaim a real holy war, against the robbers, the Anglo-French
capitalists. Now we must say that the hour has sounded when the
workers of the whole world can arouse and raise up tens and hundreds
of millions of peasants, can form a Red Army in the East as well, can
arm and organize a revolt in the rear of the British, can hurl fire
against the bandits, can poison the existence of every insolent British
officer who is lording it in Turkey, Persia, India and China.

Comrades! Brothers! The time has now come when you can set
about organizing a true people's holy war against the robbers and
oppressors. The Communist International turns today to the peoples
of the East and says to them: 'Brothers, we summon you to a holy war,
in the first place against British imperialism!' [*Tumultuous applause,*

prolonged shouts of 'Hurrah'. Members of the Congress stand up, brandishing their weapons. The speaker is unable to continue for some time. All the delegates stand up and applaud. Shouts of 'We swear it.']

May this declaration made today be heard in London, in Paris, and in all the cities where the capitalists are still in power. May they heed this solemn oath sworn by the representatives of tens of millions of toilers of the East, that the rule of the British oppressors shall be no more in the East, that the oppression of the toilers of the East by the capitalists shall cease!

Long live the fraternal alliance of the peoples of the East with the Communist International! May capital perish, and long live the reign of labour! *[Burst of applause.]*

Voices: 'Long live the rebirth of the East!' *[Shouts of 'Hurrah.' Applause.]*

Voices: 'Long live the Third, Communist International!' *[Shouts of 'Hurrah.' Applause.]*

Voices: 'Long live those who have united the East, our honoured leaders, our dear Red Army!' *[Shouts of 'Hurrah'. Applause.]*

Chairman: Please calm down and resume your seats. Comrade Buniat-Zade will translate Comrade Zinoviev's speech.

[Buniat-Zade translates into Turkic and another interpreter translates into Persian.]

Chairman: It has been reported that the Kabardian comrades want a translation into their language. Is there an interpreter here who can do that? No.

[An interpreter translates into Turkish. At 11.50 p.m. there is a break, and the congress reassembles at 12.15.]

Chairman: Tomorrow at 10 a.m. exactly there will be a meeting of the non-Party comrades at the Workers' Club. Everyone is to attend. Some very important questions will be decided. Please pass this on to those who are not present: this request applies to both non-Party and Party comrades. *[Translation.]*

Tomorrow at 10 a.m. there will be a Communist fraction meeting at the Army Club. Everyone is to attend.

The Congress of Peoples of the East will resume at 5 p.m. tomorrow. *[Translation.]*

The session concluded at 1.10 a.m.

Second Session

September 2

The session opened at 6.55 p.m. Comrade Zinoviev took the chair.

Chairman: I declare the second session of the Congress of the Peoples of the East open. In agreement with the Communist and non-Party fractions, we propose to merge two questions which are on the agenda and proceed immediately to hear reports on the second of these questions — that of the international situation and the tasks of the Eastern peoples — and then after this to open the discussion on yesterday's and today's reports, taken together. Since this has been agreed by the overwhelming majority of delegates to the Congress I shall allow myself to treat the decision as adopted, without further discussion, and invite the comrade reporting to address us. Please translate. [*Translations.*]

So, then, we proceed to the report on the international situation and the tasks of the working masses in the East. The report is given by Comrade Radek.

Radek: Comrades, yesterday we witnessed a scene which deserves the epithet 'historic', in the full sense of that word. When the representatives, assembled here, of the labouring masses of the Near East heard the representative of the European workers in revolt tell them that the proletariat of Europe is ready to fight to the death against the capitalists of the whole world, who have until now oppressed not only the European workers but also the masses of the people in the East — the representatives of those masses here present, all moved by the same emotion, rose and swore an oath to wage a holy war, shoulder to shoulder with the workers of Europe, against the oppressors of the world of labour. But, comrades, in this war which lies ahead of us

38

what will be required is not only enthusiasm, not only hatred of the oppressors. The popular masses of the East need to have a good knowledge of the direction taken by world politics, they need to know with precision the strength of the enemy and also his weak sides, they need to know how to make use of every fissure that appears in the enemy's ranks, so as to carry the struggle against him into his own camp. The international proletariat keeps a sharp watch on the changes in international politics. This familiarity with the international situation renders it a tremendous service in the developing war of the proletariat against capital. The working masses of the Near East must attain the same level in this respect as the mass of the workers in Europe. They must watch the enemy vigilantly and be able to choose the moment for attack. And this is why we are not prepared to rest content with our common urge to fight against world capital but have put on the agenda a report on the international situation and the tasks facing you.

The grey-haired East, of which Comrade Narimanov spoke with sorrow, has been suffering from the oppression of the capitalists of Europe for more than a few decades. For over a hundred years the peoples of the East have been subject to exploitation and to political oppression, have been made victims of war by the capitalist powers, the capitalist plunderers. Until now they have been only such victims, until now they have not been able to give the world brigands the rebuff they would have wished to give them, with their own forces. The entire history of the nineteenth century is filled with the struggle between British capitalism and the landlord-capitalist Tsarist Government of Russia for the mastery of Turkey, Persia and Central Asia. Russian Tsarism tried to seize Persia and Turkey. It wanted to capture and enslave the peasants of Turkey, to find an outlet to the Mediterranean, in order to measure its strength there against British capital. It went into Persia and enslaved the Persian peasants so as to be able through Persia to get at India, that pillar of the rule of British capital, that fabulous India which nourishes with the blood of the Indian peasantry the capitalists of Britain, the London Stock-Exchange, and which enables the younger sons of the British bourgeoisie to acquire millions and then, thanks to these millions, to lead the lives of parasites back in their own country. In this struggle, 'humane' British capitalism, the British lords, were fully the equals of barbarous Russian Tsarism. When it suited the convenience of the British capitalists, they came forward in defence of Turkey and Persia

against Tsarism. In so doing they advanced the banner of humanity
and a human attitude to the peoples of the East, and reproached
Tsarism for wanting to swallow up these peoples in order to coerce
and exploit them. But it was enough for British capitalism to reach an
agreement with Tsarism for it to raise the slogan of the annihilation of
Turkey, to raise the old slogan of the British minister Gladstone —
'dismember Turkey!' I will recall, comrades, just this fact, that the
Anglo-Russian struggle for Persia, the struggle between Tsarism and
British capitalism, ended in 1907 with an amicable agreement to
partition Persia, after which the British capitalists watched calmly
while the Tsarist Cossack General Lyakhov destroyed the infant
freedom of Persia, while the Cossack brigades dispersed the Mejlis,
while the representatives of the revolutionary Persian people were
hanged in the streets of Teheran and Tabriz. The British capitalists
washed their hands, saying that all this had nothing to do with them.
But, despite the fact that the British capitalists held Tsarism in their
grip — for Russian Tsarism was completely dependent financially on
British capital — they did not stir a finger to defend the Persian
people. Furthermore, the British Foreign Minister, Lord Grey[30]
instructed Buchanan, the British ambassador in Petrograd, to inform
the Tsarist Government that Britain would not oppose the Russian
aggression provided that Tsarism did not send its troops beyond the
limits of Northern Persia. The rival robbers agreed to divide Persia
into two parts. Northern Persia was handed over to Lyakhov's hangmen, while the South was to be held by the British and serve as a
barrier against a Russian incursion into India.

The struggle between Britain and Russia over the peoples of the
East was replaced in the last ten years by a different world-wide
struggle, that between the Entente group, British and French capital,
with Tsarism arm in arm with them, and a group headed by Germany.
And we have again seen, this time too, how the British, on the one
hand, and the German capitalists, on the other, said that their purpose
in going into the Near East was to bring civilization to that region, to
bring literacy to the people and teach them to use machinery, whereas
in fact the struggle between these groups was being waged for conquest of the people's wealth in Turkey and Persia — it was a struggle
between common-or-garden robbers. The British decided to strike
down and partition Turkey before that country could strengthen itself
after the Young-Turk revolt. Seeing that the Young-Turk Government was trying to form an army and to introduce a progressive

system of taxation and administration, the British capitalists resolved to break Turkey in pieces as soon as possible, for Turkey was enormously important to them. The world power of Britain extends all over the globe. British capital rules in Africa, holding in its grip both the mines of South Africa and the fertile fields of Egypt. At the same time, the second pillar of British world domination is India, where more than 300 million peasants work for the British capitalists. Between India and the African possessions of British capitalism lay Turkey, and therefore Turkey had to be destroyed, so that the British capitalists might unite, by means of a railway extending across Arabia and Mesopotamia, their possessions in Africa with their possessions in Egypt and in India, so that British capital, ruling over hundreds of millions of African and Asian nationalities, might freely transfer its troops from one part of the world to another, and ruthlessly suppress the slightest attempts at resistance on the part of the peoples of the East. British capital condemned Turkey to death so as to be able freely to put down the revolutionary movement that was beginning in India. On the other hand, German capital, which came forward as a liberator, as a defender of the popular masses, did this merely because it was opposed to an open partition of Turkey, since it was hard for Germany to get at you from the North Sea. German capitalism did not want to dismember Persia, because it had no free access to that country: what it strove for was to take all of Turkey and all of Persia into its economic grasp, and under cover of the Young-Turk and Persian Governments to exploit these peoples.

The world war of 1914, which led to the deaths of tens of millions of workers and peasants, which left behind millions of cripples and tens of millions of widows and orphans, that world war was fought in order to decide which group — the Anglo-French one or the German one — should rule the world, should be in a position to enslave hundreds of millions of workers and peasants of the peoples of Asia. This war was waged on both sides under the slogan of liberation for oppressed nations. The British capitalists who in 1908 hailed the advent of the Young Turks, expecting to be able to proceed in alliance with them, now suddenly discovered in their hearts a tremendous hatred for the Young Turks, and declared that the Turkish Government must be destroyed and the Turkish people torn in pieces, that it was necessary to liberate the cultured peoples of the East — the Arabs, Syrians and Armenians. The war was fought in the name of smashing the absolutism of the Sultan and the Young Turks and liberating the cultured peoples of the East! How did this war end? Comrades, it ended with the rout of German capitalism, something for which no worker or peasant of the East need shed a tear. But it also ended in the victory of British imperialism. What does this victory mean? The peoples of the East have already learnt this. It means that the British navy has seized Constantinople and is holding the Straits, it means that a British expeditionary force has occupied Arabia and Mesopotamia, that French forces have occupied Syria, that Greek forces have occupied the western part of Asia Minor, including Smyrna. It means that French and Italian troops have occupied Southern Anatolia, and have done this not just for the moment, not just while the absolutism of the Sultan is being liquidated, but in order to stay there, in order to dismember Turkey in the form of creating free, independent states of Syria, Mesopotamia and Arabia. What this freedom looks like we have very good evidence, comrades, from the French and British press. France promised to establish a free Syria, and found her hireling in the person of the Emir Feisal. As soon, however, as he stopped dancing to the tune of the French capitalists, French troops occupied Damascus, drove Feisal away, and now they quite openly hold Syria, expelling therefrom everyone whom the French capitalists dislike, and dictating their laws to the Syrian people.

The British talked about independence for Mesopotamia, and what a spectacle we behold. In order to create an independent state with a population of two-and-a-half millions, British capital has spend a quarter of a million pounds sterling in a single year. The question arose: why this generosity on the part of the British? A quarrel between French and British capital revealed the answer. When Lloyd George, the British Prime Minister, was asked in Parliament whether Britain was taking over the wealth of Mesopotamia, and whether British capital held some concessions in Mesopotamia, which might have impelled the British Government to spend such huge sums, Lloyd George replied that Britain had no concessions and asked for nothing from the Mesopotamians, but kept only those concessions which had already been granted to British capitalists by the Sultan's government. But when it was explained what this means — a task undertaken by none other than the French Foreign Minister, Monsieur Pichon — it turned out that the British capitalists control all the petroleum in Mesopotamia — the only wealth belonging to the Arabs of that country. This petroleum was the property of German capitalists and the Turkish Government. Now, the British have allowed the French 25 per cent of the petroleum, keeping 75 per cent for themselves. The peoples of the East are known to be very courteous, so I will not say at this congress of the peoples of the East that Mr Lloyd George is a liar and a cheat, but merely that he does not regard it as a statesman's duty to re-establish the truth when the truth is that British capitalism has grabbed Mesopotamia not in order to liberate the Arabs from Turkish oppression, but to liberate the Arabs from the petroleum which might have made them a rich nationality in the East. [*Applause.*] If, comrades, we inquire how the British, French and Americans have liberated the unfortunate Armenians, whom they ceaselessly incited, for so many decades, to fight against the Turks and Kurds, and to whom they promised freedom and cultural development — if we ask how they have stood up for the rights of Armenia, for the answer I can refer to the official organ of the Armenians in America, which very authoritatively describes what form this liberation has taken. This organ, *New Armenia,* which is published in New York, tells how the French induced the Armenians to send volunteers to Marash, to defend that province, alongside the French, against the Turks, promising them that in return they should have Alexandretta. But when the decisive battle took place, the French expeditionary force abandoned Marash, and 20,000 Armenians were left at the mercy of the army of Kemal Pasha — which, seeing in them so many enemies of Turkey fighting on the French side, spared the life of not a single one of them.[31] America has recently begun to play the role of Armenia's saviour and has incited the Armenians to go to war against those peoples among whom historical fate has decreed that the Armenians live. From time to time the Americans have sent to Armenia a ship with food inadequate to save the Armenians from hunger and cold. You know that the Armenian Republic, which is full of hatred for the Bolshevism of Soviet Russia, led as it is by bourgeois intrigues in the service of the Entente, this Armenian Republic has now been obliged to make peace with Soviet Russia, for it realizes that no salvation is to be expected from the Entente. Why don't the British, who keep 80,000 soldiers in Mesopotamia, in order to liberate the Arabs from their petroleum, who don't they send their troops to Armenia? A leading British newspaper, the *Manchester Guardian,* spoke frankly about this in an article published on May 12. It said that there is no petroleum in Armenia, nothing from which the Armenians can be 'liberated': it is impossible to rob the Armenians, so one can leave them to be robbed. And it said that if one compares the viewpoint of the British Government regarding Mesopotamian petroleum with the viewpoint of the Armenians regarding Armenian blood, then this comparison covers the British Government with shame and infamy. This is what was said by a British bourgeois newspaper — not a newspaper of the British workers in revolt, but one which, despite the weight of its criticism, is close to Lloyd George.[32]

How are the British capitalists liberating Persia since Russian Tsarism and Russian capitalism, despite all the efforts of the Allies, have been destroyed by the hands of the Russian workers and peasants? The British capitalists always said that their task in relation to Persia consisted solely in liberating that country. And Britain's present Foreign Minister, Lord Curzon, in his book on Persia published thirty years ago, said: the task of British policy in relation to Persia is to uphold the independence and freedom of Persia. The Anglo-Persian treaty of August last year shows the sort of freedom British capitalism wants to bring to Persia. For £2,000,000 in gold the British capitalist government has bought the whole of Persia from the Persian Government — that is, from its own lackeys. For these £2,500,000 [sic] in gold the British have secured control of Persia's finances and customs and of the organization of the Persian army. And regarding this policy I can again quote a very authoritative testimony, that of the French Government newspaper Le Temps of August 17 last year, which said: 'Since the Persian Government has handed over its army command by British officers, and its finances to control by British specialists, it has no longer any independent force or independent resources by which it could exercise sovereignty.' Those are the words of the French government's paper.[33]

Comrades, what does all this mean? It means no more and no less than that Entente capital, headed by France, having struck down its German competitor, the German brigand, has obtained control of the hundreds of millions who make up the peoples of the East, in order to enslave them. For the peasant in the East it means that, whereas previously he had to pay tribute in order to maintain the Sultan's clique and all manner of Shahs, Emirs and Khans, now he has to pay twice as much: to pay his own exploiters, and to pay for the bayonets of the French and British forces who will defend his exploitation by the local exploiters. This means that, whereas in Turkey there are natural resources by developing which the Turkish people might replace the wooden ploughs they use at present with iron ploughs and steam ploughs, and might have their own schools, now, when the British and French capitalists grab the riches of the Near East, the riches of Turkey and Persia, they will exploit these not in order to develop the culture of the Eastern peoples but for their own profit, so that the bankers of London and Paris may obtain even bigger profits than they enjoy already thanks to their exploitation of the European workers. [*Applause.*] Comrades, as a result of the victory of the Entente there is danger that hundreds of millions in the East may be reduced to absolute slavery. The dream is a dreadful one, but God is merciful. This danger will pass away like a bad dream if the toiling masses of the East rise up together with the workers of Europe, for the victors of the world war are themselves covered with wounds from which they are dying.

Comrades, if you look at the situation of victorious capital, if you look at the economic situation of the principal victors of this war, you will see that, in order to vanquish German capital, they have taken upon their shoulders and backs such huge burdens that under these burdens their spines too must crack. [*Applause.*] I have figures here showing the size of the state debts which the victorious countries have incurred. The French Government borrowed 200 milliard francs during the war. The British Government borrowed 160 milliard. The Italian Government borrowed 200 milliard. This means that all the victorious capitalist countries, with the exception of America, have lost in the war, by firing it off into the air, between a half and three-quarters of all the wealth belonging to these very rich countries. This means that none of these governments is able to find the resources to save itself from financial bankruptcy. If these governments wanted to pay their debts they would have to confiscate as much as two-thirds of the wealth that exists in their countries. That would mean leaving the mass of the people in those countries only one-third of what they had to live on previously. This it is not possible for them to do. And we see how the victorious powers are arguing amongst themselves how to get out of the difficulty. The weakest of the victor powers — the Italian and French Governments — are calling on the British and American capitalists to lump all these debts together and pay them jointly, so that whichever power is richest shall be the one to pay first and foremost. But the British and American capitalists decline to pay the debts of the Italian and French capitalists — they are unable to pay their own debts. The British and American capitalists were very willing to shed other people's blood, ordering the Russian peasants, the French peasants and the Italian workers to go and die in a war for the benefit of the British capitalists, but when the question of paying debts arises, they now say: friendship is friendship, but a ledger is something different, so pay your own debts. [*Applause.*] And we see, comrades, how, thanks to the fact that the victorious capitalists are trying to crush Russia, which until now was a principal outlet for their goods and supplied them with an enormous quantity of raw material, and thanks to the fact that they are trying to destroy the technically most advanced nation in Europe, namely, Germany, they are tearing up the roots of their own existence. We know that the British and American capitalists are confronted with the fact that the Eastern peoples, in their millions, are hungry for goods of all kinds, are hungry for manufactures and for machines, and the British and American capitalists are looking for markets, but they are not in a position to sell because these peoples have nothing with which to pay for the goods. As a result, the whole of world imperialism is choking in the process of a tremendous crisis, gripped by frightful convulsions. At the same time as hundreds of millions of people are unable to buy trousers and boots, in America and Britain products are piling up, and America and Britain are threatened with the closing of their factories.

And the worker masses, who see all this happening, the worker masses, whom they hounded to the slaughter during four years, telling them: in this war you are destroying the absolutism of the Kaiser and the Sultan of Turkey, and you will gain from it justice, bread and freedom — the masses of the people now see themselves faced with the threat of hunger and cold. These masses are rising in revolt and advancing their demands. And never in its long history has Britain seen such a huge wave of strikes and mighty workers' demonstrations as we are now witnessing. None other than the British Prime Minister, the shrewdest of bourgeois politicians, Lloyd George, in a speech he made in April in the British Parliament, frankly declared that Britain faces the threat of social revolution. This is not a statement made by the British Communists, whose hearts long for such a revolution. It is a warning from the British Prime Minister, who in this warning of his called upon the bourgeoisie to unite against the workers. In America we also see a wave of strikes. In Italy, in one of the Allied countries, we see not only a mounting struggle — we see Italy literally on the threshold of revolution. The Italian Government maintains itself only by the power of its bayonets; it is having every day to shoot down workers in the streets of its cities. Monsieur Clemenceau said, after the victory over German absolutism, that Bolshevism was not a danger to France, because she had emerged victorious from the war, and Bolshevism was a disease affecting defeated peoples only. Yet now we see the French Government filling its prisons with French Communists. We see the French Government shooting its sailors so as by the fear of death to hold back its armed forces from mutiny and revolution. And at this time, when the proletarians of Europe and America are rising in revolt to overthrow capitalism and to establish the reign of freedom, brotherhood and labour, at this same time, comrades, we see how, under the nose of British imperialism, in Ireland, in Egypt and in India, there is a growing movement of revolutionary struggle of the peoples whom Britain has enslaved.

Comrades, Ireland is a conquered country. In Ireland the British Government has been obliged to set up a fortress against the Irish people. In Ireland dozens of British policemen and soldiers of the expeditionary force are killed every day in the streets of the cities. In Egypt not only professional intellectual workers, not only students, not only civil servants are taking to the streets — the demonstrations have led to strikes by the fellahin whom the British used as beasts of burden during the war, and to strikes by railway workers and telegraph workers. And India is seeing not only a terrorist struggle, not only tremendous agitation among the intelligentsia, but also tremendous strikes involving 300,000 men, strikes of Indian workers who unite the struggle for their emancipation from the yoke of capital with the struggle for their national emancipation.

Comrades, in a book which is a sort of Koran for British imperialism, a book by Professor Seeley which was published many years ago, and which is used in the education of British officers when they are sent to India, and used to educate British Governors[34] — in this book, Seeley, a learned advocate of British imperialism, discusses the question: How is it that a little handful of British are able to keep under their heel hundreds of millions of Indians? And he answers that there is no magic in this. In India one part of the population fights against another on behalf of the rule of British capital. If a revolt breaks out in the North, we mobilize the Indian peasants in the South, make soldiers of them, and with their aid suppress the revolt in the North. If the Indians in the West revolt, we throw in Indians from the

East, and thus, by using some Indians against others, we keep them all under our control. And when, this advocate of British imperialism goes on, people tell us that there is bound to be a revolution, for the Indians are dying of hunger, I reply: that is quite unconvincing. 'If they cannot live, they die', but it does not follow from this that there will be a revolution. Everyone in Britain has freedom to die of hunger, and if people do not want to do this, that does not mean that there will be a revolution.

For a revolution to take place it is necessary, he says, that the people 'look up', that they have hope of liberation, and that they feel their strength. Comrades, we are sure that the moment is coming when the peoples of the East will prove to the British capitalists, the British vampires, that they do not want to die, that they have hope, and that they feel their strength. Comrades, until now every people which revolted has felt its weakness, for nobody had yet seen workers and peasants conquering their exploiters, nobody had seen workers and peasants setting their foot on the chest of British imperialism. But you, comrades, have seen that it is possible to conquer even British imperialism.

When the workers and peasants of Russia rose up, when they overthrew the power of the Tsar, overthrew the power of the bourgeoisie and landlords, and established a workers' and peasants' government, the bourgeois in all countries were sure that they would be able to crush Soviet Russia and place their yoke once more on the neck of the Russian workers and peasants. They set about hiring Russian officers, capitalists and landlords, they sent them uniforms, ammunition and military instructors, and launched one campaign after another against Soviet Russia. You remember how they bought the deceived Czechoslovak soldiers and hurled 50,000 of them against Soviet Russia. You remember how they sent against Soviet Russia Kaledin and Kornilov, and then Kolchak, Yudenich and Denikin. With the help of British tanks, gas-bombs and shells, Denikin and Kolchak formed an army half-a-million strong and waged a campaign against Soviet Russia. All capitalist Europe had its eyes on Kolchak and helped him with all its power. Russia was cut off, it was unable to get a single shell from abroad, it could not even get medical supplies with which to care for its maimed sons. In spite of all this, the workers and peasants of Russia rose up, arms in hand, and created the victorious Red Army. [*Applause.*] They smashed Yudenich, Kolchak and Denikin. I remember the day when, in a German prison in Berlin, I read in a newspaper: 'Tomorrow, Tuesday, in the chapel of the former Russian Embassy, there will be a solemn service of prayer for General Yudenich, who has set out for Petrograd.' But Yudenich was beaten before Petrograd, and Denikin was beaten before Orel. The workers' and peasants' army drove them back. Now Kolchak, Denikin, Yudenich are all gone. And now the workers' and peasants' power is finishing its business with the last of these detachments — with Wrangel and with White Poland. And in all this it has given a tremendous example to the peoples of the East who are rising in revolt.

If the workers and peasants of the East want to be free from exploitation, they too can win victory, because their adversary is cracking up, is suffering economic collapse, and because their adversary has been beaten by the Red workers' and peasants' Soviet Russia. Victory for the workers and peasants of the Near East depends only upon their own consciousness and will. No enemy will daunt you, no-one will hold back the flood of the workers and peasants of Persia, Turkey and India, if they unite with Soviet Russia. Soviet Russia was surrounded by enemies, but now it can produce weapons with which not only to arm its own workers and peasants but also to arm the peasants of India, Persia and Anatolia, all the oppressed, and lead them to a common struggle and a common victory. [*Applause.*]

When the capitalists came to the East to exploit the masses, they talked to them about 'liberation', and so we understand why there is a certain distrust among the backward sections of the workers and peasants, who have learnt from harsh experience of deception. They ask themselves: Are the precepts of Soviet Russia sincere, will it carry out its promises? Comrades, it is useless to answer such questions with protestations, they have to be answered with rational arguments. Soviet Russia arose in order that there might be no more slaves and masters, no more rich and poor. Soviet Russia is a huge, well-endowed country, which can feed itself, now that it has thrown out the lice, parasites and vampires that sucked the blood of Russian peasants and workers. It can with its own forces raise the Russian people to a height never before known. The Russian peasant and the Russian workers do not need to seek bread in other lands, for their own produces enough of it,[35] they do not need to go in search of metals, for in the depths of their own land there is an unheard-of treasure-house of these. The Russian worker and peasant are moved by desire for freedom for themselves, and have no need to enslave other peoples.

The Russian worker and peasant know very well that either they will crush world capital or world capital will crush them, that it is impossible for workers' and peasants' Soviet Russia to exist for a long time side by side with the capitalist countries. The Russian workers and peasants know that if they do not strike down the British capitalists, if they do not crush the French capitalists, then they themselves will be crushed. The Russian worker can seek peace and concord with them for a time, he can try to obtain a breathing space in which the revolution will grow stronger in other countries, but permanent peace between the country of labour and the countries of exploitation is impossible.

And for this reason the Eastern policy of the Soviet Government is no diplomatic manoeuvre, no pushing of the peoples of the East into the firing line so that the Russian Soviet Republic may gain some advantage by betraying them. We sacrificed our own territory, our own peasants and workers when, at Brest-Litovsk, German imperialism, armed from head to foot, dictated its terms to us and we were then unable to defend ourselves. Workers and peasants of the East, moments may come when we shall advise you not to go forward to utter defeat but instead to throw a sop to the wild beast that seeks to tear you in pieces. We ourselves may experience such moments, but we are bound to you by destiny: either we unite with the peoples of the East and hasten the victory of the West-European proletariat, or we shall perish and you will be slaves. Therefore, comrades, what is at issue here is not an alliance such as people conclude who may tomorrow break with each other and become enemies, but a fight fought in common and to the death. Yesterday you swore an oath to fight that fight. With our combined efforts we must win. Comrades, for this common victory common sacrifices are needed. The worker masses of Russia have been starving for three years, waiting for victory over world capital. And so, when you greet the Red Army, when you hail its victory, do you think about the fact that its victory and its weapons were forged by the blood and sweat of millions of Russian workers and peasants who sacrificed themselves in these last years? Understand that your own victory will not be won without sacrifices. Many will have to go hungry, or to shed their blood. You will have to look upon Soviet Russia and upon your countries in revolt as forming a single army which must strengthen themselves together, arm themselves together, make sacrifices together, for their common cause. And whoever says that this is

Bolshevik 'imperialism', that we are going to the East for purposes of conquest and to get food for our army, is consciously spreading lies between the workers and peasants, so as to divide them, in order that the lords of the world may crush them separately. For us it is a matter of common sacrifices, common burdens, and the victory will be common to us all. This will not be a victory of one people over another but the victory of the labouring masses of all peoples over the handful who have hitherto exploited the whole world.

Comrades, in issuing the call for a holy war against the Entente, and in the first place against British capital, we know that victory will not be ours today, that we shall have to go on fighting for a long time yet, precisely because the masses of the East will be slow in developing. News of the victories of the Red Army, of the struggle of the British, French and Italian proletariat must wander for a long time over plains and desert hills before it reaches the peasant in India and Egypt, and brings him its message: Stand up, rise, working people! In entering upon this hard struggle, we strive to enable these huge countries, these peoples, to develop their forces, develop their capacity for combined work to reconstruct mankind on a new basis of freedom, where there will not be people of different-coloured skins with different rights and duties, where all men will share the same rights and duties. The capitalists of the whole world talk of the menace from the East, saying that when 300 million Indian and 400 million Chinese peasants revolt, that will be the moment of doom for human civilization. We have seen that civilization, seen it in the glare of bursts of shrapnel over battlefields, in ruined homes and cities. Capitalist civilization means death to every kind of civilization. Capitalism is unable to ensure for you even the lot of an animal that is at least fed. The sooner that that civilization perishes, the better. [*Applause.*] And when we, comrades, hand to you the banner of struggle in common against a common enemy, we know very well that, together with you, we shall create a civilization a hundred times better than the one created by the slave-owners of the West. The East, subjected to oppression by capitalists and property-owners, has developed a philosophy of resignation. We appeal, comrades, to the warlike feelings which once inspired the peoples of the East when these peoples, led by their great conquerors, advanced upon Europe. We know, comrades, that our enemies will say that we are appealing to the memory of Genghis-Khan and to the memory of the great conquering Caliphs of Islam. But we are convinced that yesterday you drew your

daggers and your revolvers not for aims of conquest, not to turn
Europe into a graveyard — you lifted them in order, together with the
workers of the whole world, to create a new civilization, that of the
free worker. And so, when the capitalists of Europe say that a new
wave of barbarism threatens, a new horde of Huns, we answer them:
Long live the Red East, which together with the workers of Europe
will create a new civilization under the banner of Communism!
[*Tumultuous applause.*]

Chairman: We shall proceed to the translations. The first will be into
Turkic. Comrade Buniat-Zade will give it.

[*A five minute interval is announced. The session resumes at 8.40 p.m.*]

Narimanov: The session will continue. Let the translations be given.

[*Interpreters translate into Turkic, Uzbek and Chechen. Kartmyzov translates into Kumyk, and, from the Communist fraction, Buniat Zade, speaks
in Turkic.*]

Chairman: Please be seated.

Voices: 'Comrade Chairman, please let us have a translation into
Uzbek.'

[*The Chairman speaks in Uzbek.*]

Voices: 'We have understood. Please continue.'

Chairman: Will the Uzbek comrades who understood please raise
their hands.

Voices: 'A majority. A minority. Please go on. Call an interpreter.' [*An
interpreter translates into Uzbek. Artmasov* [36] *speaks in Turkic.*]

Chairman: Comrades, the Communist and non-Party fractions propose that a general discussion be opened on the two reports we have
heard. But, so that the discussion shall not take up too much time, we
need to decide straight away that only six speakers be called, and, in
addition, that the representatives of the Parties of Britain, France,
Bulgaria and America and a few others be given the opportunity to
speak on these reports, so that we hear not only from the peoples of the
East but also from the workers of the countries whose bourgeoisies
oppress the peoples of the East: We put this proposal to you and hope
that the Congress will give its approval. [*Applause.*]

[*Buniat-Zade speaks in Turkic. The interpreters translate.*]

Chairman: I call on Comrade Buniat-Zade, from the Communist fraction.

Then *Narimanov* also speaks in Turkic.

Chairman: Comrade Musa-Zade will give the translation.

Musa-Zade: Comrade Buniat-Zade says, regarding Comrade Radek's report, that the East has for a very long time been an apple of discord between the imperialists of the West, and in order to get control of the East and to exploit it the predators of Europe have applied themselves to forming a comprehensive alliance. This was the basis on which the Triple Entente and the Triple Alliance were formed, for these groupings both had the same aspiration to become masters of the East, to exploit the peoples of the East for the benefit of their robber members. A result of this alliance, or of this Triple Entente, was the Italo-Turkish War, which was promoted by Britain.[37] The unprovoked attack by Italy upon Karakalise was prepared by the British Cabinet. Hardly had this war in Tripolitania ended that Russia promoted and formed an alliance between the Balkan States and started a new war in the Balkans with the same aim as before, to get control of the Turkish Straits. Furthermore, the Triple Alliance and the Triple Entente sent their troops for the same purpose into unfortunate old Persia, where they pursued the same aim of subjecting and exploiting the country.

After the Russian Revolution of 1905 the revolution made its way into Persia. The oppressed peoples rose up, as the Russian workers had done, proclaimed Soviet power (*'Gandzhamina'*), but the defeat of the Russian revolution entailed the burial of the Persian revolution as well, by the hand of General Lyakhov and the other generals sent by Nicholas into Persia. The Persian revolution was crushed as well as the Russian.

Comrade Buniat-Zade described vividly how the first Persian revolutionaries, expelled from their country by the Persian tyrant Mahomet Ali Shah, were executed here. With the aim of partitioning the unfortunate, benighted East, tireless activity was carried on by the Western powers and the plunderers of the West. At the same time as war was being waged in Tripoli and in the Balkans, France was pushing into Morocco and strangling that unfortunate independent Eastern state. These aggressive strivings and actions were, of course, activities of the Triple Entente, which could not be watched with indifference by the Triple Alliance — the German group. At the same time unprecedented intrigue, aimed against the Entente, was being carried on by the German group, in the countries of the East. And then came the international war of 1914, aimed at completely subjecting the East. It ended with the great Russian revolution. After the fall of the bourgeois republic of Kerensky, power in Russia passed into the hands of the proletarians, the peasants and workers. The peasants and workers of Russia, after taking power, addressed the peoples of the world, and especially the peoples of the East, and said: 'We have stopped the war, we extend the hand of brotherhood to you, and we urge you to stop the war that has been started against us.' Since then the Russian workers and peasants have directed their attention towards the East. In concluding his speech, the comrade said that this Eastern orientation has now been crowned with success, and the risen East is today going forward hand in hand with the Russian proletariat, with combined forces, and will put an end to all the outrages which have been committed up to now. [*Uproar. Voices:* 'The translations are incomplete, we want a full translation.']

Chairman: Comrade Efendiyev will now deal with those parts of the speech which were omitted by the first interpreter.

Efendiyev: Comrade Buniat-Zade spoke at length about the events which took place in 1917 in Caucasia, and this is what was mainly omitted in the translation given by the previous interpreter. Buniat-Zade said that the imperialists of Turkey, various Envers and suchlike, yielded to incitement by Germany, which looked upon Turkey and the East as a tasty morsel that it wanted to enjoy and treat itself to. This was already included in Bismarck's programme. In bringing about independence [*sic*] in the East, the Germans were guided by the well-known slogan: *Drang nach Osten.*

And so the Turkish forces, helped by German bayonets and with the aid of the German imperialists, conquered Azerbaidzhan, the richest part of Transcaucasia, with its resources of petroleum, that precious liquid which was what enticed the imperialists to come here. But in Caucasia there were groups and parties which understood this war in a different sense. They considered that Turkey, with Enver Pasha at its head, had come here in order to save the people, in order to deliver the Azerbaidzhanis from Russian imperialism, in order to bring to this territory a republic, self-determination, independence, and so on. Comrade Buniat-Zade said that this was not true, that it was a lie, because Turkey liberated Azerbaidzhan from one imperialism, Russian imperialism, and at the same time handed it over to another imperialism. This was a one-sided liberation, which, after driving out the British, sat itself in their place, in order to suck the lifeblood of these countries. This was a mistake, a delusion which is now passing. This intoxication is now passing, and the masses of Transcaucasia, of Azerbaidzhàn, are waking up and beginning to understand things better and more correctly. Now, when the Soviet forces, when the Communist Party has assumed the initiative in liberating Caucasia from these groups promoted by the Turkish and German imperialists, the masses have at once begun to find their bearings with regard to what has happened and to evaluate better what is happening. Today Soviet Azerbaidzhan has been freed from these groups, these parties, these puppets put up by Turkish and German imperialism, and it is now the threshold [*sic*] of Soviet policy in the East. Azerbaidzhan is bound to play a tremendous role in that respect.

Culturally and materially it is one of the best and richest countries in the East. All this while the masses are turning one-hundred-percent towards Soviet power, and the experience which the masses have had in the last few years has taught them something and is a political guarantee that these masses will in the future close ranks absolutely with the Communist Party, and adjust their political line to the line of the Soviets, and make every effort to ensure that Soviet power triumphs throughout the East.

Chairman: The second speaker will be Comrade Bahaeddin Shakir.

Interpreter [*rendering Comrade Shakir's (Turkish) speech into Russian*]: I begin without comments and give only the essentials. When the European war began, Turkey went to war with no intention of conquest. It entered the war of necessity, to defend itself. There was only one issue at stake for Turkey, namely: either to safeguard its freedom or to fall under the yoke of one of the coalitions, either the German or the British. Before joining in the war, the Turks thought for a long time. If they did not enter the war, then, when one of the contending sides proved victorious, that would mean the end of Turkey's freedom. Even earlier Turkey did not follow a policy of conquest and had no predatory aims.

In our country, in Turkey, the officers belong to a different category from the Russian or European officers. The Turkish officer is a genuine proletarian. He has not been brought up in the spirit in which officers in Europe and in Russia were brought up. The view that

Turkey had a plan worked out beforehand, and had already come to an understanding with Germany, is false.

The agrarian question in our country, in Anatolia, also has special features. It is a very simple question. There are no landlords there, no large landowners. Turkey has, in general, no powerful bourgeois class, and so neither the Turkish Government nor the Turkish people could pursue a merely aggressive policy. They had only one policy: 'Don't trouble us and we won't trouble you.'

Comrades, I prove this by the fact that when the war had continued for a long time, and the German coalition felt that it was winning, the Turkish people and the Turkish Government wanted to establish buffer states, that is to say, an Armenian, an Azerbaidzhani and a Georgian state. If it is said that Turkey was pursuing an aggressive policy, how can it be explained that the Turkish people and the Turkish Government held to this policy alone, that they wanted to protect themselves by establishing buffer states between Russia and Turkey? No, neither in the West nor in the East did Turkey intend to annex other people's lands, and, in general, Turkey did not pursue an aggressive policy.

That is what Comrade Shakir said in his long speech. I have translated the essence of it.

[*The same interpreter translates the speech into other languages.*]

Voice from the hall [*in Turkic*]: 'The comrade interpreter did not warn us that he was translating the speech of the previous speaker, it was as though he was expressing his own views.'

Narimanov: Yes, it was a translation. Where is the Persian interpreter?

[*An interpreter translates the speech into Persian.*]

Zinoviev: The next speaker will be Comrade Gaidarkhanov[38] from the Communist fraction.

[*Gaidarkhanov speaks in Turkic and translates his own speech into Persian.*]

An interpreter translates the speech into Russian: Comrades, first and foremost I call your attention to that part of the speeches by Comrades Zinoviev and Radek in which Comrade Zinoviev said that we have come here frankly and sincerely to extend our hands to our brothers in the East, and do not want to employ any diplomacy here. Comrade

Radek also said that we have come here to offer our hand, and if we die, we die along with you, and if we live we live along with you. This is of enormous importance for the peoples of the East, for the peoples of the East have not heard this for 200 years. All that time they saw and heard how European capital was slaughtering them. I want to give you a few examples of how European capital sought to stifle the liberation movement of the Eastern peoples. Let us take Persia. A revolution broke out there, and this revolution was put down by the European capitalists, headed by Tsarist Russia and British imperialism. India too, in the same way, with its 350 million inhabitants, and without even a penknife in its pocket, was also deprived of the ability to defend itself and continually exploited in an inhuman way by British capital. The Indians are dying of hunger, but the British capitalists are living in splendid palaces at their expense. I want to say the same thing about Turkey. A comrade spoke here saying that Turkey waged a defensive war, that Turkey was not a tool in the hands of German imperialism and had no imperialistic aspiration of its own. This does not square with the facts, comrades. Turkey had great imperialistic aspirations. It acted wholly as a tool in the hands of European imperialists. If Turkey had not involved itself in this war with imperialists who were striving for conquest, then at the present time the European imperialists would not be tearing to pieces the working peasantry of Turkey. Comrades, as you see, the East has already woken up, a revolution has broken out in Persia itself against Britain, just as a certain movement has begun in India, and also in Turkey.

Gathered here are representatives of these and other peoples who are hostile to British and every other kind of imperialism. I am sure that these peoples will reach agreement here and will organise a rebuff to the British and other imperialists and liberate the East from the yoke of the capitalists. [*Applause.*]

Chairman: We are now going to close the session, but first there is an announcement. Both fractions have agreed to set up four sections: on the agrarian question, on the national and colonial question, on the question of the Soviet structure, and on the organisational question. These four sections are to be made up as follows: each group of 20 delegates will choose one representative to join each section. This will mean approximately 90 members to a section. It would be desirable that the elections take place tomorrow, as the Congress will not be meeting then — there will be a parade.[39] The elections will have to

take place in the hostels, so that each hostel elects one representative
per 20 delegates. If there are any left over, they must be grouped. If
any have to be eliminated, the Presidium will see to that. So, then, we
ask you to ensure that, tomorrow, all these sections are completed.
[*Translation.*]

The session was closed at 12.02 a.m.

Third Session

September 4

The session opened at 12.13 p.m. Comrade Zinoviev took the chair.

Chairman: I declare the third session of the Congress of the Peoples of the East open. We will continue with discussion of the first two reports. I call on Comrade Narbutabekov.

Narbutabekov: Comrades, before making my speech I must warn you that, having only fifteen minutes . . . [*Voices:* 'Can't hear.']

Chairman: Please be quiet: the comrade is a bit hoarse.

Narbutabekov: My time is limited. In fifteen minutes it is, of course, impossible fully to describe the international situation of the working masses of the East. I shall be brief and I ask you to listen to me with attention and not to interrupt, as I have no voice left.

Comrade Zinoviev described the tasks before this Congress clearly and distinctly in his speech. I shall not touch on that. As far as the situation of the working masses in the East is concerned, that is a question of extraordinary importance not only for us, the peoples of the East, but also for the Soviet power itself, for any power which definitely sets itself the task of achieving certain aims among the many millions of the East, where there are so many languages and dialects (about 53),[40] needs to listen to the voice of these peoples, and our duty as delegates is to put certain demands to the Soviet power, precisely and clearly. We declare that our Moslem peoples and peoples of the East want no other power but the Soviet power. We have no choice. It is either the British capitalists or the working masses of Russia and the whole world. One of these two things must be, as Comrade Radek said: the Soviet power must either perish, and all become slaves, or it must conquer, and then we shall be free. In order that these words may be put into practice, we the peoples of the East must make it quite clear that there are two worlds: the world of the West and the world of the East.

You know that the West has, during the many centuries in its historical development, several times changed its form of state structure, from the most despotic forms to liberal-democratic republics, whereas in the East the form of the state structure has not altered. Russia is the first of the European states to have brought forward a new form of state structure, the form of Soviet power. Comrades, the world of the East and the world of the West are complete opposites in this respect. The East is in a special situation, in its psychological, cultural, economic and religious aspects as in its social forms and the forms of its everyday life, and these peculiarities have got to be reckoned with. Nicholas II and other plunderers of the working people never took account of these peculiarities. Our interests were always trampled on. In the first days of the revolution, when the Bolsheviks put forward the slogan of 'self-determination for the nationalities' in opposition to Kerensky's capitalist slogan of 'war to the victorious end', all 53 nations of the Russian state echoed it. This was one of the principal reasons why Kerensky's capitalist slogan failed. We, the peoples of the East, had faith in that slogan of 'self-determination for the nationalities', and to this day we have faith, faith in the ideological guides and leaders of the world proletariat — Comrades Lenin, Trotsky, Zinoviev and others; but at the same time we must say to the Congress that what we want is for the voice of the Moslem working people and the peoples of the East to be heard. If this voice is heard, the state power will find it easier to carry out its tasks and aims in implementing the great principles of the social revolution in the East.

We demand genuine realization of the principles of freedom, equality and brotherhood, in fact and not merely on paper. I am sure that if that were done, not a single Moslem would venture to raise his hand against the Soviet power. You all know, comrades, that in the East from time immemorial, beginning with Genghis-Khan and Timur and ending with the bloody Abdul Hamid, there has been no other form of government but despotism: in heaven there is Almighty God, and on earth the Sultan. The state structure has not altered as it has in the West. When the great Russian Revolution burst upon the world, we were utterly unprepared for it. We were unable immediately to adapt the entire mass of our habits and ways of living to the framework of Communism. It must be said that, apart from the Soviet power there is no other kind of power acceptable to the East, which can save the working masses of the peoples of the East from the hands of the capitalists. Everyone knows that the East is utterly different from the West, that its ideas are different — and so a rigid application of the ideas of Communism will meet with resistance there. Accordingly, if we want the four hundred millions in the Moslem world to join the Soviet power, we need to apply a special yardstick in their case. The declaration the non-Party comrades want to make is this, that the diverse interests and special features that exist in Caucasia and Turkestan and in all the former borderlands of the Russian state must be resolutely defended, and it is the duty of the Congress to stress them, to say to our government: Comrades, the Moslems will not abandon the Soviet power, but this is on condition that the peculiarities of the Eastern peoples be recognized, and the measures adopted by the Soviet power in this direction must be implemented not on paper but in fact. [*Applause.*]

Comrade Radek said that the Soviet power is accused by the West-European *Kulturträger*, the West European brigands, of carrying out a policy of Red imperialism. In order to refute this charge it is necessary that our comrades, the leaders of the Communist Party and the Soviet power, shall declare that this is not so and will not be so. We Turkestanis state that we have never before seen Comrade Zinoviev, or Comrade Radek, or the other leaders of the Revolution. They should come and see for themselves what is happening in Turkestan, what exactly is being done by the local authorities there, whose policy is such that it is antagonizing the working masses against the Soviet power. I regard it as my duty as a delegate to say this, because I am staunchly in favour of the platform of Soviet power.

I will be brief, for time is short. This congress is made up not of creatures of the bourgeoisie but of genuine representatives of the working masses, who must support the Soviet power. Whether you are a Chechen, a Daghestani, an Adzharian, a Kirghiz or a Kazakh, everyone at this Congress must clearly and definitely state to the Soviet power what our needs are, and say: 'Comrades, do not waver, go straight ahead along the road laid down by the working masses of the people, for there is no other road, no other way out. Even if the West European proletariat does not support the Soviet power it will be supported by the Moslems and the peoples of the East.'

For this reason I declare that the Soviet power can find no better ally at the present time than the working people of the East, for during the three years that our comrades, the best leaders of the world revolution, have been appealing to them, up to now the West European proletariat has shown no active support.

The well-known failure of the July 21 strike proved that the West European proletariat, owing to the conditions in which it carries on its political life, cannot help;[41] therefore, without wasting time, it is necessary to organize the East in the proper way, in accordance with its religious and socio-economic conditions. There is no other road for the Soviet power to take. [*Applause*.]

We Turkestanis say that, from the moment of the October Revolution the toiling masses of Turkestan rallied to the Soviet power just like their Russian comrades. Shedding our blood on the Turkestan fronts against the enemies of the Soviet power, we bound up our lives closely with the toiling masses of all Russia, and the accusations of chauvinist tendencies brought against Turkestani activists must be rejected, for our workers have proved the contrary with their blood.

During three years the working people of Turkestan have acquitted themselves with honour in this struggle. But what was needed to ensure this? Very little. Only the paying of close attention to the life of the Eastern peoples and the application of those principles which delegates have advocated. There is no question of counter-revolution here, any more than of chauvinism, for we, the representatives of our working people, have suppressed our narrow nationalistic tendencies; and we, the first revolutionaries of Turkestan, have no fear of any *ulemas*, of any Black Hundreds of the mullahs. We were the first to raise the standard against them [*applause*] and we shall not lower that standard, to the very end: we shall either perish or conquer. I tell you, comrades, our Turkestani masses have to fight on two fronts. On the one hand against the reactionary mullahs in our own midst, and on the other against the narrow nationalist inclinations of the local Europeans. Neither Comrade Zinoviev, nor Comrade Lenin, nor Comrade Trotsky knows the real situation, knows what has been going on in Turkestan these last three years. We must speak out frankly and draw a true picture of the state of affairs in Turkestan, and then the eyes of our leaders will be opened. They will come to Turkestan and set things right.[42]

I throw this out to all, both the non-Party and the Party comrades from Turkestan.

So that what has happened in Turkestan shall not be repeated in other parts of the Moslem world, I warn our government that we know all the shortcomings of the policy which has been pursued in these three years, and we say: Remove your counter-revolutionaries, remove your alien elements who spread national discord, remove your colonizers who are now working behind the mask of Communism! [*Tumultuous applause, cries of* 'Bravo'.]

Comrades, I will not say much, but will confine myself to recalling the sacred words of the world's leader Comrade Lenin, when he said that he is on his own and we must help him in every possible way.

You have his famous words before you and you keep them in your heart — and after these words nobody can say that the Soviet power wishes us ill. It may be that among its representatives there are provocateurs and demagogues, but these must be ruthlessly destroyed, just like counter-revolutionaries.

We are not afraid of open counter-revolutionaries, we have encountered them on the war fronts. But, comrades, there are among us persons who, behind the mask of Communism, are bringing ruin upon the Soviet power as a whole, spoiling the entire Soviet policy in the East, and we must declare, fearlessly: Down with these provocateurs and demagogues who corrupt the fundamental idea of Soviet power! [*Tumultuous applause, shouts of:* 'Down with them!']

Now, after what I have said I must go on to say the following. The theoretical position of the Soviet power in relation to the East was set out with the greatest clarity in the appeal to all the toiling Moslems of Russia and the East. The Council of People's Commissars issued in November 1917, over Comrade Lenin's signature, a special appeal to all the toiling Moslems of Russia and the Easy. In this historic appeal, besides the statement that the treaty which provided for partitioning Turkey and taking Armenia away from her had been torn up and annulled, and that Constantinople must remain in the hands of the Moslems, the following appeared: 'Henceforward your beliefs and customs, your national and cultural institutions are declared free and inviolable. Build your national life freely and without hindrance. It is your right. You yourselves must be masters in your own country. You yourselves must build your lives in your image and likeness.'

After these words, is it conceivable that we should turn our backs on the Soviet power?

But now, as we travel about, Moslems come up to us and say that our beliefs are being trampled on, that we are not allowed to pray, not allowed to bury our dead in accordance with our customs and religion. What is this? It is nothing but a sowing of counter-revolution among the toiling masses.

It may be that the same thing is happening in other places too, but I declare, in the name of the non-Party delegates, and perhaps the Communists also will join in this, that with the remarkable congress we are holding today our Soviet power should introduce a definite policy in relation to the East. Then the Eastern peoples will rally to the Soviet power not only on paper but in arms, and then no power in the world will be able to resist the pressure of the many-millioned masses of the peoples of the East, together with the proletariat and peasantry of Russia.

Long live the oppressed East!

Long live those real Communists who, without reservation, want to put these principles into practice!

Long live our leaders, the leaders of the world proletariat — Comrades Lenin, Trotsky, Zinoviev and the others.

[*Tadzhayev translates into Turkic and other interpreters translate into Turkish, Persian and Chechen.*]

Korkmasov: Comrades, I am taking the floor to join in the discussion and will have to speak in Russian and then translate my own words into Kumyk, so that to translate another speaker now into Kumyk is, owing to my state of health, too much for me. I ask Comrade Aliyev to take my place.

[*An interpreter translates into Kumyk.*]

Chairman: The last of the speakers on the list, Comrade Korkmasov, will now address us.

Korkmasov: Comrades, the fervent, inspiring call with which Comrade Zinoviev summoned us to struggle against world imperialism aroused in the hearts of all members of the Congress the feelings which already earlier filled the hearts of the Highland poor.[43] When they drew their sabres and daggers, only lately wiped clean of Volunteers' blood, the Highland poor showed that today as always they are ready to follow their great leaders in order to join in the bloody decisive, final battle with the brigands and scoundrels of world imperialism for the sake of the emancipation of the oppressed peoples of West and East. [*Tumultuous applause.*]

Comrades, what speeches can be made, what discussion can take place after this decisive demonstration you have given? It would be incomprehensible and alien to the Highland poor.

Assembled in their own congress a month ago, the Highland poor, and even the *ulemas*,[44] issued a call for a *ghazavat*, a holy war, against all the oppressors of the East: not to lay down our arms until the enemy of all the poor of the world and the working people of all nations has perished! [*Applause.*]

The Highland poor do not need any words. From the beginning of the great social revolution they have waged a ceaseless struggle not only against the internal counter-revolutionaries — the Imam, the Highland Government, but also against the external ones — the Turks, the British and the hirelings of the latter, Bicherakov's[45] and Denikin's men. And, naturally, comrades, after experiencing all this incredibly hard struggle, the Highland poor cannot utter any equivocal words here or lodge any complaints.

But let me tell you, comrades, in a few words, what has happened in these three years, so that these facts from the life of our region, from the life of the working masses of the North Caucasus, may form a living bridge between East and West, illustrating the great truths that have been expressed here regarding international politics and the struggle against international imperialism, by our comrades Zinoviev and Radek.

Thanks to their self-sacrificing struggle, comrades, after a struggle such as not a single revolution, not a single people has known, the Russian workers and peasants won freedom and they presented this freedom, as though on a plate, to the peoples of the East.

And what happened? It turned out that the ruling classes — the princes, the Khans, the Beys, the rich, the mullahs — thought they would erect a wall between the great social revolution and the harassed Highland poor. Then these parasites, thanks to the intrigues of the Turkish imperialists and the British, brought on to the scene an idol, the Imam, as a religious weapon with which to oppress the toiling masses.

What a farce! After the great Shamil, who defended the Highland poor against the Khans, the agents of the autocracy,[46] Najmuddin Gotsinsky, a common criminal who was put in prison even by the Tsarist Government, was raised to the dignity of Imam. How did the Highland poor react to this farce, did they stand for it? No, the Highland poor launched a civil war. None of the efforts of the Pan-

Islamists and the Pan-Turkists and none of the attempts made by the British and the agents of Nicholas was successful, however. After less than a year had passed, the Imam was overthrown even by those who had particularly supported him: he was nicknamed 'not Imam but Ivan'.[47] The poor of Daghestan, led by their own socialists, having linked up with the Red forces, proclaimed Soviet power in Daghestan. It is hard to convey to you the joy that was felt by the working people. This power is our own, the power of the poor, they said. After this, is it possible for us to utter words such as those that were uttered here just now? Such complaints are alien to our poor.

Comrades, nevertheless, sustained by the counter-revolution which was raging in Russia, the Highland princes, generals and landlords, having been beaten in the mountains in their gamble on the Imamate, and knowing that there was strong sympathy with the Turkish people among the masses, turned their gaze towards that Turkey where various Pashas, Beys and so on ruled, sitting on the backs of the working people. Would they help in crushing the Highland poor? Turks did actually come in. I am very sorry not to see here a leader who was very active in organizing the counter-revolution in the mountains — Enver Pasha, who in the palace of the old Sultans, forgetting the ideals of the original Young Turks, organized along with Chervomoyev,[48] Kotsov and other generals of Nicholas II a counter-revolution to crush the Soviet power. [Applause.]

Turks appeared — and what did they do? The Young Turks Yusuf Izet Pasha, Nuri Pasha and various other Pasha-mashas and Beys, who ought to have won victories on various fronts of the imperialist wars dear to their hearts, but did not, turned up in Daghestan in order to establish a front against the working people and, thanks to help from Bicherakov's Cossacks and officers of Nicholas's army, they were able for a time to subvert Soviet power in Daghestan.

But what did they give to the poor of Daghestan instead of that power? The one-man dictatorship of Prince Tarkovsky.[49] That was how the ideology of the Young Turks had developed at the great moment of the social revolution. They found no other way of solving their problems. Around this counter-revolutionary, around this traitor to his own people, all sorts of rascals subsequently gathered — Kotsovs, Chervomoyevs and suchlike — and proclaimed the mythical Highland Republic. But only a few months had passed when, after plundering the working people and selling the weapons left behind by the Turks, who had fled for home before a stronger imperialist, the

British imperialist, having nothing more left to plunder, this gang of adventurers handed over the Highland people to be victims of the Volunteer bands. That was how the wretched farce under the title of the 'Highland Government' was played out. The Volunteers, finding that the Turks and their creatures had not finished the job of crushing the Bolsheviks, and backed, on the other hand, by the British, launched a furious campaign against all adherents of the Soviet power, both particular individuals and whole communities. The Turks had arrested Bolsheviks and exacted contributions from Bolshevik settlements, but the Volunteers decided that they had not done enough, that counter-revolutionaries must do still more, and opened a real front against the Highland poor. This heroic struggle, which lasted nearly a year, is known to you, comrades: it has dyed Daghestan in the colour of its own blood, shed for the glorious Red flag. [*A storm of applause.*]

You also know, comrades, how the Highland poor in those same long months of struggle had to repulse Musavatist agents as well, and Turkish counter-revolutionaries who opened an internal front, in the person of Nuri Pasha, another counter-revolutionary, the brother of Enver Pasha. The struggle was a tragic one. Comrades, the Highlanders wanted to make their small contribution to helping the great Red Army, which was also there fighting the counter-revolution on the steppes of Russia. The struggle was crowned with victory. At the end of twelve months the Red Highland partisans had captured the towns of Temir-Khan-Shura, Derbent and Petrovsk, and greeted with red banners the first detachments of the great Red Army. And so, comrades, for the Highland poor there can be no talking about some detailed matters or other, some domestic affairs, such as the Turkestani comrade talked about, when what is at stake is the world revolution. What faces us is a great world war. We must say, and we do say, to the scoundrelly world imperialists of France, Britain and America that, even before the Congress of the Peoples of the East, before the call issued by our leaders, we began a *ghazavat*, a holy war, against you, and tomorrow we shall go into action against you, arms in hand! [*Tumultuous applause.*] And so, comrades, let me end with the call:

Long live the oppressed peoples of the East!

Long live the oppressed working masses of the West!

Long live their alliance under the red banner of the Third International! [*Shouts and applause.*]

Long live their fraternal alliance under the guidance of our great leaders, Comrades Lenin, Trotsky and Zinoviev, to smash the enemy, world imperialism and capitalism! [*Applause.*]

[*Korkmasov translates his own speech into Kumyk.*]

Chairman: Please pay attention, a Turkic translation will now be given. [*Voice:* 'The Turkic speakers understood — only a Persian translation is needed.']

Chairman: The point is that the previous speech was translated into Turkic but delegates told us that they didn't understand, and so they asked that this speech be translated into Turkic, so we shall have a translation. Please pay attention.[50]

[*Buniat-Zade translates the speech into Turkic.*]

Zinoviev: Comrades, I have to announce that we need to complete the elections to the sections. Far from all the hostels have carried out these elections, and this must be done without delay. The next session will begin at 6 p.m. And now we shall break for lunch. [*Translation.*]

The session was closed at 3 p.m.

Fourth Session

September 4

The session opened at 8 p.m. Comrade Zinoviev took the chair.

Chairman: I declare the fourth session of the Congress of the Peoples of the East open.

Before proceeding to our ordinary business I wish to inform you of a decision which has just been taken by the Presidium of our Congress. The Presidium has discussed the question of the time during which the congress should carry on its work, so that we may conclude this work according to a definite plan. The Presidium has arrived at the view that our work should be finished by the 9th of this month, so that we have five days and nights at our disposal. In order that our work may be completed within this period, the Presidium finds it necessary to take some steps to cut our discussions short and has therefore decided, in the first place, to reduce the number of guest-speakers. We should, of course, be very pleased if all the foreign comrades who have come here could address us, but, unfortunately, the Congress has not time enough to hear all of them. Accordingly, we shall call on the British and French comrades only, while the speeches of the representatives of America, the Balkans, Spain, Holland, Austria, Japan and other countries will be printed in the newspapers and included in the report of our Congress.[51] Further, the Presidium proposes that speeches be translated only into the three official languages: Russian, Azerbaidzhani-Turkish,[52] and Persian. Next, the Presidium requests the comrade delegates who do not understand any of these languages to do as we did in Moscow at the Congress of the Communist International: let the comrades who do not understand the speaker's language sit

69

together and try to arrange to have among them a comrade who does understand the language in question and can explain to them what is being said. In case of necessity, while a translation into one of the official languages is being given in the hall, they can give their translations either in the corridors or out in the street. This is awkward, of course, but it would be even more awkward to drag the Congress out interminably. Today only two speakers have spoken, for fifteen minutes each, while the rest of the time has been spent in giving translations, and an entire session has been spent like that. In addition, the Presidium has decided that the comrade interpreters shall abridge when they translate, conveying what was said in such a way that the translation takes only a quarter of the time taken by the speech itself. Hitherto matters have proceeded differently: the interpreter's speech has taken a great deal longer than the original. We consider that at such a huge Congress as this we must proceed more economically. I call on the interpreters to translate. [*Translation.*]

Comrades, the Presidium has one other announcement to make. It proposes that the Congress agree to select from among the members of the Presidium two comrades to act as chairman: for its part, the Presidium proposes that these comrades be Narbutabekov and Narimanov. Then, the Presidium requests the Congress to confirm the appointment of two women as representatives of the women delegates to the Congress.

In order to speed up the proceedings, the Presidium has decided that plenary sessions of the Congress shall take place each day, starting at five o'clock, these plenums to continue until 11; and then, from 11 to 2, meetings either of the sections or of the fractions. Finally, I want to inform you of a rule proposed by the Presidium. A rapporteur will be allowed one hour and a co-rapporteur 30 minutes. For a concluding speech fifteen minutes, and for speeches other than those of the rapporteurs, 10 minutes. Speakers will not be allowed to speak more than twice. One will be called upon to speak 'for', and another to speak 'against'. A rapporteur will reply at once to all questions which have been handed in. Opportunity for personal questions will be given at the end of the session. Questions will be called upon only on receipt of written requests. Statements will be submitted in writing. [*Translation.*]

Chairman: Comrades, in view of the fact that all these proposals have been adopted unanimously by the Presidium, I allow myself to ask the

Congress to confirm them. Will anyone who is against the Presidium's proposals please raise his hand.

[*An interpreter translates into Turkic.*]

Chairman: Those in favour of confirming the Presidium's proposal, please raise your hands after the translation. [*Translation.*] Please put your hands down. Who is against? Nobody. Accepted unanimously. We shall proceed to next business. First of all, I call upon the delegate from the United Communist Party of Great Britain, Comrade Quelch.

[*Quelch speaks in English.*]

Chairman: The Russian translation will be given by Comrade Petrov.

Petrov: Comrade Quelch began his speech with a quotation from Marx. Karl Marx said that the British working class would be free only when the peoples of the British colonies were free. That is why he is here, representing the British Communist Party, because that Party recognizes that the truth of what Karl Marx said is beyond any doubt.

Comrade Quelch says that the enemy of the British working class, the British capitalist class, is at the same time the enemy of the peoples of the East, the oppressed East.

Therefore, the struggle of the British working class against British capitalism is at the same time your struggle, the struggle of the oppressed peoples of the East.

British imperialism is today oppressing and plundering hundreds of millions of people in Ireland, India and other countries. In Ireland at present there is a serious situation, a decisive struggle is taking place. The Irish people are fighting for their independence. In spite of the presence in Ireland of a huge number of British soldiers, the Irish people are fighting heroically and successfully for their independence. The same thing is happening, says Comrade Quelch, in India, which has been oppressed for centuries by British capitalism: to this day the British capitalists are sucking all the wealth out of wretched, starving India.

Moreover, so as to safeguard its rule in India, British imperialism is seizing Central Asia, extending its rule over the whole of Asia.[53] British imperialism, says Comrade Quelch, is like a monster which can never be satiated. It is greedy, and grabs more and more territory, and oppresses the people who live there.

The British working class knows this, and has at its own congresses frequently protested against this policy of British imperialism. The organized workers of Britain have demanded and are demanding at their congresses that the right of self-determination be accorded to all peoples and nationalities. [*Applause.*] They are striving for complete liberation for all the peoples who are today oppressed by British imperialism. Comrade Quelch continues: recognizing that the struggle of the British working class is directed against those who are your enemies too, that is, against British imperialism, the British Communist Party has sent a representative to Russia and to the Congress. But the moment will soon be here when the representatives of the British proletariat will be able to render more serious help in our struggle for liberation from British imperialism.

British imperialism costs the British proletariat very dear. The frontiers of the British empire are strewn with the bones of British workers killed for the glory of British imperialism.

The RSFSR stands at the head of all the workers and oppressed peoples and wages a decisive struggle for the complete liberation of mankind.

It is therefore natural that British, French, German and Austrian workers, and workers in other countries, are rallying in even greater numbers under the banner of the RSFSR, under the banner of Communism.

At the present time, Soviet Russia is negotiating with the British capitalist government, but the British workers know that these negotiations, and the temporary peace which the Russian Republic is trying to obtain, are only intended to win new positions for the continuance of this struggle. The workers of Britain and the other countries of Western Europe have complete confidence in the Russian Soviet Republic and support it in all the steps it takes, in its entire policy.

This great Congress, says Comrade Quelch, shows that you too, the peoples of the East, are marching behind the Russian Soviet Republic in its struggle for the liberation of mankind. He says that in Britain the working class is getting ready to take political power, that in Britain the social revolution is imminent [*Applause*], and he is sure that the peoples of the East will go forward together with the revolutionary proletariat under the banner of the Communist International right up to complete victory and the destruction of the old world, in order to create a new world of freedom and happiness for mankind.

He ended his speech with these slogans: Down with international imperialism, long live the Russian Soviet Republic! Long live the World Soviet Republic! Long live the International! [*Applause.*]

[*Translations into Turkic and Persian.*]

Chairman: The next speaker will be the representative of the French workers, the delegate of the Paris Committee of the Third International, Comrade Rosmer. [*Applause.*]

[*Rosmer speaks in French.*]

Chairman: I call on Comrade Pavlovich.

Pavlovich: I came to Russia, says Comrade Rosmer, to attend the Second Congress of the Communist International. I considered it my duty to come here, to Baku, to bring greetings from the workers and peasants of France to the oppressed peoples of the East.

When the world war began, the bourgeois press of all countries asserted that this world war would bring freedom to the oppressed nations, in opposition to barbarous Germany. But if that was so, says Rosmer, why did the great powers not begin by freeing the peoples they themselves oppressed? Why did Britain not give freedom to Ireland? Why did it keep the three hundred million people of India under its yoke? Why did France, which said it was fighting against German barbarism, oppress and hold down Morocco, Tunisia and Algeria and other Moslem countries?[54]

When the war ended, France and Britain tried to take back from these peoples even the miserable crumbs they had given them. When it was necessary to fight the Germans, when hundreds of thousands of Algerians, Tunisians and Moroccans had to be mobilized, they were promised various freedoms; but the very day after Germany had been defeated all these miserable freedoms were withdrawn, and when the representatives of Tunisia sent a delegation to France and pointed out that 45,000 Tunisians had fallen on the battlefield, and recalled the promises that had been made to them, these delegates were themselves put in prison, and those native newspapers which took the liberty of publishing the fact were closed down and confiscated.

That is how they behave in France, and in Britain too, that is how all the great powers treat the countries whose blood they made use of in order to defend themselves against German imperialism. But how are we to account for the fact that now, after the war, the European states are obliged to exploit the population of Africa and Asia as never before? This is very easy to explain. As a result of the war, bankruptcy and ruin, the productivity of labour has fallen, the French worker does not want to work for the capitalist as he used to, and it is impossible to force him to work. And so they have thought of a way: they want to squeeze the native population of Asia and Africa still harder, to turn them into slaves who will be forced to work not only for themselves but also for the French and British workers. The native world must understand the danger which threatens it. It must unite around Soviet Russia, that palladium of the independence of the peoples of the East, and raise the banner of revolt and holy war against the capitalist world.

Long live the Third International! [*Applause.*]

Chairman: Comrade Korkmasov will give a brief translation.

[*Korkmasov translates.*]

Chairman: The last speaker will be the representative of India, Comrade Fazli Kadyr.

[*Fazli Kadyr speaks in Farsi.*[55]]

Interpreter: Comrades, the representative of India greets the first Congress of the Peoples of the East and says that the Indian peoples who are languishing under the yoke of British capitalism look for help from you and from Soviet Russia, which carries forward the revolutionary banner of the world proletariat, and, he says, we have long looked forward to the Congress, looked forward to the day when all the peoples of the East would unite and free ourselves from world imperialism.

He ends his speech with: Long live the world revolution, long live the unity of all the peoples of the East!

Declaration by the Indian Revolutionary Organisation in Turkestan:
To the comrade delegates to the Second Congress of the Communist International, in Baku.

The Indian Revolutionary Organization in Turkestan asks, on behalf of the three hundred million oppressed people in India, that the delegates to this congress and the representatives of Soviet Russia gathered here with the aim of liberating mankind, may help India, which is in such great need of their help. All who are striving for liberation hope that this help will be given without any interference in the internal and religious life of those who await liberation from the yoke of capitalism and imperialism. All revolutionaries appeal for help to Russia in their struggle to put their national programmes into effect. In the Eastern Question as a whole, one important fact especially stands out, the importance of which cannot be denied, namely, that India, and India alone is the real cause of serious conflicts in this world. History has shown more than once that freedom for India means freedom for the world and an end to all wars. From the huge population of India the brutal British forcibly take men for their army in order to attack other nations.

The Indian Revolutionary Organization is in a position to prove this fact, and to do this before the First Congress of the Peoples of the East in Baku. The organization asks that the Congress give it as soon as possible the very great help which India so much needs.

Chairman of the Indian Revolutionary Organization,
Mahomed Abdur Rabe Berk
Tashkent, August 10, 1920

Chairman: In conclusion Comrade Shablin will give a brief statement on behalf of the Communist Party of the Balkans.[56]

Shablin: Comrades, on behalf of the Balkan Communist Federation, to which belong the Bulgarian, Yugoslav, Greek and Romanian Communist Parties, I am authorized to say to you, delegates of the peoples of the East, that we, the Balkan peoples, are also oppressed and enslaved by the world bandits of Britain and France, just like you, that your struggle means our liberation as well.

The victorious Russian revolution, which is becoming a world revolution, shows us the path of the great struggle for liberation, once and for all, from exploitation of man by man.

Against the united front of the imperialist oppressors we bring forward the united front of the oppressed and enslaved peoples of the whole world.

Long live great proletarian solidarity!

Long live the liberation of the East!

Long live the alliance of the working people of the whole world!

Chairman: We have been obliged, unfortunately, to refrain from hearing from the comrade representatives from America, Japan, Spain, Holland and Austria, owing to lack of time, and we ask permission for their speeches to be printed in the newspapers and also in the report of our Congress. [*Voices:* 'Please, please.']

Next, comrades, two prominent Turkish leaders, not delegates to our Congress, who are here in Baku, have sent the Presidium state-

ments in writing, and as these statements are of great political importance, the Presidium has decided to make them public, both from this
tribune and in the press. One of these statements is by Enver Pasha
and the other by Ibrahim Tali, the representative of the Turkish
People's Government of Anatolia. We shall now read both of those
statements. ['Please, please.' *Translation.*]

Chairman: I call upon Comrade Ostrovsky to read the statements.
[*Uproar, exclamations.*] Comrades, please be absolutely quiet.

Enver Pasha's Declaration:[57]

Comrades, I thank on my own behalf and on that of my comrades
the Third International and its Presidium, who have enabled us
fighters against world imperialism and capitalism to assemble in Baku
today.

Comrades, we consider ourselves fortunate that, in opposition to
imperialism and capitalism, which is not satisfied with robbing us and
stripping us naked but is trying to drink our blood and destroy us, and
in opposition to the lying politicians of Europe, we today stand
shoulder to shoulder with a true and honest ally, the Third International.

Comrades, when Turkey entered the war, the world was divided
into two camps. In one was imperialist and capitalist old Tsarist
Russia and its allies, and in the other Germany, also imperialist and
capitalist, with its allies. Of these two groups, we, fighting against
Tsarist Russia, Britain and their friends, who wanted to strangle and
destroy us utterly, took the side of Germany, which at least agreed to
let us live.

German imperialism used us for its bandit aims. But our desire was
only to safeguard our independence.

Comrades, the sentiment which caused us to leave a calm, refuge-
seeking life[58] for the burning deserts of Tripoli and the poor tents of
the Beduin, and forced us to spend there the most difficult time of our
lives, was no sentiment of imperialism. We were trying to save Tripoli
for the Tripolitanians,[59] and we are glad that now, after nine years of
war, they have succeeded in driving out the Italian imperialists. Nor
did we have any different intention where Azerbaidzhan was concerned. We consider that Azerbaidzhan belongs to the Azerbaidzhanis. If we fell into a false situation, that was our bad luck.

Comrades, during the world war I occupied a very important post. I
assure you that I regret that we were obliged to fight on the side of

German imperialism. I hate and curse German imperialism and the German imperialists just as much as I hate and curse British imperialism and the British imperialists. In my view, all who have made it their aim to enrich those who do not work deserve to be destroyed. That is my viewpoint where imperialism is concerned.

Comrades, I assure you that if the Russia of today had been in existence then, and had been fighting the war with its present aims, we should have been fighting on your side, just as today, with all our energy. So as to show more clearly that my idea is correct, I will tell you that when we decided to act together with Soviet Russia, and did so, Yudenich's army was near Petrograd, Kolchak held the Urals, and Denikin was approaching Moscow from the South. The Entente, advancing its forces and regarding the game as already won, was showing its predatory teeth and rubbing its hands with glee. That was the situation when we began to be friends with Russia. Had the Black Sea storms not forced me back, breaking the mast of my vessel, if the bars of the prisons of Kovno and Riga, and crashes by the aeroplanes in which I was flying, had not delayed me, I should have been with you in Russia's most difficult hour, and it would not have been necessary to relate these personal details in order to explain matters to certain comrades.

Comrades, you know that in the imperialist conflict of this world war we were defeated. But from the standpoint of the war of the oppressed I do not regard us as having been defeated, for Turkey, as a result of the closing of her Straits, became one of the factors which brought about the collapse of insatiable Tsarist Russia and its replacement by the natural ally of all the oppressed, Soviet Russia. Thereby Turkey helped to bring it about that a new road has been opened for the salvation of the world. From the standpoint of the oppressed I see this as a victory.[60]

Comrades, the army which at the present time is waging a heroic struggle against imperialism and which draws its strength from the peasantry, was, as I have said, not defeated, it only temporarily laid down its arms. And now, after fighting against the same enemy for 15 years it is still, despite the greatest privations, fighting on for another year. It is impossible to compare the present struggle with the previous one. Seeing that, now, the Eastern world has come forward in alliance with the Third International, and the oppressed of the whole world support its just claims, this struggle is filled with resolute hope of victory.

Comrades, the intense phase of imperialist war, which began at the time of the Transvaal war, continued with the war between the imperialists from 1914 to 1917, which has now ended. But the war at the present time has entered a decisive period, and it will certainly end in victory for us, that is, victory for the oppressed, and not just with imperialism and capitalism piling their arms, but with their complete destruction.

The present congress brings fresh strength to the Red Army, which has shed its blood in defence of the oppressed, and also to the Turkish fighters. In the same way, this congress contributes to ensure that the struggle will end in our victory, that is, in the victory of justice. It is not only our endeavour to find support in the struggle we have begun that has caused us to draw near to the Third International. It may be that another factor is the similarity of our principles. We have always drawn our revolutionary strength from the people, that is, from the peasants. If our factory workers had been a strong force, I should have mentioned them first. However, they too were with us. They worked with us, body and soul. That is how it is now, too. Consequently, we base ourselves upon the oppressed section of the people. We feel their pain, and we live and die along with them.

Comrades, taking account of the people's desires, we stand for recognizing their right to self-determination. We consider ourselves bound by the strongest ties for the whole of our lives to those who want to live together with us: as for those who do not want to do this, we are willing to recognize their right to decide their fate for themselves. That is our view on the national question.

Comrades, we are against war, that is, we are against people strangling each other for the sake of power. And in order to achieve permanent peace we march with the Third International, and therefore we are now, despite all obstacles, waging a bloody struggle and shall continue this struggle.

Comrades, we want happiness for the working people, that is, we are against speculators, whether foreign or native, profiting by the fruits of others' labour. It is necessary to oppose that without any hesitation. We want our country to enjoy the fruits of common labour through the development of agriculture and industry on a large scale. That is what we think about the economic question.

Comrades, we are convinced that only a conscious people can achieve happiness and freedom. We want sound knowledge, associated with labour and guaranteeing us genuine freedom, to bring enlightenment to our country, and in this matter we recognize no distinction between men and women. That is what we think about social policy.

Comrades, I declare to you that the union of revolutionary organizations of Morocco, Algeria, Tunisia, Tripoli, Egypt, Arabia and India, which has sent me here as its representative, is in full solidarity with you in this respect.[61] It is fully convinced that, by using all revolutionary means, it will succeed in breaking the teeth of the wild beasts and depriving them of their strength for good.

Comrades, the hands raised for this purpose reach out to each other. I shake the hands of all those who will work with us to the conclusion of this struggle, which will go on for a long time, but which will end in our victory. I wish them success.

Long live the alliance of the oppressed!

Down with the oppressors, who tremble before this alliance!

Chairman: I call upon Comrade Mehmet Emin to translate Enver Pasha's statement into Turkish.[62]

[Mehmet Emin translates.]

Chairman: Comrade Ostrovsky will now read the statement by the representative of the Ankara Government, Ibrahim Tali.

Statement by Ibrahim Tali:

World imperialism, having exploded in Central Europe and stretched out its hands to the vital arteries of Turkey, at the end of four years had brought Turkey to a state of complete breakdown.

The Turkish peasant who, when he took up arms, had no other aim than to protect his national frontiers and defend his productive forces from foreign exploitation, believed the promises of the lying American professor when he said that now every people would be ensured the right to life and freedom and that all workers would be happy, and he laid down his arms.

But then, when he saw that these arms were being turned against him, that they were beginning to destroy all his sacred rights for the benefit of the Western capitalists, and that they wanted to take from him his last crust of bread, this Turkish peasant at once became angry, and rebelled.

Comrades, I will here explain to you the causes and factors which led to this revolt, and also its essential character, and the story of how the Government born of this revolt came into being. The Anatolian revolt was due to causes of two kinds, external and internal. The external ones were these: the Turkish peasant, who had for four years been fighting on more than eleven fronts against the most powerful bourgeois states, at last felt a strong desire to eat in peace the bread he had won with the sweat of his brow and to live in peace in his own village. But the Western capitalists decided to send against this Turkish peasant, who had laid down his arms, the myrmidons in their service — from the West the Venizelist Greeks and from the East the Dashnak Armenians. The Turkish peasant knew that the imperialists and their myrmidons acted with fire and sword and bombs wherever they went, and that these were robbers, a small group of whom were seizing by force the fruits of the labour of the working class. But, thinking that this monstrous decision would not be put into practice, the Turkish peasantry remained calm for a while. However, France, which had said that it was fighting for the freedom of the peoples, not satisfied with having taken Syria, seized in addition, amid conflagrations and acts of violence, Adana, Marash and Yurknesh. At the same time the French Prime Minister, who had said that he was acting in the interests of civilization, after he had made sure of victory over our country, threw off the mask and announced in the Palais Bourbon, for all to hear: 'In order to safeguard her economic interests in the East, France must have control of all the mineral resources situated in the zone extending to Mosul. And so we consider it necessary to continue our advance as far as Mardin. We must take into account the importance of the natural resources to be found there, from the standpoint of France's industry.'

Comrades, as a result, there began an offensive against our only outlet to the Mediterranean Sea, against Smyrna, which brought about a union of the defenders of national rights, in the West and in the East, against the robbers. After the seizure of Smyrna, in the East, on the initiative of the opponents of the imperialists, that is, on the initiative of the population of Erzerum and Trebizond, a national assembly was convened in Erzerum, at which it was resolved to defend our rights. Subsequently, at congresses in Sivas and Ankara, this decision was reiterated and confirmed.

The internal causes were these. The poor peasant of Anatolia had for centuries suffered from the violence and tyranny of the bourgeoisie, he was oppressed, he was worn out by the disease that came from Stambul — the bureaucracy, the dictatorship both of the Sultan's government and of the aristocrats, and also the parasitic officials sent to him by the Government, and now there awakened in him a feeling of holy anger against those aristocrats and Pashas who had never spent one day of their lives with him when the peasant was working in his fields and dying of hunger, but, in splendid palaces and villas on the shore of the Bosphorus, had given themselves up to the vilest pleasures, consuming the results of the work of the poor class and always acting provocatively towards the peasantry. By this revolt the peasant made it clear that in future he would give not a single crust of his bread to Stambul, its Pashas and Beys and their parasitical hangers-on. There, comrades, are the causes and factors of the recent revolution in Anatolia, so that this is not in the least a movement based on the bourgeoisie, as is supposed in the West. Speaking frankly, I can tell you that since the accomplices of Western capitalism in the East — the Dashnaks, the supporters of Venizelos, and the old courtier Pashas too, their tools, who have used the Sultan's court in the interests of British capitalism — since these have thrown themselves into the arms of the Entente, the Anatolian revolutionaries have turned to the East, where the Red revolution has risen like the dawn. The classes whose interests are endangered by this popular movement have striven with their combined forces to advance the counter-revolution everywhere. And the counter-revolutionaries — parasites upon the people like Sheikh-Redjeb in Sivas, Sheikh-Eshref in Baiburt, and also the Chaban-Oglu family, who have been used for centuries to leading a carefree, debauched life at the expense of the poor people, and likewise Yuzgada and other such persons — all these together organized a revolt in Stambul, where it seemed natural to them for the Anatolian peasant to live in slavery, and along with Anzavur Pasha set themselves to defend religion.[63]

Comrades, the Anatolian peasants and the revolutionaries who had remained among these criminals and brigands reacted with enthusiasm and rejoicing to the international revolution, which they felt sure would bring liberation and happiness to all mankind, and they are convinced that their destiny is bound up with that of the Third International.

The revolutionary people's government organized (after the dispersal of the parliament by the imperialists) by the defenders of the people's rights and the national congresses, confirmed this through the delegation they sent to Moscow. They are happy that the hand sincerely extended from Anatolia has been clasped with the same sincerity, and they are ready to utilize the social and moral results of this revolution, the principles of which they consider salutary for mankind.

Comrades, from these explanations it is clear that Anatolia, on the road to developing enlightenment, has resolved to defend its fate and its independence to the last breath of the last of its sons. And it accepts with complete sincerity the hand of friendship extended to it by Soviet Russia.

Long live revolutionary Russia which has set out on this road, and revolutionary Russia's backer — the revolutionary East!

Zinoviev: In connection with the declarations we have just heard, the Presidium proposes that a resolution be adopted. The text of this resolution will be presented to you by our Hungarian comrade, Béla Kun.

Béla Kun: The Presidium of the Congress of the Peoples of the East has unanimously resolved to present this resolution to you:

'Having heard Enver Pasha's statement on the Turkish national movement, the Congress of the Peoples of the East adopts the following resolution:

'1. The Congress expresses its sympathy with all Turkish fighters in combat against world imperialism, the oppressor and exploiter of the Eastern peoples, which holds in slavery the working people of the whole world, and first and foremost against the British and French imperialist bandits. Like the Second Congress of the Communist International, the First Congress of the Peoples of the East declares that it will support those general-national revolutionary movements which seek to free the oppressed peoples of the East from the yoke of foreign imperialists.

'2. However, the Congress notes that the general-national revolutionary movement in Turkey is directed only against foreign oppressors, and that success for this movement would not in the least signify the emancipation of the Turkish peasants and workers from oppression and exploitation of every kind. The success of this movement would not entail the solution of questions which are of the greatest importance for the Turkish toiling classes, namely, the agrarian question and the question of taxes, and would not eliminate the principal obstacles to the liberation of the East, namely, national discords.

'3. The Congress finds it necessary to show particular caution in relation to those leaders of the movement who in the past led the

Turkish peasants and workers to the slaughter in the interests of one of the imperialist groups and thereby subjected the toiling masses of Turkey to twofold ruin in the interests of a small group of rich men and high-ranking officers. The Congress proposes to these leaders that they prove in deeds that they are now ready to serve the toiling people and make amends for their false steps in the past. In calling on the toiling masses of Turkey and the entire East to support the general-national revolutionary movement in Turkey, the Congress urges the peasants and workers of Turkey to come together in independent organizations, to be ready to carry the cause of emancipation through to the end, and not to allow the foreign imperialists who are trying to hinder the work of emancipation to make use of their connections and influence among the Turkish rich, kulaks, bureaucrats and generals (the Pashas, Derebeileri, and so on). Only in this way can the toiling people of Turkey succeed in freeing themselves from all their oppressors and exploiters, and only then will the land, the factories, the mines, and all the country's wealth be put at the service of the toilers and the toilers alone. And only in this way.'

[*Izmail Hakki translated the resolution.*]

Chairman: I now put to the vote the resolution which the Presidium has unanimously recommended to you. [*Uproar. A voice:* 'I want to speak.']

The Presidium proposes that the vote be taken without discussion, and according to the rule you should have handed up a note. [*A voice:* 'I did hand up a note.' *The vote is taken.*] All in favour of the resolution that was read to you, please raise your hands. [*Uproar. Voices:* 'I handed up a note.' 'Let me reveal the truth.']

Please do not make a row. There are 1,800 of us here. It is impossible to carry on like this. Please put your hands down. Who is against? Any abstentions? The resolution is carried. [*Applause.*]

Comrades, we have thereby disposed of the first two points on the agenda. We propose that the Congress empower the Presidium to apply itself to drawing up two appeals. One appeal will be addressed to the peoples of the East, in which, on behalf of our Congress, the situation in the East will be described, the oppression to which the peoples of the East are subjected by British imperialism. This appeal will conclude with a call to a holy war of the toiling masses against the robbers of the East — the French and British imperialists. [*Loud applause. Shouts of* 'Hurrah'.]

The second appeal we propose to address to the toiling masses of Europe and America, to the workers, our brothers in labour. In this we shall first show, on behalf of the Congress of the Peoples of the East, how vilely the bourgeoisie of their countries have dealt with you, and, finally, we shall call upon them to give their attention to this situation in the East, call upon the British workers to support not only Soviet Russia but also the peoples of the East, oppressed by the British Government. We are sure that this appeal, in the name of tens of millions of toilers of the East, to the workers of Britain, America and France will be listened to, and printed in workers' newspapers throughout the world, and the workers of the whole world will understand what a tremendous duty is incumbent upon them, and they will strive to fulfil this duty to the peoples of the East. [*Applause.*]

Comrades! These two appeals have been composed. In a day or two, tomorrow or the day after, proofs of them will be issued to you. These appeals will have to appear over the signatures of all the members of the Presidium you have elected. [*Applause.*]

[*An interpreter translates. Applause.*]

Chairman: Will all those who agree that these two appeals be issued on behalf of the Congress please raise their hands. Please put your hands down. Who is against? Any abstentions? None.

The Congress will meet tomorrow at 5 p.m.

The next question on the agenda is the colonial-national question. At 11 a.m. the agrarian section is due to meet at the Army Club. If the elections have not been carried out, this will have to be seen to, and at 11 a.m. the agrarian section will meet at the Army Club. The Congress of the Peoples will reassemble at 5 p.m.

The session was closed at 11 p.m.

Appendix to the report of the Fourth Session

John Reed's speech:

I represent here the revolutionary workers of one of the great imperialist powers, the United States of America, which exploits and oppresses the peoples of the colonies.

You, the peoples of the East, the peoples of Asia, have not yet experienced for yourselves the rule of America. You know and hate the British, French and Italian imperialists, and probably you think that 'free America' will govern better, will liberate the peoples of the colonies, will feed and defend them.

No. The workers and peasants of the Philippines, the peoples of Central America and the islands of the Caribbean, they know what it means to live under the rule of 'free America'.

Take, for example, the peoples of the Philippines. In 1898 the Filipinos rebelled against the cruel colonial government of Spain, and the Americans helped them. But after the Spaniards had been driven out the Americans did not want to go away.

Then the Filipinos rose against the Americans, and this time the 'liberators' started to kill them, their wives and children: they tortured them and eventually conquered them. They seized their land and forced them to work and make profits for American capitalists.

The Americans have promised the Filipinos independence. Soon an independent Filipino republic will be proclaimed. But this does not mean that the American capitalists will leave or that the Filipinos will not continue to work to make profits for them. The American capitalists have given the Filipino leaders a share of their profits — they have given them government jobs, land and money — they have created a Filipino capitalist class which also lives on the profits created by the workers — and in whose interest it is to keep the Filipinos in slavery.

This has also happened in Cuba, which was freed from Spanish rule with the help of the Americans. It is now an independent Republic. But American millionaire trusts own all the sugar plantations, apart from some small tracts which they have let the Cuban capitalists have: the latter also administer the country. And the moment that the workers of Cuba try to elect a government which is not in the interests of the American capitalists, the United States of America sends soldiers into Cuba to compel the people to vote for their oppressors.

Or let us take the example of the republics of Haiti and San Domingo, where the peoples won freedom a century ago. Since this island was fertile and the people living on it could be put to use by the American capitalists, the government of the US sent soldiers and sailors there on the pretext of maintaining order and smashed these two republics, setting up in their place a military dictatorship worse than the British tyrants.

Mexico is another rich country which is close to the USA. In Mexico live a backward people who were enslaved for centuries, first by the Spaniards and then by foreign capitalists. There, after many years of civil war, the people formed their own government, not a proletarian government but a democratic one, which wanted to keep the wealth of Mexico for the Mexicans and tax the foreign capitalists. The American capitalists did not concern themselves with sending bread to the hungry Mexicans. No, they initiated a counter-revolution in Mexico, in which Madero, the first revolutionary President, was killed. Then, after a three-year struggle, the revolutionary regime was restored, with Carranza as President. The American capitalists made another counter-revolution and killed Carranza, establishing once more a government friendly to themselves.

In North America itself there are ten million Negroes who possess neither political or civil rights, despite the fact that by law they are equal citizens. With the purpose of distracting the attention of the American workers from the capitalists, their exploiters, the latter stir up hatred against the Negroes, provoking war between the white and black races. The Negroes, whom they lawlessly burn alive, are beginning to see that their only hope lies in armed resistance to the white bandits.

At the present time the American capitalists are addressing friendly words to the peoples of the East, with a promise of aid and food. This applies especially to Armenia. Millions of dollars have been collected by the American millionaires in order to send bread to the starving Armenians. And many Armenians are now looking for help to Uncle Sam.

These same American capitalists incite the American workers and farmers against each other: they starve and exploit the peoples of Cuba and the Philippines, they savagely kill and burn alive American Negroes, and in America itself American workers are obliged to work under frightful conditions, receiving low wages for a long work-day. When they are exhausted they are thrown out on to the street, where they die of hunger.

The same gentleman who is now in charge of bringing aid to the starving Armenians, Mr. Cleveland Dodge,[64] who writes emotional articles about how the Turks have driven the Armenians into the desert, is the owner of big copper mines where thousands of American workers are exploited, and when these workers dared to go on strike the guards protecting Mr. Dodge's mines drove them at the point of the bayonet out into the desert — just as was done to the Armenians.

Many Armenians are grateful to America for its attitude to the Armenians who suffered from the brutality of the Turks during the war. But what has America done for the Armenians apart from issuing wordy declarations? Nothing. I was in Constantinople at that time, in 1915, and I know that the missionaries refused to make any serious protest against the atrocities, saying that they had a lot of property in Turkey and so did not want to bring pressure to bear on the Turks. The American ambassador, Mr. Strauss, himself a millionaire who exploited thousands of workers in his enterprises in America, proposed that the entire Armenian people be shipped to America, and himself donated quite a large sum for this project to be carried out; but his plan was to make the Armenians work in American factories and provide cheap labour so as to increase the profits of Mr. Strauss and his friends.

But why do the American capitalists promise aid and food to Armenia? Is it out of pure philanthropy? If so, let them feed the peoples of Central America and help the Negroes of America itself.

No. The main reason is that there is mineral wealth in Armenia, and that it is a big reservoir of cheap labour which can be exploited by American capitalists.[65]

The American capitalists want to win the confidence of the Armenians with a view to getting their claws into Armenia and enslaving the Armenian nation. It is with this aim that American missionaries have established schools in the Near East.

But there is also another very important reason: the American capitalists, together with the other capitalist nations, united in the League of Nations, are afraid that the workers and peasants of Armenia will follow the example of Soviet Russia and Soviet Azerbaidzhan, will take power and their country's resources into their own hands, and will work for themselves, making a united front with the workers and peasants of the whole world against world imperialism. The American capitalists are afraid of a revolution in the East.

Promising food to starving peoples and at the same time organizing a blockade of the Soviet Republics — that is the policy of the United States. The blockade of Soviet Russia has starved to death thousands of Russian women and children. This same method of blockade was applied in order to turn the Hungarian people against their Soviet Government. The·same tactic is now being used in order to draw the people of White Hungary into war against Soviet Russia. This method is also being used in the small countries bordering on Russia — Finland, Estonia, Latvia. But now all these small countries have been obliged to make peace with Soviet Russia: they are bankrupt and starving. Now the American Government no longer offers them food; they are no longer of any use to America, and so their peoples can starve.

The American capitalists promise bread to Armenia. This is an old trick. They promise bread but they never give it. Did Hungary get bread after the fall of the Soviet Government? No. The Hungarian people are still starving today. Did the Baltic countries get bread? No. At a time when the starving Estonians had nothing but potatoes, the American capitalists sent them ships laden with rotten potatoes which could not be sold at a profit in America. No, comrades, Uncle Sam is not one ever to give anybody something for nothing. He comes along with a sack stuffed with straw in one hand and a whip in the other. Whoever takes Uncle Sam's promises at their face value will find himself obliged to pay for them with blood and sweat. The American workers are demanding an ever larger share of the product of their labour; with a view to preventing revolution at home, the American capitalists are forced to seek out colonial peoples to exploit, peoples who will furnish sufficient profit to keep the American workers in obedience and so make them participants in the exploitation of the Armenians. I represent thousands of revolutionary American workers who know this, and who understand that, acting together with the Armenian workers and peasants, with the toiling masses of the whole world, they will overthrow capitalism. World capitalism will be destroyed, and all the peoples will be free. We appreciate the need for solidarity between all the oppressed and toiling peoples, for unity of the revolutionary workers of all the countries of Europe and America under the leadership of the Russian Bolsheviks, in the Communist International. And we say to you, peoples of the East: Do not believe the promises of the American capitalists!

There is only one road to freedom. Unite with the Russian workers and peasants who have overthrown their capitalists and whose Red Army has beaten the foreign imperialists! Follow the red star of the Communist International!

Fifth Session

September 5

The session began at 7.15 p.m. Comrade Zinoviev took the chair.

Chairman: I declare the fifth session of the Congress of the Peoples of the East open. The Presidium proposes that we now deal with the national and colonial questions. Comrade Pavlovich will give the report.

Pavlovich: Comrades, questions of colonial and national policy have played a very big part in world history. The last world war was the result of a clash between great world powers and their attempts to gain possession of the black and, above all, the yellow continent. On the eve of the war I formulated the essence of the colonial conflicts between the European powers when I said that these conflicts could be reduced to the conflicts between three groups of letters: B-B-B, C-C-C and P-P. Germany was advancing a project for a great Berlin-Byzantium-Baghdad railway which was to bind to the German Empire, with a steel chain, the whole of the Ottoman Empire, and especially Asia Minor, and through the latter to open for German imperialism a road to Persia, India, Egypt — that is, a road to possession of the black and yellow continents. To Germany's three Bs Britain counterposed three Cs: Capetown-Cairo-Calcutta — a railway which was to unite into one the whole of East Africa from South to North, and then Arabia, Mesopotamia, Southern Persia and India. Against these two projects Russia put forward its own Petersburg-to-the-Persian-Gulf project. In all of these schemes we see the struggle between the world powers for the mastery of Asia and Africa.

These questions of (predominantly) colonial policy which brought about the world war of 1914-1918 now threaten to give rise to armed conflict between the allies of yesterday: America and Japan, America and Britain, and, finally, Britain and France.

From the revelations published in the French press in connection with the debates in the Senate on the occasion of Clemenceau's resignation[66] it emerges that at the most critical moment of the war with the Triple Alliance Britain and France were preparing to tear each other's throats out over the division of Asia Minor, and that Clemenceau had to give up his post in connection with very serious clashes with Britain over Syria. At the present time relations between France and Britain are extremely strained. But for fear of Soviet Russia and Bolshevism it must be supposed that the world war of 1914-1918 would long since have been transformed, as happened with the first Balkan war, into a war to the death between the victor powers. The possibility of armed conflict between France and Britain, Britain and America, or America and Japan is not at all out of the question, so long as the fates of the peoples remain in the hands of the bourgeoisie. America and Japan confront each other, armed to the teeth, over the question of hegemony in the Far East. If America is expanding its Navy with feverish speed, setting itself the aim of possessing by 1925 a Navy of equal strength to that of Britain, the mistress of the seas, it is doing this in order to deprive Britain of maritime hegemony and to strengthen the influence of the US in the East. If Britain is taking all possible measures against a strengthening of the maritime power of France and not allowing the submarines captured from Germany to be added to the French Navy, it is doing this because of the danger that, in the event of an armed conflict, France, possessing as it does excellent naval bases in the Mediterranean would be able, if not completely to sever, then at least to hamper gravely Britain's communications, through this great sea-road, with Egypt, Asia Minor, the Persian Gulf, India — in short, with the East.

This colonial question, the question of the partition of Asia, is the mainspring of this bitter war which the capitalist world has been waging since the first day of the October Revolution against Soviet Russia. Russia inspires fear in the countries of the capitalist world not only as a beacon, a guiding star, which summons all people of courage to the struggle for a new order, not only as a country with many millions of inhabitants and extraordinarily rich in natural endowments and sources of raw material which is no longer content to remain, as it was under the Tsars, a semi-colony of Anglo-Franco-Belgian capital — Soviet Russia inspires fear and dread in world imperialism as a colony which has freed itself from foreign oppression and which not only by its very example summons the enslaved East to fight for freedom, which not only by its whole internal policy towards the backward nations contributes to the awakening and development in the East of a striving for national self-determination, but which also renders real aid to the backward and oppressed peoples living outside the borders of Russia, in their struggle against predatory international capital. [*Applause.*]

One of the non-Party comrades expressed his admiration for the leaders of the Communist Party, Comrades Lenin, Zinoviev and Trotsky, emphasizing the unbounded confidence placed in these highest representatives and leaders of the Soviet power by all the nationalities inhabiting Russia, and mentioned with bitterness that some representatives of the Communist Party, pseudo-Communists, as he called them, behave in the borderlands otherwise than as they should, discrediting the Soviet power and by their conduct inciting the native population against the very idea of Soviet power. We know this. All this is possible, or rather, it is inevitable. When in the storm and stress of mighty historical events an order collapses which has stood for entire millennia, when what is involved is the abolition of such institutions as capitalist property, which has for whole centuries been striking deep roots in the soil of society, it is natural that such a geological (so to speak) revolution, the transition to a new form of life cannot take place painlessly, without unavoidable deformities and deviations, which bear only a temporary character and are of only transitory significance. But the essence of the matter consists not in the abuses committed by some unworthy individual representatives of the Soviet power and the Communist Party. The essence of the matter consists in the general direction, the basic tendency of Soviet policy in relation to the particular nations which inhabit the territory of the former Tsarist empire.

The capitalist world understands very well what this general tendency of Soviet policy is in relation to the nations which were formerly oppressed by Tsardom and those which are now oppressed by the whole capitalist world and just because the capitalist powers understand our policy so well, they have, in the interests of safeguarding their role over the peoples they exploit, declared a war to the death against Soviet Russia. [*Applause.*]

Who cannot see the difference between our workers' and peasants' socialist federation and the brigand capitalist empires? The 'free constitution' of Britain holds in harsh slavery and strangles the 300 million people of India, who have for so long groaned under the British yoke. Republican France cruelly suppresses the slightest manifestation of desire for freedom and national self-determination in Morocco, in Algeria, in Indochina, in all its colonies. The great Transatlantic republic, the United States, still refuses to recognize the independence of Cuba and the Philippines, for whose 'liberation' the war with Spain was allegedly begun in 1898.

At the same time the Government and the worker and peasant masses of the Russian Socialist Federal Republic joyfully greet the formation on the borders of the former Tsarist Empire — where, as in all capitalist countries, every striving for national self-determination was stifled and suppressed — of the autonomous Bashkir Soviet Republic, the autonomous Tatar Socialist Soviet Republic, and so on. In all capitalist states without exception, both big and small, in France, Britain, Japan, America, Holland, Belgium, Poland and the rest, we see crude violence being used against national minorities and sometimes the transformation into nations of slaves and serfs of huge communities of hundreds of millions of people who have fallen under the rule of a more organized, more 'civilized' minority, as we see in the case of the enslaved 300 millions of India, ruled over by capitalist Britain, armed to the teeth. At one pole, in the capitalist countries there is savage suppression of national minorities, and sometimes of national majorities too, where a national minority holds the reins of government. At the other pole, in the republic of Soviets, there is the most solicitous, most fraternal feeling and attitude shown not only towards more or less big national entities but also towards the very smallest of them.

Under the first Ukrainian People's Republic it was the Austro-German imperialists and General Skoropadsky who ruled in the Ukraine. That was the time when, by agreement with the Germans and Austrians, Petlyura's Ukraine was obliged to supply Austria and Germany with 75 million poods of grain, 11 million poods of cattle on the hoof, and so on.

Under the second Ukrainian People's Republic the Ukraine was a colony of French capital, in accordance with the agreement which the mercenary Petlyura signed in Odessa with the French General D'Anselme. By this agreement nearly all the Ukraine's railways and the country's financial and military enterprises were handed over to the French stockbrokers.

The third Ukrainian People's Republic, promised by the same Petlyura, was merely a screen for the establishment in the Ukraine of the hated evil rule of the Polish gentry.[67]

The whole history of the Ukraine cries out against this fresh act of betrayal by Petlyura. That history is one of heroic exploits and great defeats of the Ukrainian peasantry, the Ukrainian 'cattle' in a struggle over many centuries against the Polish gentry. On the other hand, the whole history of the Poland of the gentry is a long series of wars against the Ukraine aimed at enslaving that country. Ukrainian literature, the immortal works of Shevchenko, Ukrainian folk-poetry, reflect this page of the long-suffering history of the Ukrainian people, whose entire development proceeded through bloody struggle against the Polish lords. All the Cossack revolts, the whole struggle of the Zaporozhian Camp,[68] the struggle of Bogdan Khmelnitsky,[69] were, fundamentally, a struggle of the Ukrainian peasants against the yoke of the Polish landowners, a struggle against the Polonizers, the enemies of the Ukrainian national language and Ukrainian culture.

And Petlyura, as a condottiere and hired bandit, offering his bloody services to anyone who will agree to pay him well, wanted to surrender the Ukrainian land, the Ukrainian language, all Ukrainian culture, to the Polish gendarme, to the insolent Polonizers, who, for example, closed Byelorussian schools and proclaimed Polish the state language even in the regions where the Polish population made up only an insignificant percentage. The Polish gentry, the Polish *Kulturträger*, are already trying to Polonize Byelorussia, Volhynia and Podolia, and intend to do the same in all the regions of the Ukraine that they manage to conquer.

Tens of hundreds of honest Ukrainians, sincerely desiring the national and cultural rebirth of the Ukraine, including two pillars of Ukrainian national public opinion like Hrushevsky and Vinnichenko,[70] have become convinced that only Soviet power can now fulfil to the end the role of liberator of the Ukraine from all forms of oppression.

On May 27 the Presidium of the All-Russia Central Executive Committee confirmed the decision to establish an autonomous Tatar Socialist Soviet Republic with as its centre the city of Kazan. This news evoked a mighty echo throughout the many-millioned Moslem world, in Persia, Afghanistan, Turkey and India and was, in the eyes of our Moslem brothers, the workers and peasants of the East, a fresh example of those great principles which underlie the national policy of the Russian Federal Republic. But this is not to the liking of the capitalist governments.

Let two or three decades pass and we shall see how, together with the spread of popular education in the republic of Soviets, together with the opening of thousands and thousands of schools, evening courses, academies and so on, together with the complete ending of illiteracy in Russia and in the Ukraine alone, alongside the wonderful old monuments of Russian and Ukrainian literature, with the works of Pushkin, Lermontov, Tolstoy, Gogol and Shevchenko, great new works will appear, composed by brilliant new poets, men of letters and so on, who will have sprung from the ranks of the workers and peasants. Tatar, Bashkir, Kirghiz, etc., poetry and literature, which have only just awakened to life, will flourish luxuriantly, and all the separate streams, tributaries, rivulets and great rivers, will inter-mingle in a fantastic and harmonious way, merging and feeding with their living waters one common international ocean of the poetry and learning of toiling humanity, freed for the first time from national and class oppression, and will shine with such unprecedented, incomparable beauty as neither classical Greece, with all its amazing works of art, could give the world, nor the civilization of the medieval and capitalist epochs, with all their blazing galaxy of immortal poets, artists, thinkers and scholars.

Yes, all this will be! But before we reach this wished-for future, much blood will flow and many thousands of fighters for the new order will fall beneath the enemy's blows upon the battlefields, many tens and hundreds of thousands of women and children will die in their homes, or beside ruined *auls*,[71] from hunger and cold. All this is inevitable, alas, and it happens not by our fault but through the criminal will of the capitalists, who do not want to give up their profits. But all fighters for a better future have to suffer in this way, and not merely the representatives of the small nations, not only the population of the borderlands. Come and see what is happening in Petrograd, Moscow, Tula, in a whole number of our cities, where, because of the criminal blockade and the bloody war that was forced upon us, hundreds of thousands of workers are faint from hunger and cold and yet have not lost heart, but march off in their thousands to the front, to lay down their lives for the Soviet power. [*Applause.*] They know, these heroes, that they will not die in vain, for they have given their blood for the sake of their comrades' happiness, for a better future for their children and the generations to come.

The war against Soviet Russia is a war against the East.

In the giant struggle we have begun, the peoples of the East will henceforth be our loyal allies. For a war against Soviet Russia is a war against the revolutionary East, and, contrariwise, a war against the East is a war against Soviet Russia. [*Applause.*]

Why are Britain and France so interested in supporting Wrangel? Because Wrangel holds the Crimea, and so the rear of revolutionary Turkey is cut off, and Soviet Russia cannot bring aid to the Turkish revolutionaries. On the other hand, so long as Asia Minor is occupied by the Allies, by their expeditionary forces, *our* rear is threatened. The Greek occupation of Thrace and Adrianople is aimed at isolating revolutionary Turkey and Soviet Russia from the revolutionary Balkans. Finally, if European imperialism is supporting Dashnak Armenia and Menshevik Georgia with arms, money and bread, this is being done in order to support these countries as a barrier separating revolutionary Russia and Caucasia from revolutionary Turkey, Persia and India. Imperialism is everywhere raising up these artificial barriers against us, but they will all collapse under the blows of the masses in the Crimea, Georgia, Armenia, Thrace and Greece. At the same moment that the Polish mad dog was unleashed against Soviet Russia, the Greece of Venizelos was let loose on revolutionary Turkey. And now we read in the Greek papers which have reached here that an attempt has been made on Venizelos's life and he has been wounded with seven bullets.[72]

Who made this attempt? Turks, Bulgars, Russians? No, two Greeks! [*Applause.*]

Does not this attempt show that in Greece itself, transformed from a poor country of four million people into a big military power with a population of twelve millions, discontent is growing against the imperialist policy of Venizelos, which is urging the country towards the abyss of ultimate ruin? Capitalism is digging its own grave, but in order to hasten the death of capitalism the peoples of the East must, shoulder to shoulder with Soviet Russia, strike the final blows at the world bourgeoisie. The revolutionary East must conclude a close alliance with Soviet Russia. The transitional form to complete union of the toiling masses is a federation of Soviet states.

The Turkish comrades expressed the view, in their appeal to Soviet Russia, that the question of the Dardanelles should be decided by the states bordering on the Black Sea, excluding participation by Wrangel and the Entente. We warmly welcome this idea, the realization of which would be a first and decisive step towards a federation of all the peoples and countries whose territories adjoin the Black Sea. [*Applause.*]

The renegade Hervé, in one of his articles in defence of the Poland of the gentry which has attacked Soviet Russia, howled: 'If the first defence-line which European civilization established against Asiatic barbarism by creating Poland is broken, the Governments of Europe will have to concentrate all their forces on the second and last defence-line, which runs, close to Paris, Brussels and London, along the Rhine, in order to protect European culture from the invasion of Asiatic cholera, yellow plague, vodka-inflamed savagery and fanaticism which is advancing, in the shape of the Red Army, upon the whole civilized world.'

The Russian Communists are proud of all these attacks made against them. One of the fundamental features of the Third International is that it sides with the revolutionary movement of the oppressed peoples not in words but in deeds, and makes it a duty for the Communist Parties of all countries, especially the oppressor countries, to give most active aid to the national-revolutionary movement in the more backward states and nations. [*Applause.*]

The leader of the Georgian Mensheviks, Zhordania, counterposes to the Asiatic policy of the Bolsheviks the so-called European line of the Mensheviks; the Mensheviks, he says, are European socialists we, says Zhordania of himself and his friends, are bearers of culture and civilization, whereas Muscovy means Asia with its inertia of fanaticism.

We can now reply to Zhordania that the entire Third International shares at the present time the viewpoint of the Bolsheviks, that all Communists — Russian, French, British, Italians and so on — have now become Asians, and are resolved to help every revolutionary movement in the East and in Africa. The workers now know that when in Britain a decision is taken regarding Persia, India or Asia Minor, or merely affecting one province of Turkey, or when what is involved is Anatolia, Syria or Arabia, this directly affects the fate of the Italian, British, American and the whole world-wide working-class movement, and that all these questions call for their immediate intervention and action. The French, British and Italian workers who march under the banner of Communism must not allow European troops to be sent to Anatolia, Syria, Mesopotamia, Constantinople and so on; and we can hope that the day is not far off when the whole international proletariat will fight as vigorously against the strangling of the East as it is now fighting against the strangling and blockading of Soviet Russia. [*Applause.*] The Third International, that is, the Communists of the whole world, take as their basic task to explain this simple truth, that so long as the yellow and black continents are oppressed, so long as European mercenaries are killing Turks, Persians, Arabs, Egyptians and so on, the European worker will be unable to cast off his own chains and will remain a slave of the capitalist. For this reason the Third International calls on the European workers to fight for the liberation of the East.

This is not the attitude to the colonial question taken by the Second International, this is not the current line of action of the yellow traitor International headed by Kautsky, Renaudel, Vandervelde and other agents of imperialism.

By its very nature, that International was incapable of supporting the revolutionary movement among the oppressed peoples in Morocco, Algeria, Tunisia, Asia Minor, Persia, India, Egypt and so forth. Even less was it capable of taking the initiative in bringing revolution to the black and yellow continents or even simply in making propaganda for ideas of liberation among the suffering masses of Asia and Africa. The Second International did not and does not want to know the East from that angle. Of course, the leaders of the Second International have allowed themselves to discuss the colonial policy of their governments and sometimes they even publish, in Paris, London or Berlin, books and pamphlets on these themes, such as the book by Charles Dumas and so on;[73] but these gentlemen have not translated their books and pamphlets into the native languages, and have written on colonial matters merely so as to attract attention to themselves in the metropolitan countries, either in parliamentary circles generally or in the socialist parties in particular, and in fact all these fervent defenders of the natives support the colonial policies of their Governments. When the news was received of the pogroms against the Armenians in Turkey, the European Socialists eagerly organized demonstrations and big meetings to protest against the bloody Sultan. But when the French Government sent, year after year, ever-increasing numbers of troops to Morocco and massacred Moslem tribesmen, then the socialists remained silent, as they did also in relation to the cruelties committed in India, the strangling of Persia, the enslavement of Egypt, and the mass exterminations and bloody orgies carried out by the British troops in the black continent.

Moreover, there are socialists such as Lagrosillière,[74] Party members, delegates to all manner of socialist congresses, national and international, who openly defend colonial policy, justifying it by the need to bring the natives the blessings of civilization and progress.

The Second International did not want to know about the East, was not interested in the fate of the peoples of the black and yellow continents. True, when the news came about the anti-Armenian pogroms in Turkey the whole press of the Second International printed indignant articles in favour of the Armenians and impressive demonstrations were held. But all this was done merely for the benefit of the capitalist governments, who obtained a fresh occasion for interfering in Turkish affairs. The socialists had one attitude to the anti-Armenian pogroms and another to the pogroms, slaughter and extermination of the native population in Morocco, Algeria, India, etc.

We condemn anti-Armenian pogroms and will fight against them, but at the same time we make it a duty of members of the Third International, representatives of the French and British Parties, to fight with all their power, and not just in words but in deeds, against colonial policy generally, against the oppression and extermination of the inhabitants of Morocco, India, Indochina, Algeria and Turkestan.

The best illustration of the Second International's policy on the colonial question is the fact that at their congress in Geneva not a single word was uttered about the East.

As Comrade Zinoviev showed you, the world war has resulted in the whole world being divided into two groups of nations, with a small group of privileged, exploiting, 'first-class' nations, numbering a quarter of a milliard people, separated off from the rest.

As a consequence of this state of affairs, class contradictions have been still further intensified throughout the world, both in the metropolitan countries and in the colonies.

Poverty has been intensified to an extreme degree among the population of the victor countries. The value of money has fallen, goods have become more expensive, the productivity of labour has declined. Britain, France, even America, are going through a profound economic crisis. In America 2,000 strikes broke out in one month alone. Throughout the capitalist world the workers are not what they were before. Bourgeois economists complain that the proletariat has been engulfed by a wave of laziness and work-shyness, that the working class is suffering from a paralysis of the will. Yes, in a certain sense this is true. The European worker is already psychologically incapable of working for the capitalist as he used to. He wants to suffer and undergo torments, like the Russian worker, for his *own* interests, for the interests of his *own* class, and not for the sake of the dividends and profits of the exploiting class. [*Applause.*]

And so we come to the recent efforts directed at intensified exploitation of black and yellow labour. But the East does not want to be a means of enrichment for the capitalists of Europe. It not only does not want to be exploited more than before, but does not want to be an object of exploitation at all. [*Applause.*] The East is no longer what it used to be, either economically or spiritually.

On the one hand, in some eastern countries (such as, for example, India), during recent decades and especially during the world war, when the metropolis was unable to cope with the demands of the army and navy, a fairly well-developed industry came into existence. In sugar-production India holds a very prominent place on the world market (three million tons, out of the world's production of 16 million). The tobacco, tea and jute industries, and the textile industry in general are strongly developed in India. Altogether, there are about 15 million factory workers and weavers in the country. For the length of its railway network India holds fourth place in the world, being surpassed only by the USA, Germany and Russia. Consequently, there is a numerous railway proletariat in India.

Together with this development of industry in India and some parts of China we see a more extreme intensification of poverty and of class contradictions throughout the East. In India, China, Persia, Bukhara and elsewhere the rich have become still richer and the poor still poorer.

In Bukhara the peasants (*dekkhans*) drag out a very miserable existence. Their situation recalls the dark days of serfdom. They are robbed by everyone, from the *mirza*[75] to the Emir, and in recent years the burden of taxation in Bukhara has grown markedly heavier. Not long ago, fifty *dekkhans* sold all their cattle and farm implements in order to pay their taxes. Many sold their houses and their plots of land. Cotton is sown only by the rich, and owing to their lack of seed the poor peasants have this year sown only one-tenth of the area they sowed previously.

In Persia all the peasants are landless and all the land belongs to two or three thousand big landowners (*molkadars*).[76]

Many people have asserted that the Eastern peoples must necessarily pass through the stage of capitalism before reaching communism. The Third International has come to the conclusion, as the result of the debates at its Second Congress, that, with the aid of the advanced proletarian countries, the backward peoples can go over to the Soviet system and pass through a certain stage to communism, missing out the capitalist phase of development. [*Applause.*]

The popular masses of the East are not so well educated as the working masses of the West, but the heart of the man of the East, awakened by the thunder of the revolutionary events in Russia, is filled with self-sacrificing zeal and burns with a bright fire of hatred for the oppressors, a sacred fire of struggle.

The entire East is saturated with the bacteria of revolution. Millions of the suffering masses of the East are gripped by the spirit of protest and are straining to go into battle.

If into this compound which is densely saturated with revolutionary bacteria we introduce a crystal in the form of peasant soviets, soviets of the toilers, the resulting crystallization will proceed with rapid strides, and we shall significantly advance the cause of the revolutionary education and organization of the masses of the East in the struggle against the world of the predators, the struggle for a new social order. [*Applause.*]

The idea of Soviet organization, as Comrade Lenin has rightly said, can be applied not only to proletarian but also to feudal and semifeudal relations. Peasant soviets, toilers' soviets are a means appropriate not only for capitalist countries but also for countries where pre-capitalist relations prevail.

Formation of such soviets facilitates the struggle of the toiling masses both against their own exploiters — the landlords, capitalists and speculators — and against world imperialism, whose agents and accomplices all these *molkadars, zemindars, Khans, Beys, Pashas* and so on are. [*Applause.*]

The working masses of the East must rise up against their enemies, both internal and external, but the Eastern peoples cannot by their own strength, without the help of the revolutionary world proletariat, liberate themselves from the yoke of the aggressors.

The history of the Russian revolution of 1905 and of the Persian, Turkish and Chinese revolutions of 1908-1910,[77] which were suppressed by the power of international capitalism — for the Russian revolution of 1905 was overcome thanks to the French Bourse, which supplied the Tsar with milliards of francs — and the history of Soviet

Russia, victoriously defending itself against the onslaught of world imperialism, show at one and the same time both all the difficulty of the struggle against world capitalism and the conditions for victory over it.

Comrades, it is necessary not to lose sight of the simple truth that the peoples of the East will not achieve their freedom unless they unite with the proletariat of all countries. Britain, that mighty military and economic organism, against which we are beginning a decisive war with our joint efforts, can be overcome only with the co-operation of the British proletariat itself.

Where lies the strength of Soviet Russia in its struggle against the capitalist powers? How is the fact to be explained that this country, gripped by a chain of hunger and cold, blockaded on all sides, sustained for three years a war with the most powerful states in the world? The explanation is that a considerable part, the best part of the British, Spanish, French and Italian proletariat, whose representatives you see here, that this part is with us, that it refuses to help its own capitalist governments strangle Soviet Russia.

The source of Soviet Russia's might is the sympathy of the international proletariat. And what is the reason for this sympathy? The fact that Russia is the land of the proletariat, of Soviet power. The European Governments are no longer able to send their own troops against Russia, but have to hire mercenaries in the shape of the Polish landlords, the Czechoslovaks, and so on.

If the Eastern peoples want to have the benefit of the sympathy of the international proletariat, they too must fight for Soviet power, for the principles proclaimed by Soviet Russia.

If the capitalist states, which have millions of men under arms, are not in a position to despatch troops against Russia, this is because for the European workers fighting against Soviet Russia is equivalent to fighting not only against the Russian proletariat but against the proletariat of their own countries. Fighting against Russia means, from the standpoint of the French and British workers, committing class suicide. [*Applause.*]

But the British workers who organize Councils of Action to oppose their own government in its fight against Soviet Russia react very feebly to the events in Ireland, where a war to the death is being waged against the British bourgeoisie for national self-determination.

At best the rank-and-file British worker can only feel sympathy with the Irish in their hard fight for self-determination, but the Irish epic does not kindle the enthusiasm in the breast of the British, French and Italian proletariat, does not touch those strings which are plucked by the gigantic struggle of the Russian people against world imperialism.

Indeed, suppose the Irish separatists succeed in their aim and realize their cherished ideal of an independent Irish people. The very next day, independent Ireland would fall under the yoke of American capital or of the French Bourse, and, perhaps, within a year or two Ireland would be fighting against Britain or some other states in alliance with one of the world predators, for markets, for coal-mines, for iron-mines, for bits of territory in Africa, and once again hundreds of thousands of British, Irish, American and other workers would die in this war.

The example of Poland, whose bourgeois and landlord representatives bewailed for decades, up and down the scale, the partition of the old Rzeczpospolita, and wrote ardent articles about respect for the national rights of peoples — the example of this bourgeois Poland, which is now behaving as a hangman towards the national minorities on its own territory, and serving as the gendarme of international capitalism for struggle against the workers and peasants of Russia; or the example of the Balkan states — Bulgaria, Serbia, Montenegro, Greece — squabbling amongst themselves over the division of the booty and over their desire to annex to their own territory some nation which was only yesterday under the Turkish yoke; and a whole number of other facts of the same sort show that the formation of national states in the East, in which power has passed from the foreign rulers who have been driven out into the hands of the local capitalists and landlords, does not in itself constitute a great step forward in the matter of improving the position of the popular masses.

Within the framework of the capitalist system, any newly-formed state which does not express the interests of the toiling masses but serves the interests of the bourgeoisie is a new instrument of oppression and coercion, a new factor of war and violence.

If the struggle in Persia, India and Turkey were to lead merely to the capitalists and landlords of those countries, with their national parliaments and senates, coming to power, the masses of the people would have gained nothing.

Every newly-formed state would be rapidly drawn, by the very course of events and the iron logic of the laws of capitalist economy, into the vicious circle of militarism and imperialist politics, and after a few decades we should witness another world war, the horrors of which would make the war of 1914-1918 pale into insignificance, for there would take part in it not tens but hundreds of millions of soldiers, armed to the teeth, from the black, yellow and white continents — another war for the interests of the French, German, British, Indian, Chinese, Persian and Turkish bankers and factory-owners. [*Applause.*]

What will be the result of the formation of a re-born, powerful Turkey, if power remains in the hands of the rich, the speculators and the landlords? The examples provided by the recent past — the warlike policy of Enver's Turkey, and the behaviour of newly free and independent bourgeois states such as Georgia and Armenia — provide abundant illustrations of what I have said.

The Turkey of Enver Pasha made an alliance with the Germany of that same Wilhelm who proclaimed the need for a union of all the Western peoples for war against the East. The behaviour of the Turkish representatives at the Brest conference was disgraceful. Yet the Turkish nationalists were not content with the conditions of the monstrous Brest peace.

Turkey seized Ardahan, Kars and Batum. Moreover, the Turkish forces advanced still further and seized Akhaltsykh and Alexandropol.[78] Georgia was spared only through the intervention of Germany. Then the Turks threw themselves upon Azerbaidzhan and seized Baku. The two-months' rule of the Turks in Baku was the blackest page in the history of that long-suffering city, the stronghold of the proletariat in Caucasia.

The Georgia of Noah Ramishvili and Zhordania is ravaging and plundering Southern Ossetia, razing its *auls* to the ground, and terrorizing the population, forcing them to flee into Soviet Russia. Georgian punitive expeditions under the command of the monarchist Colonel Tukhareli are burning entire villages in Abkhazia.[79]

Georgia lays claim to Azerbaidzhanian territory, and in 1918 it began a war with Armenia which was stopped only by the intervention of Britain.

Armenia claims Karabagh and Zangezur (the secret letter of General Dro about the occupation of these territories, dated August 4, 1920, has become well-known).[80] Furthermore, the Georgian imperialists have put forward truly megalomaniac plans for the annexation of Van, Trebizond, Bitlis, Erzerum and Diarbekr, with outlets to the sea. Armenia wants to become a great Mediterranean power, ruling over territories in which Armenians constitute at most 50 per cent of the population. The Armenian papers invite the Greece of Venizelos to occupy Trebizond — a regular provocation.

The masses must rise up against their enslavers, both native and foreign. If the national revolutionary movement were to lead merely to the formation of new, powerful Eastern states in which the local bourgeoisie ruled, with Indian, Persian, etc., parliaments, then within decades we should have another frightful world war, in comparison with which all the horrors of the war of 1914-1918 would seem trivial.

From all this let us draw the following conclusions. The Communist International recognizes no colonial policy of any sort. The peoples of the East will take this proposition of the Third International and put it into effect by force of arms. There ought not to be any colonies. All nations have equal rights. Out with the British violators from India, Egypt, Persia and Mesopotamia! Out with the French bandits from Syria, and with the Greek bandits from Cilicia, Smyrna, etc.! The peoples of the East will brand the Second International with shame and will join with the Third International in saying: 'Traitors, renegades, hirelings of capital, get out of the ranks of the International!' The fact that the whole world has up to now been divided into two groups of nations — the oppressors and the oppressed — is due, first, to the crude violence of the bourgeois governments, which have put down with fire and sword any manifestation of striving for national self-determination; second, to dissension among the toiling masses of the East; and, third, to the traitorous conduct of the native rich, the landlords, of whom there are plenty in any Eastern country. All these Moroccan, Algerian, Persian, Turkish, Indian and Bukharan rich men and landowners — *mulaygafis, hadjis, pashas, beys, mirzas, emirs, shahs, khans, maharajas, molkadars, zemindars* — are agents of international imperialism, supporting the power of foreign capitalists, of the world bourgeoisie.

The revolutionary national movement will improve the position of the masses of the people only if it constitutes a decisive stage towards a profound and far-reaching socialist movement.

The main guarantee of victory for the Eastern peoples in the struggle against the monster of world imperialism, against that fire-breathing dragon compared with which all the fantastic, fabulous creatures of terror created by folk-imagination seem wretched pigmies and dwarfs, is unity of the toiling masses not only of the entire

East but also of the West. This war can end successfully only if it be waged on both fronts — against foreign capital and against one's own bourgeoisie.

In order that this condition may be fulfilled by the revolutionary masses of the East, they must organize around peasant soviets, soviets of the working people.

The Eastern masses can win victory in the struggle for freedom only by rapprochement with the working masses of the West. How can this rapprochement be hastened? The first step towards it must be a close alliance between all the peoples of the East and Soviet Russia, in which the entire international proletariat sees the advance-guard, the pioneer of the world revolution. The transitional form to full unity of the toiling masses of the different nations is a federation of Soviet states of the East for struggle both against the plans of conquest of the imperialist powers and against the machinations of the internal enemies.

Accordingly, in order to put an end to the fratricidal war between the Georgian, Armenian and Turkish workers and peasants it is necessary first and foremost to establish Soviet power in all these countries, and then to form a federation of the peoples who inhabit them.

In order to settle the question of the Dardanelles it is necessary to form a Black Sea federation. The principle of federation has shown its viability in external relations by the example of the former Red Hungary, of the Ukraine, and so on, and in internal policy in connection with the Tatar and Bashkir republics.

Only the dictatorship of the proletariat and, in general, of the working masses, liberated from foreign oppression and having overthrown capital completely, will provide the backward countries with a guarantee that these countries will not, like the states formed from fragments of the Austro-Hungarian empire and Tsarist Russia — Poland, White Hungary, Czechoslovakia, Georgia, Armenia — or formed from fragments of Turkey — Venizelist Greece and the rest — be new instruments for war, plunder and coercion.

Only the complete triumph of labour over capital reduced to dust will guarantee peace between the toilers of all countries.

Arise, peoples of the East! The Third International summons you to a holy war against the carrion-crows of capitalism. Comrade delegates, develop the class-consciousness of the popular masses, organize them around peasant soviets, soviets of the toilers, summon all the toilers to ally themselves with Soviet Russia, propagate the idea of a federation of oppressed nations, and, finally, create a union of the proletarians and peasants of all countries, religions and languages.

We must by the united efforts of the working people of all lands put an end to world imperialism and the coercion of one nation by another. We must put an end to the colonial policy of the capitalist powers and enable all countries to live in freedom and independence.

For this it is necessary to take the revolutionary road and prepare for the decisive battle, prepare the masses for immediate armed offensive, in serried ranks and close columns. Make haste, for one cannot postpone the revolution! Delay means death! [*Applause.*]

Otherwise, economic ruin will spread, the economic abyss will become wider and deeper, want will increase, decay will be intensified.

For six years now the bourgeoisie has been exclusively occupied with war and plunder, and it will not cease from this work of destruction, having become transformed into a highway robber.

There was a time when the bourgeoisie, in spite of everything, carried mankind forward, at any rate in the field of industrial progress, of the growth of the productive forces. Now it is dragging mankind back in every field, pushing it towards final destruction. Post-war capitalism has all the robber habits of the newly-rich upstart, while at the same time it shivers with fits of fever and organic convulsions, being undermined by every sort of excess and standing on the brink of death. Is it surprising that even the most moderate and recently peace-loving bourgeois of the pre-war epoch, poisoned by all the miasmas with which the atmosphere of imaginary wealth and merely outward-seeming prosperity is thick, trembling before the spectre of imminent bankruptcy which rises up at every moment, have literally lost their heads and have become transformed into raging beasts, capable only of hurling themselves upon the creatures around them, biting and tearing them to pieces?

The world bourgeoisie, like a badly wounded beast, is thrashing about in convulsions, in fury, striking blows with its teeth and claws not only at living creatures but at whatever inanimate objects it can reach in its convulsive leaps.

This badly wounded beast must not be allowed to recover. The working masses of the East must rise as one man and, in alliance with the proletariat of Russia and the revolutionary elements of all Europe and America launch an attack upon the imperialist predator, the evil vampire which holds in slavery hundreds and hundreds of millions of people in the white, yellow and black continents.

To us revolutionaries there is nobody, after the hangman, more contemptible than the latter's victim who submissively and without a struggle yields himself to suffering and torture.

This final duel which we are beginning to fight will require of us bloody sacrifices and hard efforts, but we shall win. We shall march forward, never looking back.

Comrades, Oriental fantasy has created a fable which shows symbolically, so to speak, the conditions under which a man or a people, having undertaken a certain task, can succeed in accomplishing it. This fable tells of three wonders of nature which are situated on the summit of a magic mountain. Many brave heroes have set out to win these treasures, but as soon as anyone approaches the magic mountain, voices begin to resound, calling on the brave man to turn back. They are either the plaintive moans and cries of children, wives, fathers and mothers, appealing to the bold spirit to return and not to risk his life for a chimera, or else terrible shouts which resemble the frightful howling of a storm, or claps of thunder. Thousands and thousands of daring fellows failed the test — they looked back to where these sounds were coming from, and were transformed into stone statues. And the whole mountain, from foot to summit, became strewn with these lifeless figures of stone into which living men had been transformed. But then a courageous and strong-willed man came along. He began to climb the mountain paying no attention either to the tender prayers of his kinsfolk or to the terrible shouts and frightening voices which sounded from behind him, threatening him with all the plagues of Egypt and a most painful death. He did not look back, but marched forward, fastening his gaze upon the summit of the mountain. And he achieved his aim, gaining possession of the treasures that were on the mountaintop.

And now comrades, you are beginning your ascent of the mountain in order to win all the treasures of the world. And you will hear the voices of those who are near to you, appealing to you not to risk your lives, you will hear the terrifying cries of all sorts of Moslem bigots, Pan-Turkic and Pan-Islamic fanatics, Georgian and Armenian Mensheviks and Dashnaks, who will threaten you with all sorts of bogies, but you will march forward, ignoring these cries, will climb the mountain, arms in hand, without looking back — otherwise you will be transformed into images of stone. [*Applause.*]

But you will reach the mountain-top, you will gain possession of the wonders of the world, you will see the realm of brotherhood, freedom, real equality of nations, the realm of labour. [*Applause.*]

Lond live the offensive military alliance of the working masses of East and West!

Long live the international Soviet republic of labour, in which there will be no enslaved, no oppressed peoples!

Long live Soviet power throughout the world!

Long live the Third, Communist International! [*Applause.*]

Chairman: Comrades, before proceeding to the translation, we should like to put a proposal to you. In order to underline the aspirations of the Congress and hasten the emancipation of women in the East, we ask you to confirm the inclusion in the Presidium of these three women: Bulach, from Daghestan, Nadjia Hanum, from Turkey, and Shabanova, from Azerbaidzhan. [*Voices:* 'Please, please.' *Applause, rising to an ovation.*]

Comrade Nadjia Hanum will say a few words.

[*Nadjia Hanum speaks in Turkish. – Loud and prolonged applause.*]

Chairman: Long live the emancipation of the women of the East! [*Loud applause. Shouts of* 'Hurrah!' *All stand. Ovation.*]

Chairman: Yashasun shargin azad hanum lari![81]

Shabanova: Long live our comrades Lenin, Zinoviev and Trotsky! [*Shouts of* 'Hurrah!' *Applause. Ovation. Exclamations in various languages resound through the hall, covered by the roar of clapping.*]

Chairman: I call for the translation of Comrade Pavlovich's speech. The translation must be brief, in accordance with our decision of yesterday. I call on Comrade Sultan Zade to give the translation.

[*Sultan Zade translates.*]

Zinoviev: In view of the fact that the Congress is very tired, both fractions propose that we confine ourselves to hearing two speakers only, one from each fraction. The speakers nominated are Comrades Mutushev and Ryskulov. These comrades will be allowed ten minutes each, and we shall then take the vote. Please translate. [*Translation.*]

I call upon Comrade Mutushev.

Mutushev (Communist): Comrades, my time is very limited, so I request your co-operation as regards silence and attention. The picture of the national and colonial question as it stands today has been drawn for you so far as its general features are concerned. It is fitting to add to the strokes drawn by the comrade who gave the report a few words about national-colonial *policy* — to look at the question, so to speak, in movement, from a definite point of view.

Comrades, we have to approach this serious question in a realistic way. It is not a question that is raised merely for effect, but an extremely vital one, on the correct solution of which the entire fate of the revolution depends. In the short time which I have at my disposal I shall try to give you a brief account of the actual, objective situation.

What is the East? The division between East and West has its own history, but, in the last analysis, we mean by the East today the countries of Asia and of the north coast of Africa, mainly Egypt. In particular, by the Moslem East we mean: Turkey, Persia, Baluchistan, Afghanistan, Bukhara, Khiva and all the regions of Turkestan, India, and part of China. That is what is meant by the Moslem East. Naturally, in such an extensive territory as this there is tremendous heterogeneity, an enormous exotic bouquet of nationalities, speaking a variety of languages, but they are all united by common features in their culture — by Islam.

It is, of course, impossible in ten minutes, to embrace this ocean of concepts called the East. Accordingly, in speaking about national-colonial policy, we shall examine this question within the limits of our programme.

Comrades, taking stock of an objective situation means making an assessment of reality which is realistic and as accurate as possible, looking to see how property is distributed, what the means of production are, and what the production relations are; furthermore, it means taking into account the colossal ideological stock of spiritual culture which has been conditioned by the given economic basis. That is, strictly speaking, what is meant by taking stock of an objective situation, and to do that I unfortunately lack the time. By developing revolutionary tactics the Soviet power, which heads and inspires the revolutionary movement in the East, gives guidance to this movement and brings to the East the totality of its proletarian Soviet culture. Is there such a culture, is there a proletarian culture, and, if so, what is it? I take it as my task to show to you that, in the situation which has come about, the only way out for the peoples of the East is through very close alliance and living contact with Soviet Russia, as the leader of the revolutionary movement on the world scale. Let us first of all note what exists in the areas concerned before we proceed to what is entering the East. In the East we have masses of peasants and, with rare exceptions, an almost complete absence of a factory proletariat. We ask ourselves, where is the centre, where is that main point around which the social revolution in the East has to be accomplished? The answer is: the peasant masses, agrarian relations, the barbarous despotism of the local rulers, and the imperialism of the West. And we understand the revolutionary movement in the East as meaning: organization of the peasantry against the feudal survivals with which the sad life of the East is so filled, and overthrow of the shameless, predatory imperialism of the West. Just as in past times the movement of the peoples from East to West was agrarian, concerned with land, so also now, in the twentieth century, the movement of the revolution from West to East will be basically a movement concerned with land. We bring to the East emancipation of the land and of the working peasantry.

Let us look at Turkey, which has played so big a role throughout the East. It is a striking picture, at which we have only to glance in order to feel the social ghastliness of rural life as led by the Turkish peasantry. Twelve years of unbroken rule in Turkey by the party of 'Disunion and Regress',[82] crowning the previous nightmare history of the Sultans' absolutism, has brought the Anatolian peasants to a state of pauperism. Here is the picture. Far off on the horizon we see a Turkish *aul*. In the foreground a grey-haired old Turk is ploughing the land: he has harnessed to the plough, along with his one and only ox, his own daughter. The tremendous social significance of this picture is clear. All the young men have been taken away from productive work to fight in wars, and almost all the draught animals have been killed. This is the economic dead-end into which Turkish absolutism, with the benevolent co-operation of Western imperialism, has led the Turkish peasantry. This is the fulcrum upon which the lever of the revolution must accomplish social revolution in Turkey. There is, however, a spark of proletarian organization in Turkey, there are Communist cells which carry on propaganda both legal and illegal. Mustafa Kemal's movement is a national-liberation movement. We support it; but as soon as the struggle against imperialism is concluded we are sure that this movement will advance to a social revolution. Let us proceed to Persia. The dreadful situation of unheard-of poverty in which the Persian peasants live has lasted for many years. It is enough to look round in the streets of Baku and you will see a mass of people who are dragging out a most miserable existence — products of an inhuman capitalist economy, the so-called *ambali*. [83] When you look at these human beings who have been deprived of the elementary meaning of life, who spend the whole day engaged in the heaviest labour merely so as not to die of hunger that same night, you realise that in Persia there is 'an excess of working population', that the soil exists there for social revolution. It is not hard to appreciate what goes on farther off, in Afghanistan, Baluchistan and India, under the 'paternal' care of British imperialism. From India the European brigands extort countless treasures, while the legitimate owners of these treasures — the workers and peasants of India — die like flies from hunger and epidemics. I think that everyone understands that the whole essence of our work at this Congress is to explain that Soviet power and the dictatorship of the proletariat, awareness of the common interests and tasks of the whole of toiling mankind, is the *sine qua non* for the victory of labour over capital and the emancipation of the oppressed masses of mankind from the yoke of imperialism.

What cultural assets does the proletariat possess and what does it bring to the East? The scientific basis of Communism is furnished by the works of Marx, Engels and many other learned men. This trend in social science is called Marxism, historical materialism. Thus, in working out their proletarian conception of the world the toilers possess a scientific asset to which the bourgeoisie has no equal. It must be added that the proletariat sees itself as a class which cannot free itself from the yoke of capital without also freeing all the other classes of society. From this it is clear that the proletariat is the only class which strives to realize a culture truly common to all mankind. It brings to the East not disunity but the unity of all the working people of the human race, towards which purpose it has created great cultural assets in the shape of the trades unions and co-operatives. This is the outstanding strength of the proletariat, expressed in the mutual solidarity it has established — mutual confidence and firm determination to go forward together to the final, life-and-death battle with capital. Moreover, the proletariat has created an unprecedented form of governmental organization — Soviet power. This is a very great achievement by the proletariat in the political field: very simple in structure, brilliant in concept. These are the cultural assets which the proletariat is bringing to the East in the name of the emancipation and liberation of the oppressed masses. Of course, every human movement has its shortcomings: here too, matters do not proceed without unevenness, and so it is necessary to say a few words about the peculiar features of proletarian culture, so that you may realize that shortcomings are inevitable, that it is pointless to talk about some shortcomings, and that, finally, there are and will be shortcomings about which it is dishonest to remain silent.

The famous Christian theologian Thomas Aquinas distinguished between the church militant, fighting for its place in the world arena, and the church triumphant in its victory. The former is romantic, the latter classical. But it is not only the church that experiences this fate — the same is true of art and culture. Every culture is at first a militant culture, a culture fighting for the right to exist. Proletarian culture is a culture of struggle, of quest for the true roads by which mankind must advance: it is a romantic and not yet a classical culture. There is no triumphant tranquillity in it, it is all passion and fervour, and this is why it includes both mistakes and shortcomings. Do not forget, either, that the class struggle, the social revolution, is a life-and-death battle between two irreconcilable camps. From this battle either labour or capital will emerge victorious, or else they will both perish. The salvation of the East lies in the victory of the proletariat, and so our only road is that of contact with Soviet Russia. Under its leadership and instruction, along with it, we must go forward against the common enemy — world capital. I have briefly spoken to you about what exists in the East and what is entering the East. The policy of the proletariat on the national and colonial question is expressed in the resolutions of the Eighth Congress of the Russian Communist Party, the main burden of which is as follows: unity of the proletariat and semi-proletariat of all countries and all nations, that is, what we see before us in the shape of the Third International; and abolition of the privileges and domination of one nation over another, with federation as the transitional form of the union of all the working people . . .

The Chairman announces that the time allowed for the speech is up. [*Voices:* 'Please continue.'] The comrade has spoken for 20 minutes. That's more than ten minutes, but, if the Congress is willing, he can, of course, be allowed to finish his speech. [*Voices:* 'Please, please.']

Will those in favour of Comrade Mutushev finishing his speech please raise their hands? Who is against? There is a majority 'for'. So, then, the Congress wants Comrade Mutushev to go on with his speech. Comrade Mutushev, please continue.

Mutushev: [*Applause.*] Comrades, I was interrupted and I don't remember what I was saying at that moment. Although I have been enabled to continue, it is not possible to enlarge very much owing to the lack of time.

My only desire is that you may take away from this Congress one simple idea, one firm consciousness, namely, that we shall either perish together with Soviet Russia or shall together with Soviet Russia live a bright new life based on Communist principles — that there are on our planet two centres: the centre of bourgeois domination, Versailles, and the centre of proletarian struggle, Red Moscow.

Comrades, I should like to remind you that our ancestors at one time advanced from the East to the West as predatory conquerors, and while there is distrust among the oppressed peoples of the East towards the oppressor countries of the West, there is also the same distrust, as a survival from the past, in the countries of the West towards the peoples of the East. The days of Tamerlane and Genghis Khan have not been forgotten. The working masses of the East and the West must not permit such mutual distrust to continue, for they have a common foe — world capital and imperialism. Let me remind you of some lines from the verses of the great Lermontov: ' "The East shall not affright my ease," Kazbek made answer fair; "Already nine long centuries the race of men sleeps there." ' [84] Today we can say with pride that the East is awakening from its sleep of centuries and coming out on to the common human road of social construction in fraternal unity and contact with the proletariat of the West, embodied in Red Russia. I should like to draw for you one sharp stroke so as to portray in your imaginations that 'culture and civilization' which Western imperialism is bringing to the East, to the colonies. The poet Gorodetsky expressed in his poem 'Coffee', which was published in the Baku workers' paper *Voyenmor*,[85] the whole power of poetic protest against this 'culture'. On the island of Java a native girl with a dark-red skin is picking coffee. On the quay a Britisher, whip in hand, is supervising the packing of the coffee, and when the work slackens however slightly he urges the slaves on with cruel blows of his 'civilized knout'. And on the island of Java wounds and groans poison life for the dark-red native girl. The poem continues. The coffee has been picked and sent off to Europe and America. In restaurants in Paris, London or Chicago, the bourgeois, accompanied by prostitutes, guzzles on profit extracted from the sweat and blood of the proletariat. And he drinks the coffee that the Britisher got from Java. The poet writes, inspired by all the power of his poet's heart: 'This is why, when the black coffee bubbles with a golden glint in the porcelain cup, there rises to the brain a wave of desire for violent actions, and the heart suddenly yearns for catastrophe. Blow up Europe! Sweep away with fierce will the evil shamelessness of buying and selling! No whip is needed for the flowers of the magnolia, no guard for the sun that shines on the ocean.' [*Applause.*]

Chairman: Please take your seats. I call upon Comrade Ryskulov. [*Applause.*][86]

Ryskulov: The colonial and national questions, which we are discussing today, are of very great importance for us. These questions are also very important for the capitalist system.

The last half-century of the existence of the capitalist system has been mainly based on this colonial, national policy. If we follow the activity of the capitalist powers during the last half-century we see that this last stage is a completely new form of the capitalist system, what Comrade Lenin has called monopoly capitalism, that is, the stage of capitalism in which large markets have been concentrated in the hands of separate alliances of capitalists, trusts, and in which competition proceeds between these separate alliances and groups.

As a result of this policy, this competition, we see the frenzied grabbing of colonies and of particular markets, and the forcible transformation of the inhabitants of these colonies into slaves subject to inhuman exploitation.

We see that the territories of the black continent of Africa and of Asia have been more and more completely divided up between particular big states. As a result of this colonial policy, the world powers which are at the head of this policy clashed in their interests, formed two coalitions, and brought about the five-years' war which we have experienced, and this has resulted in the social revolution which has taken place in Europe and has begun in the East.

At the present time it is quite pointless to dwell upon the different features of particular forms of colonial exploitation, for we have left this period behind us.

When the Second International existed, colonial policy was discussed, but only on paper, in words. Essentially, the Second International endorsed the striving of the great powers for conquest. Today the Eastern question presents itself in quite a different way.

With the establishment of the dictatorship of the proletariat in Russia, with the victory of the Communist Party, we see that light has been thrown upon the colonial question from a different angle. There is no longer that fear which the leaders of the Second International entertained that the peoples of the East would destroy the culture of Europe. The leaders of the Second International feared this. They feared to offend the feelings of their bourgeois rulers. But there is nothing of this, nothing at all in the Communist Party, in the Third International.

The slogan of unity of the Western proletariat with the revolutionary tendency in the East, the peasants' and working people's movement in the East, has been firmly advanced.

Despite the fact that the Communist tendency is growing stronger in all countries, despite the fact that the Third International is a mighty force which is shaking the foundations of capitalism, despite the achievement of the victory of socialism, nevertheless the colonial question is of paramount importance for our policy, along with the agrarian question.

Correct solving of these questions is of enormous importance, and we can promote the solution of our tasks by presenting these questions correctly.

At the present time conditions in the East are completely favourable for the introduction of a revolutionary movement, for drawing the mass of the working people into the socialist movement. A precondition for this is the situation of the peasants which has come about as a result of the colonial activity of the great powers. A pre-condition for this is the legacy of the five-years' war, which has created a mass of poverty, oppression and ruin in the colonies. As a result, the working people of the colonies are prepared for revolt, prepared for a revolutionary offensive against imperialism.

But while in the West the socialist movement takes the form of a Communist movement, we certainly cannot count on a purely Communist movement. In the East the movement assumes a petty-bourgeois character, the form of a movement for national self-determination, for the unity of the East. But this movement will undoubtedly develop into a social movement, an agrarian movement. [*Applause.*]

The task of the Communist International is to wrest the working class of the West, which is still in part under the influence of the opportunists, of the compromisers, finally from under their influence, to train conscious supporters of Communism, and at the same time there is the most important task, that of uniting the scattered revolutionary movement in the East with the movement in the West. This is the most important task facing the Third International.

It is for this question that we have assembled here and this is the question we shall solve here, or rather, we shall show the way to achieve its solution, we shall show how to bring about as quickly and soundly as possible the unity of the West with the East, for the final smashing of the foundations of capitalism.

In relation to the East, the Third International proves, not only on paper, in appeals, in words, but in practice, in deeds, that 50 millions of the peoples of the East have joined the Soviet power. We see that Soviet republics have been formed from the former colonies, in Turkestan, Caucasia and other countries with a Moslem population, and these Soviet republics are entering as federal units into Soviet Russia; and now these Soviet republics, inhabited by oppressed toilers, are developing culturally, raising their cultural level. They are now liberated and are building their own social life.

That is truly a great deed which the Communist International has performed. The break which these borderlands, these republics, have experienced, what has happened there, must serve as an example to the entire East. Let all the working people not just hearken to our appeals, to our ideas — let them look at these republics, which are examples for them. In these borderlands the Communist Party has shown that its programme is applicable not only for the Western proletariat but also in the East.

However much the supporters of the Second International and the compromisers may have argued that the colonies of the East are inhabited by slaves who can never come up to the level of Europe, who are so backward that no labour, no effort can make them progress, despite such views as these, we see that this East, held in such low esteem by bourgeois Europe, has shown that it can join forces with Communism and Soviet power precisely among these backward Moslem peoples.

The forms of state structure and the methods of reforming economic life in the borderlands will undoubtedly serve as a graphic example for those countries of the East which have not yet freed themselves and which must be freed.

At the present time the movement in those countries of the East where revolutionary organizations are weak, where the organizations of the working people are weak, is assuming, of course, a bourgeois-national character. At the head of this movement stand supporters of a

petty-bourgeois revolution, supporters of democracy, but not supporters of Soviet communism. This movement, at its beginning more
united, more powerful, of course, is rendering us a great service, for
this force acts against the Entente, against world capital, and that
helps us greatly.

The Third International, the Communist Party, must, of course,
support this movement, but at the same time we have to say that it is
not this movement that will finally liberate the toiling masses. Liberation of the toiling masses can be effected only through the social
revolution. Therefore, while we see that the petty-bourgeois
revolutionaries in the East, though opposing capitalism, at the same
time have nothing in common with Communism and necessarily want
to set up their own independent national republics, these independent
republics will exist as such only on paper, but will never be really
independent. For either they must remain in the camp of the
bourgeoisie, of the capitalists, or they must enter the camp of the
world proletariat — there is no middle way between these two positions. This we can see in reality. Such states as Armenia, Finland and
Poland are examples which are all too eloquent. These states are not
distinct states. They were deliberately set up by the Allies, they are
quite simply particular organized gangs which by special assignment
from world capital are fighting against Soviet Russia. Consequently,
if, somewhere in the East, say in Turkey or in other places, supporters
of the revolutionary movement who are at the same time opponents of
Communism should try to set up such independent states, these states
would not survive: they would fall under the influence of the
imperialists, of world capital, and would turn their weapons against
the proletariat, against the working people of the East. The situation
is clear, therefore — it is clear that the working people of the East have
only this one choice: to organize themselves as quickly as possible
under the slogan and banner of the Communist International, to carry
through the agrarian revolution, to take the land and to take power
into their own hands. This is the only solution, the only way, the only
means of achieving real self-determination of the peoples, real emancipation from the yoke of world capital. [*Applause.*]

Comrade Lenin, in his theses on the colonial and national question
at the Second Congress, defined quite exactly and realistically the
tasks of the Communist Party, the tasks of the Third International in
the East. Although he has not been in the East, in his theses he
registers everything as though it has been taken from life. These

theses point, first and foremost, to the need for liberation from the yoke of world capital and for a call to struggle against world capital not only by the Communist tendency but also by the bourgeois-national tendencies. These bourgeois-national tendencies are appealed to for alliance, but at the same time it is concretely shown that they do not provide for the final emancipation of the toilers. This movement cannot bring liberation. Furthermore, the social bases for such liberation are indicated: in this respect, the principal support for this revolution is constituted by the agrarian question.

For all the toiling classes the moment has unquestionably arrived when they must, having organized themselves, go forward together with the Western proletariat, go forward resolutely against world capital. And the pre-condition for this is that the oppressed peoples of the East, crushed for centuries by capitalism, that very East which once gave light to Europe, and which was also crushed by that same Europe, must rise up. In the depths of the East are hidden mighty forces, a tremendous power, which is now rising up in one mighty stream, and which, uniting with the stream of the Communist movement, will finally smash the rule of world capital. The basis for this is the fact that many Communist Parties have been formed, which have been joined by the leaders of the working people of the East. This is shown by the fact that a number of Soviet republics have been formed out of former colonies. Our pre-condition for this is the fact that there is now in session a Congress of the Peoples of the East, of the working elements of the peoples of the East. We are on the threshold of that powerful, tremendous movement which will begin in the near future, a movement which, united in a mighty Eastern International, will, together with the Western proletariat, strike finally at the very heart of world capitalism.

Long live the Communist International, leader of the world proletariat and of all the world's toilers!

Long live the leaders of the Third International!

Long live the toilers of the East, who are now rising up powerfully and unitedly against capital! [*Applause.*]

[*Voices:* 'Gadzhiyeva! Translate into Uzbek. Gadzhiyeva.']⁸⁷

Chairman (ringing his bell): There will now be a translation.

[*An interpreter translates into Turkic.*]

Chairman: There will be an interval of five minutes. [*Translated into Turkic.*]

Chairman: The discussion of the colonial question is concluded. The Presidium does not present a special resolution on this question, assuming that the Congress identifies itself with the relevant resolution of the Second Congress of the Communist International.

The following written statements have been handed in:

(1) A declaration on Palestine by the central bureau of the Jewish sections of the Russian Communist Party.

(2) A declaration by the Jewish Communist Party (Poale-Zion)[88] on the national and colonial questions.

(3) A declaration by representatives of the working masses of Armenia.

(4) A declaration by the Mountain Jews.[89]

(5) An address by the Moslems of South-western Caucasia[90] to the Congress of the Peoples of the East. [*Translation*]

Chairman: A translation into Turkic is also needed.

[*Voice:* 'And a translation into Azerbaidzhani. Please!'] [*Translation.*]

Chairman: All these documents are very important but they are also very long, and it is unfortunately not possible to read them out and translate them. The Presidium proposes that they be appended to the report of the Congress, as documents. [*Translation.*]

Comrades, with this we now close the Congress. The next session will be tomorrow at 5 o'clock.

The session ended at 10.05 p.m.

Sixth Session

September 6

The session opened at 7.10 p.m. Comrade Zinoviev took the chair.

Chairman: I declare the sixth session of the Congress of the Peoples of the East open. Today we have on the agenda the question of Soviet construction in the East. Translation, please. [*Translation.*]

Accordingly, we shall proceed to hear the report on this question. I call on Comrade Béla Kun. [*Applause.*]

Béla Kun: Comrades, in support of theses which have been discussed in detail by the Presidium and which it now unanimously puts before you, I propose to address you as follows.

Mighty Tsarist Russia, an immediate neighbour of the peoples of the East, fell beneath the blows of the workers and the poorest peasants. This revolution did not stop half-way. It did not leave state power in the hands of those classes which more or less disliked the Tsarist regime but whose whole existence was based on oppression of the working people. This revolution did not leave intact the former structure of government, but smashed it, in order to build upon its ruins the authority of the workers and the poorest peasants, endeavouring by means of this authority to carry the struggle forward until no possibility of any sort of oppression was left. In another sense, too, this revolution did not stop half-way: it was not checked at the frontiers of the state, but, like a devouring flame, spread both westward and eastward. This spreading of the revolution to West and East threatens to bring about the final downfall of that system which, not content with exploiting the working people of its own countries, has come to flower in imperialist colonial policy and borne fruit in world

120

war. A revolution in the West and in the East must inevitably follow upon the social revolution of the workers and poorest peasants of Russia. These two revolutions are organically interconnected not only because they are directed against a common foe, world imperialism, but also because the necessary premise of their victory is common, concerted struggle. In order to subjugate the colonial peoples the imperialist exploiters have mobilized the European workers, whom they have tried to win over to their side by means of bribes — crumbs from the super-profits extorted from the colonial peoples. This happened both in Britain and in Germany. They aimed in this way to deflect the workers from the path to revolutionary understanding. On the other hand, the imperialist bourgeoisie have given much thought, especially in recent times, to using against the European workers' movements the colonial troops they have recruited, exploiting the lack of consciousness of these soldiers so as to defend their shaken state power against the working class.

I, comrades, have had the opportunity to witness personally this sort of policy on the part of the imperialist bourgeoisie. When we, the workers and poorest peasants of Hungary, seized power, the French bourgeoisie at once attempted to strangle our revolution, using the hands of Moslem colonial troops. However, despite our difficulty in communicating with these soldiers owing to the difference of language, we nevertheless managed to find a way to their minds and hearts, and they threw down their arms when they were called upon to drown our revolution in blood.

The imperialist bourgeoisie usually succeeds in finding in the colonial countries a stratum of the native population, and in the semi-colonial countries a ruling class, whose aid it can utilize so as to make its exploiting policy less difficult and less expensive than it would otherwise be, and also less costly in blood. The sultans and emirs and the ruling strata associated with them in the Eastern countries, after their own resistance has been broken, have always readily agreed to become collectors of tribute for the imperialist oppressors: thus, the Shah of Persia agreed to act as tribute-collector for Russian imperialism and for British imperialism, turn and turn about. The Young Turks skinned the Turkish peasants on behalf of the German imperialists, and now the Anglophils headed by the Sultan are depriving the Turkish peasant of his last cow in the interests of the Anglo-French imperialist bloc. The Emir Feisal, who is on the payroll of the French bankers, has agreed to break up the unity of the Turkish people and to make the Turkish peasantry accept the position of beasts of burden to the French imperialists.[91]

The imperialist bourgeoisie found allies in the colonial and semi-colonial countries of the East sooner than the revolutionary proletariat did. It helped these allies not only by giving them miserable crumbs from what it had plundered from the toiling poor of these countries, but also by training them in those methods by which it had deceived and stupefied its own working class.

Capitalism succeeded in holding in submission the rebellious worker masses of Europe only by persuading them that they too shared in state power, though this was in fact merely an instrument in the hands of the ruling class with which to oppress the working people. Similar to this was the parliamentary constitution in Turkey, drafted in accordance with the European pattern: although to the outward view it gave rights to the working people, in reality everything remained as before — domination by the pashas, tyranny of the officials, and no hindrance to the activity of the usurers who brought ruin upon the people.

The revolution of the European and American proletariat and poorest peasantry is directed precisely against those lies which aim to keep exploitation and oppression in being behind a screen of democracy, freedom and equality. The revolution of the Russian workers and poorest peasants created that form of government which puts power into the hands of the working masses not merely in words but also in deeds. This form is the Soviets of workers and peasants. Until the Russian workers and peasants took power through their Soviets the land remained in the hands of the landlords and the factories and mines in those of the capitalists. 'Freedom' merely gave the bourgeoisie freedom to squeeze sweat out of their workers and to refuse to the non-Russian nationalities the right to decide for themselves whether they wanted to remain within the Russian state or to be independent of it. The Communist revolution and the victory of the Soviet order at once transferred to the working people the land, factories and mines and, in place of the inequality between exploiters and exploited, established the equality of all working people. With the ending of exploitation there ended all interest in enslaving and exploiting other peoples. One of the first steps taken by the Soviet republic was recognition of the right to self-determination for all peoples and liberation of Russia's colonies. Just as the Tsarist regime had secured alliances with the shahs and emirs, that is, with the ruling strata of the oppressed countries, so Soviet Russia immediately proposed an alliance to those toilers whom the old Russia, both Tsarist and democratic, had kept in a colonial situation.

Only the Soviet system made it possible to transfer power to those whose interest it was that the instruments of production should not serve the interests of a tiny handful of persons but should belong to all the working people.

The Soviets, these fighting organs of the workers and peasants, organs of their authority and government, are a new form of state. The workers and poorest peasants, having disarmed the enemies of the people, organize themselves in Soviets, take up arms, and themselves promulgate laws and decide what shall be the norms of the social order. The toiling masses themselves, either directly or through their representatives, pass the laws.

No parasites or exploiters boss the workers about, no usurers lord it over the poor. All these elements have been deprived of all rights. Soviet power is in sharp contrast to what prevails in the East today. It means rule by the toilers and the poor peasants, in place of rule by the rich and the parasites. I think that there is no delegate present here who is not convinced that oppression and exploitation can be ended only by introducing this form of state power. It is clear that until now, while our beys, khans, usurers and tribute-collectors possessed political rights, while they were able to distort the truth by means of all sorts of tricks and deceptions, to interpret the law in accordance with their own interests, and to resort to force of arms whenever their cunning did not help them — until now it has been quite futile to talk of putting an end to oppression and exploitation.

The theses I am laying before you set out in brief outline the essential features of Soviet power. Soviet power is not a system which cannot be adapted to the special conditions of a particular people or a particular region. In places where the predominant element consists of industrial workers, where exploitation is carried on by factory-owners and bankers, the Soviet organization will be quite different from what it will be in places where the main part of the population is engaged in agriculture and where exploitation takes the form of usury. Whereas in Western states it is the factory-owners, bankers and big landowners who have, first and foremost, to be removed from power and stripped of rights, in the Eastern countries Soviet power must be directed, first and foremost, against usurers, kulaks, khans, beys, foreign exploiters and officials. The Eastern Soviets must, of course, be soviets of the peasant poor, and just as in Daghestan and Azerbaidzhan a method has been found for determining at what number of cattle the exploitation of others' labour begins, so in all other tribal communities it will be possible to determine rules which will ensure that Soviets so organized will really be organs of the toiling poor.

The hangers-on of the bourgeoisie know how to spread all manner of dreadful stories about the Soviet order. Those in the East who are interested in keeping the toilers of the East in slavery, either along with the Western capitalists or independently of them, have quickly learned to do the same.

Whereas, in the West, Soviet power is the expression of the dictatorship of the proletariat, in the East, in those countries where there is no industrial working class, it will be the expression of the dictatorship of the poorest peasantry. It is self-evident that where a factory exists, where there are, even if only in small numbers, some better educated and experienced industrial workers, these workers will be the leaders of the rural poor. They will not, of course, be leaders of the same sort as the previous rulers, who, concerned with their own well-being, led the poor peasants into exploitation and want, but will be leaders who, since they are themselves interested in the ending of all forms of oppression and exploitation, will act in the interests of the general good of the people.

Very briefly, I want to speak against the time-hardened view by which peoples who have not passed through a phase of capitalist development, and so through bourgeois democracy, have to experience all this before they can go over to the Soviet system. This idea is maintained for the sole purpose of keeping the poorest peasantry of the East for a still longer period in the power of the emirs, pashas, beys and foreign colonialists. There is another objection which is advanced against the formation of Soviets in the East, namely, that the dictatorship of the proletariat is impossible without an industrial proletariat, and in the East the numbers of the industrial proletariat are infinitesimal. To this we reply: 'In the West, Soviet power is indeed the form and expression of the dictatorship of the proletariat, but in the East, where the exploited element is not the industrial workers but the poorest peasantry, the latter must also be the leading element in the Soviets.'

There is yet another objection. 'The peoples of the East are not yet mature enough to decide their fate for themselves; they need to pass through the phase of bourgeois democracy in order to acquire the capacity for self-government.' Only imperialist colonialists argue like this.

In the language of the people it means: 'Wait, Moslem poor peasants, until the pashas, beys, speculators and usurers deign to teach you how to take the land and power away from them.'

I think the falsity of this is clear to all the delegates. The Moslem poor have lived for many centuries under the rule of the Sultans, pashas and so on, and then came the colonialist merchants, those oppressors: they not only did not teach the people anything, but tried to keep them in ignorance. If the people are to wait, they will wait for centuries, until these hangmen have not only plundered them but have made them quite incapable of taking power for themselves. The ability to rule, like the ability to use a weapon, demands that you make a start and get some practice in: he who never handles a rifle will never learn to shoot.

In conclusion, I want to remind you of the changes which will be brought about in the pattern of everyday life, for the peoples of both East and West, by the common victory of their revolution. Economic intercourse between West and East will certainly not cease with the victory of the revolution. On the contrary, these ties will be very much closer than before; but they will be of quite a different kind from what they are today. The East is now united with the West by bonds of oppression and the coercion exercised by colonial troops. The means of colonial rule have always been alcohol, syphilis and weapons. Officers of the British and French imperialist armies have undressed the womenfolk of the oppressed Moslems not only with their eyes. The natural resources of the fertile Eastern lands have flowed away to the West — not into the hands of the Western workers, however, but into the coffers of the Western bankers, factory-owners and landlords.

These bankers and factory-owners, the oppressors of the Western workers, have always found allies in the East. The usurer who collects the fruits of Eastern fields, the state ruler and his entourage who have obtained loans from Western capitalists and ruthlessly collect the interest on these loans from the working peoples, these have always served as tools of colonial policy.

When the revolution of the proletariat and the poorest peasantry deprives the capitalists, landlords, factory-owners and bankers of all power and sends their myrmidons — generals, officials, priests — to the devil, and when power passes to the Soviets, which represent the masses of the working people, these new workers' and peasants' states will not, of course, pursue any aggressive aims in the East. They will not seek their allies among the Sultans and emirs, among the pashas and beys, and will not allow usurers to act as intermediaries in the economic dealings that will take place between the West and the peasantry of the East. The workers of the West and the peasants of the East can regulate their economic relations only directly, through their Soviet states. The Soviet state of the workers can sell the fruits of its labour only directly to the peasants of the East, and will never consent, can never consent, to receive goods produced by the stubborn labour of Eastern peasants through the mediation of usurers who rob them. Soviet states cannot follow the example of the capitalist system, which is entirely based upon buying and selling. Fraternal aid one to another, a just distribution of the fruits of joint labour — this is what can serve as the fundamental principle in the economic relations linking West and East after the victory of the revolution. And when the Soviet system triumphs in the West and the East there will disappear that difference which has existed and exists today between colonial and metropolitan countries. Entry into an international federation, into a world union of Soviet states, will equalize, so to speak, the East with the West, and will organically rule out any possibility of exploitation of the Eastern peoples.

Whoever appreciates that the liberating revolution of the peoples of the East, like the social revolution, will lead on to socialism cannot have any view on the question of the state system to be proposed for the East other than advocacy of Soviet power. In the days when bourgeois revolutions and the bourgeois order were flourishing, endeavours by the ruling strata of the East to establish a parliamentary system for the East as well, fully corresponding to capitalism and bourgeois democracy, were quite comprehensible. Establishing a parliamentary system meant at that time trying to raise the East to the level of the West, to give economic forces the opportunity to develop freely. Strictly speaking, the idea was that the working people should allow to sit astride their necks, instead of the foreign exploiters and oppressors, the native variety of the same breed.

At the present stage of development of the international revolution it is no longer a question of who will be the oppressors, among whom and in what way the wealth created by the toiling people is to be divided up. The Soviet system means an end to all forms of exploitation. The point is that the fruits of the toilers' labour are to be enjoyed by the toilers alone.

'Whoever does not work shall not eat.' Naturally, whoever wants to see the complete emancipation of the toilers of the East cannot be for a system which seeks, by means of its organs of power, to maintain exploitation. Whoever wants the peoples of the East to be freed from all forms of exploitation and oppression, whoever wants to be liberated from foreign colonialists and from the native agents of foreign imperialists, whoever wants to replace the rule of the pashas, khans, beys, usurers and other bloodsuckers by the rule of the working masses, can take no road but that of Soviet power. Whoever wants the poor peasants to cease being subject to the tyranny of the rich and their hangers-on, whoever wants the poor to be able to settle their affairs for themselves, will, on his return from the congress to his *aul*, to his village, fight tirelessly for that peasant agrarian revolution which is being realized in the East by Soviet power and which will lead the East out of its present oppressed situation. We are sure that at the Second Congress of the Peoples of the East the representatives of the federation of Eastern Soviet states will report on how the poor of the East took power, how they are building their Soviet organs, and how they are marching onward along the road which leads to the abolition of all exploitation — to communism. I propose the adoption of the following theses.

Theses on Soviet power in the East

1. The revolution of the peoples of the East against external and internal oppression, against the foreign imperialists and the local exploiters, puts on the agenda the question of the state system in all the countries of the East. The European bourgeoisie has succeeded for a long time, by means of all sorts of intrigues, in concealing from the propertyless and those with little property, the proletarian and semi-proletarian elements, the essential nature of state power as an instrument of oppression. In contrast to this, in the states of the East the coercive nature of the ruling power is quite obvious.

The lives and all the products of the labour of the poor, who are totally without political rights, are liable to be bought and sold by various sultans, shahs, emirs and tribal leaders, and by the rich and the bureaucratic cliques associated with them. This situation prepared the way for the imperialist exploiters, who, in the colonial countries and those reduced to a semi-colonial condition, always concluded their deals with the help of the state rulers and the higher officers and officials, at the expense of the poor.

2. As in Western states, the rich exploiting strata of the population in the Near-Eastern countries have tried to give their rule an appearance of democracy. The parliamentarizing of Turkey and Persia and the transformation into democratic republics of Georgia (under the leadership of the Mensheviks), Armenia (under the leadership of the Dashnaks) and Azerbaidzhan (under the leadership of the Musavatists) took place under the slogans of freedom and equality. All these policies proved useless, however, even for creating a facade of democracy. Unheard-of poverty of the masses continues, together with prosperity for the agents of the foreign imperialists. The land remains in the power of its previous owners, the old tribute system continues, bringing immeasurable harm to the working people, and not only is usury tolerated, it is backed by the state power, to the detriment of the poor. All this has revealed the falsity of the slogans about equality put forward by the Turkish, Persian and Azerbaidzha-nian national-democratic parties, and also by the Menshevik and Dashnak parties, which operate under cover of socialist slogans.

3. The revolution of the toiling masses of the East will not come to a halt even after the rule of the foreign imperialists has been eliminated. It will not cease with a system which, under the false slogan of democracy, under cover of slogans of equality, seeks to maintain the power of the sultans, shahs, emirs, pashas and beys, seeks to maintain the oppression of the working people, inequality between the haves and the have-nots, the oppressors and the oppressed, between rich and poor, those who pay tribute and those who live on this tribute. The revolution will not halt at the estate boundaries of the landlords, proclaimed to be sacred: the Eastern peasantry, like the Russian, will develop their revolution to the dimensions of a huge agrarian peasant revolution, as a result of which the land must pass into the possession of the working people and all exploitation must disappear. Just as the Russian peasantry carried through their agrarian revolution with the support of the industrial workers under the leadership of the Com-munist Party, and, welded together in Soviets, are now defending the land they took from the landlords and the power they took from the exploiters — in the same way the oppressed peasantry of the East will in their revolutionary struggle count upon the support of the

revolutionary workers of the West, on the support of the Communist International and on that of the present and future Soviet states.

4. Soviet power and Soviet organization are not only the instrument of power and the organizational form of the industrial proletariat, but also constitute the only appropriate system whereby the working masses, after excluding from power the privileged, and consequently hostile, elements (landlords, speculators, higher officials, officers) can themselves build their own destiny. Only Soviet power gives power exclusively to the toiling poor. Unity of the Soviets, and their federation, is the only way to secure peaceful co-operation between the toiling elements of different peoples who have hitherto slaughtered each other in the East, and to help them to join forces to destroy the power of their oppressors, both foreign and native, and repel the oppressors' attempts to restore the former position.

5. So-called democratic self-government, putting the administration exclusively into the hands of the privileged strata (khans, beys, and so on) prevents the toiling masses from managing their own affairs. It deprives them of the possibility of learning to govern, stops them from acquiring the knowledge they need for this purpose. In contrast to this, experience among the peasants of Soviet Russia, Siberia, the Bashkir-Kirghiz republic[92] and Turkestan has shown that the peasants of the Eastern countries are capable of managing their own affairs.

6. The victory of the Communist Party in the West will put an end to the exploitation of the Eastern peoples. But victory for the Communist revolution in the West will not mean that East and West can then get on without mutual economic links. On the contrary, the victory of the revolution in the East and in the West will mean that in relations between different countries there will be, instead of exploitation, reciprocal support and aid. After the victory of the Communist revolution, economic intercourse will take place between states, and so the economic intercourse of those Eastern states which have not adopted the Soviet system would only serve the interests of the small group of capitalists who, having obtained corn and raw materials, would carry on trade with the Western Soviet states in exactly the same way as they do at the present time with the imperialist states — exploiting for this purpose the toiling masses of the East.

In the interests of complete liberation from imperialist exploitation, with transfer of the land to the toilers and emancipation from the power of speculator-exploiters, what is needed is removal from power of the non-working element, of all foreign colonialist elements (generals, officials, etc.) and of all privileged persons, and it is also necessary to organize the rule of the poor on Soviet principles. And all the other interests of the working people demonstrate to the East that it is imperative to establish Soviet power.

Chairman: Comrades, we now come to the vote on Comrade Béla Kun's theses, which were unanimously approved by the Presidium. Will those in favour please raise their hands. Who is against? Nobody. The theses are adopted. [*Applause.*] Let us proceed to the next question. Comrade Skachko will give the report on the agrarian question.

[*Translation.*]

Skachko: Comrades, all the Eastern countries are peasant countries. Owing to various conditions, and principally to the oppressed state in which they have been kept by the Western European capitalists, who denied them the possibility of independent development, the inhabitants of these countries have not developed their own industry and to this day they are still exclusively engaged in agricultural labour. The great mass of the entire population of the Eastern countries consists of peasants. Emancipation of the peoples of the East means emancipation of the peasants. While in the Western countries the productive class consists mainly of industrial workers, and while it is the industrial proletariat that can be called the King of the West, in the Eastern countries the sole producers of material values are the peasants. And so only they can be called the Kings of the East, and the Eastern countries should belong only to them. Let us look, comrades, at how these Kings of the East live, these men and women whose labour sustains not only all the peoples of the East but also a good part of those of the West. They live in the same wretched, pitiful, downtrodden and oppressed condition in which the peasantry of Western Europe lived many centuries ago. Though creating everything, they themselves enjoy none of it, and they bear the burden of unlimited oppression both by foreign capitalist conquerors and by their own privileged classes and despots. Various sultans, shahs, khans and beys, the masters of Eastern countries and lands, wallow in fabulous Eastern luxury while the peasants whose labour created this are dying of hunger and want, and are forced to leave their own very rich and fertile countries for alien lands, in search of the crust of bread they cannot obtain at home. Despite the fact that at the basis of the Moslem religion lay principles of religious communism, by which no man may be slave to another and not a single piece of land may be privately owned, and all religious institutions must make it their principal concern to care for the orphaned and indigent, nevertheless these religious principles have not saved the peasants from being reduced to serfdom, or preserved the land from seizure by landlords and despots. Gradually, these principles have been modified to the advantage of the ruling classes. The land, free and belonging only to God, was first declared to belong to the ruling Sultans and Shahs, and then became the property of feudalists and capitalists. The *waqf* lands,[93] which were given to the mosques and the clergy so that the income from them might support charitable institutions of value to the people, gradually lost their original function and became lands belonging to the clergy and to private persons, and the income from them, instead of being used for the benefit of the poor, was taken by the secular and ecclesiastical rulers — parasites who used these lands merely in order to exploit the poor peasants. The peasant, a free man according to the *shariat*,[94] was gradually turned into a slave, either by direct coercion on the part of the khans and beys or by economic compulsion based on the seizure of the land by the landlords. The situation of the peasantry of the Eastern peoples has not improved but constantly deteriorated, and has finally become so impossible and unbearable that no other way out is left for them but either to die a slow death from hunger or to break their servile chains and make a new life for themselves through social revolution.

How, indeed, can a man live in the conditions in which the Eastern peasant is living? Can we call a human life the existence that the wretched Persian *rayat*[95] drags out? He is not a human being, he is only the beast of burden of his landlord, the *molkadar*. This landlord has power to dispose of his life and property, to execute him or to punish him with strokes of the cane, to take the peasant's wives and daughters for his harem. Comrades, all this is going on a few hundred *versts* from Baku, over which flies the red flag of the Workers' and Peasants' Socialist Republic. A few hundred *versts* from this place, where the peasants have taken power into their own hands, other peasants are living in a state of utter slavery. The Persian peasant cannot call a single fragment of land his own: he can easily be evicted by his landlord even from his farmhouse, to die of hunger in the barren steppe. For the right to work his land, for the right to grow corn, he has to hand over to the landlord four-fifths of the crop, four-fifths of what he has produced by the labour of his hands. Of all that he gets from the land by his own work he is allowed to keep only miserable leavings, while the main part is devoured by the various parasites who sit astride his neck and make his life a sheer unbearable torment of grim slavery.

That is how things are in Persia. But the position of the peasants is no better in the other countries of the East. Even in the most advanced of the Moslem countries, Turkey, the peasant is poverty-stricken. Although serfdom has been abolished in Turkey, nevertheless even there the peasant is being reduced to a servile situation through economic conditions. The despotic government of Turkey, which always looked upon the peoples subject to its rule as conquered peoples, always pursued one aim and one alone in its administration: to extract from the population as much income as possible, taking no account at all of what it cost the population to produce this income and what frightful want was created by this barbarous, ruthless extortion. For centuries the despotic government of Turkey and its minions enforced such a frightful system of taxation and such a barbarous system of levying them, by means of tax-farming, that it completely ruined the peasantry and rendered them quite incapable of cultivating their holdings. In Turkey there are huge tracts of land, located in the most fertile vilayets, which are lying uncultivated, in utter desolation, the peasants having left the country, in search of a bite to eat. This has happened because the peasants are unable to work the abandoned land, since they have neither oxen, nor money, nor seed — they have none of the things they need in order to cultivate the land. In the southern part of Asia Minor, where also there are huge uncultivated tracts, there are more than 100,000 so-called *marabas*,[96] nomadic wage-labourers who, having neither land, nor farmsteads, nor shelter, wander in hordes all over the country, looking for miserably-paid seasonal work on the landlords' estates. Even those peasants who still have a holding of their own cultivate it not for themselves but for all manner of usurers, to whom their indebtedness obliges them to hand over four-fifths of their crop. The extent of the exploitation and the poverty-stricken situation of the Turkish peasants is shown by statistics. These figures reveal that even in peacetime the Turkish peasant never has left, out of all the corn he produces, more than six poods per year per head, or three-quarters of a pound a day. Today the Russian proletariat, ruined by many years of war and receiving, in the big centres which are worst stricken with famine, only one-and-a-half pounds of bread a day, is better supplied with bread than the Turkish peasant living in a fertile country abounding in free land! In Turkey as in Persia the position of the peasant is absolutely unbearable. It is a position of utter want, chronic hunger, endless indebtedness and work for the tribute-collectors and usurers, without any certainty regarding his title to the land and with no hope whatsoever of any improvement in his wretched situation.

This is the desperate, oppressive situation in which the peasants of other Eastern countries also find themselves. Not to speak of the Armenians, driven from their land, forced to take refuge in barren mountains, deprived of their homes and livelihoods and stripped of all they possess by the Kurdish landlords, the *aghas*, the peasants of all the other nationalities, even if not driven from their land, have little joy in their lives, for they work not for themselves but for their oppressors. In Khiva, Bukhara and Afghanistan, where agriculture can be carried on only on irrigated land, all such land has been grabbed by the landlords, the beys and khans, and the peasants are able to work it only as wage-labourers. In India the British rulers have taken nearly all the land, and, seeking to squeeze the maximum revenue from this unfortunate country, have leased it out to big capitalists, so that the peasant can gain access to the land only as a sub-tenant or a wage-labourer. Out of what the Indian peasant produces from the land he has to hand over the lion's share to the British rulers and another share to the capitalist farmer, keeping for himself only such a share as enables him to die of hunger amidst the flowering valleys of his fertile homeland, his wondrous country with its countless riches.

Everywhere, in all the countries of the East, the peasantry, who alone create all the material values which sustain their own people and others as well, themselves drag out the wretched existence of downtrodden, starving slaves. Everywhere in the countries of the East the peasant, that king and creator of riches, is starving to death and groaning beneath the whips of his own and foreign oppressors. 'Starving to death', comrades, is no mere phrase: the peasantry of the East really are starving — it has been proved statistically. In order to escape from his miserable situation, to escape from want, poverty and hunger, the peasant of the Eastern countries must throw off the centuries-old oppression both of the foreign capitalist exploiters and of his own oppressors the sultans, khans, shahs and beys. [*Applause.*] The peasantry of the East have starved long enough, they have served their various oppressors long enough — now they must free themselves and become the actual owners of their own land and the absolute masters of their fate. The many-millioned masses of peasants of the East must now rise up in all their colossal might and throw off all their oppressors, must take power into their own hands [*Applause*] by forming their own peasant Soviet government, by forming revolutionary peasant Soviets. All the sources of the oppression of the peasants must be destroyed — first and foremost, the system of landlordship which enslaves the peasant. Whoever does not work shall not eat; whoever does not till the land shall not possess it! [*Applause.*] All the land belonging to the landlords and feudalists, shahs and khans must be taken from them and given to the peasants, without any purchase-price, without any compensation to the former owners. Together with the land, all the animals and farm implements belonging to the estates of the feudalists and landlords must be taken, for the peasant must receive not only land but also the possibility of working it, and for this purpose he must seize all the instruments of production and all the wealth that his landlord oppressors possessed. Since there are in the East, besides the landlords' land, also huge tracts of state-owned land which are used by various secular and ecclesiastical institutions, officials and clergy, this land too must be taken from the ruling privileged classes and turned over to the peasants. Comrades, there is no cause to fear because some of this land belongs to the clergy. Of course the latter, who have concentrated huge tracts of land in their possession, and exploited peasant labour on this land, declare that this land belongs to God and therefore is inviolable, and the peasant dares not reach out to take it, but, comrades, this is all lies and fraud! Even according to the *shariat*, the land can belong only to him who tills it, and not to the clergy who have grabbed it, like the *mujtahids*[97] in Persia, who were the first to violate the fundamental law of the Moslem religion. They are not defenders of this religion but perverters of it. They are just such parasites and oppressors as the feudal landlords, except that they are also hypocrites who disguise their character as oppressors behind the white turban and the Holy Koran. This mask of sanctity must be torn from them, comrades, and the land they own must likewise be wrested from them and given to the working peasantry. [*Applause.*] All the confused and complicated legislation of the countries of the East, disguising private ownership under various masks and restricting the right of the possessor of a holding to use it as he pleases, preventing the peasant from cultivating his land as he wishes, must be swept away. Every peasant must have the right to utilize his land as he chooses, ignoring all such prohibitions and restrictions. [*Applause.*] Instead of the complicated and confused land laws which serve to enslave the peasant, it is necessary to establish just one land law, consisting of a single article: all land belongs to the state, and the right to use it belongs only to whoever works it with his own labour. [*Applause.*] That must be the only land law, giving the land to the toilers, to the peasants, and casting out from the land all parasites, exploiters and slaveowners. [*Tumultuous applause.*]

Then, comrades, attention must be paid to that scourge of the peasants of all the countries of the East which beats sweat and blood out of them and devastates the peasants' holdings — that fearful burden of taxes which the peasantry of Turkey, Persia and India have borne for hundreds of years. There is no need to tell you what these taxes have meant, what a fearful burden they have laid upon the peasants, how they have taken the skin, the blood, the very life of the peasants by means of a venal, corrupt administration. You know how the tithe provided for in the *shariat* has been turned into three-quarters and four-fifths of the peasant's crop, and how these taxes have reduced the peasantry of the Eastern countries to utter poverty. This scourge of taxation and the tyranny of officials and administrators associated with it must be destroyed, all taxes must be cancelled. The peasants must be freed from exploitation not only by the landlords but also by the state. [*Applause.*] But as it is clear that no human organization can exist without incurring certain expenses, the newly-formed Soviet Government of the peasants will also need to have a certain amount of revenue at its disposal, and so the peasants will have to give their government a certain portion of what they produce, which will be needed to support the urban workers, the state machine and the Red Army which defends the peasants' freedom. However, this levy, its amount and the actual way it is to be collected will be decided and put into effect not by venal, bloodsucking officials but by the peasants' Soviets. [*Applause.*] Relieved of taxes, the peasantry must also be relieved of debts. You know, comrades, how burdened with debt the Eastern peasant is; you know that he is always in debt to a neighbouring landlord, or to some kulak, trader or usurer; you know that without contracting loans the Eastern peasant cannot carry on cultivating his exhausted holding, and is therefore always up to his ears in debt. This indebtedness of the peasants makes them serfs to the usurers and obliges them to work, their whole lives through, for the enrichment of a moneylender. If the land were to be taken over, but the power of the old debts were left pressing upon the peasants, it would mean that the latter would have escaped from the claws of the landlords merely to fall into those of the usurers. This heavy yoke of debt which harnesses the peasantry to the old world of slavery must be left behind in that old world, and one of the first steps taken by the risen revolutionary peasantry must be a complete and categorical cancellation of all peasant debts whatsoever — to the state, to land banks, to landlords, to traders, to usurers. All the debt liabilities of the peasants must be declared invalid. The new revolutionary world must tell the old world of the usurers that the peasants of the Eastern countries no longer owe anyone so much as a kopeck. [*Applause.*]

I have mentioned these, comrades, as the first steps to be taken by the revolutionary peasants in the countries of the East. I have indicated the measures which the peasants will need to take at once. When you return home you will advise the peasants what they must do. They must annihilate their feudalists and landlords, overthrow the power of the despots who rule them, take power into the hands of peasant Soviets, take possession of all landlords' land, state-owned land and *waqf* land, with all the animals and implements belonging to those lands, share them out among the peasant poor, stop paying taxes, cancel debts, and thereby free the peasantry from all exploitation from any and every quarter.

Then, when the peasants of the East have succeeded in casting off the yoke of the foreign capitalists and of their own oppressors, when the peasants of the East have succeeded in forming Soviet republics, closely linked with the Soviet republics of the West — then, with the aid of the friendly republics of the industrial proletariat, it will be necessary to organize on a wide scale the supply to the peasants of all the means and instruments of production needed for agriculture, so that agriculture may flourish in the Eastern countries, so that the land in these countries, which is rich and abundant, and which was once the cradle of all mankind, may again bloom with splendid flowers and again bring forth all the wealth of former times, and even more. The furnishing of these supplies will be the concern of the governments of the Eastern Soviet republics and of the proletariat of the Soviet republics of the West.

As well as supplying the peasants with means of production, with machines of tremendous power such as the East has not yet seen, it will be necessary to teach the peasants how to use them collectively, for these machines, which are extremely productive, easing the peasants' labour tenfold, are not suitable for work on small holdings — they are adapted only to large areas and entail the need for joint cultivation of the peasants' land, the need to merge scattered labour into joint, collective labour, properly organized and shared. Only such joint, collective, properly-organized labour can transform the convict labour of the cultivator into labour which is sufficiently easy and pleasant. And it is for you, comrades, to show the peasantry the need to go over from scattered labour to joint labour. It is for you to show that the way of life of separate little economic cells, separate households, has always meant for the peasants and will continue to mean for them, the disintegration which makes possible their enslavement and oppression. In order that the peasantry may become a mighty force, they must merge into the close, organized unity into which the proletariat of the industrial countries of the West has merged. In order to achieve this unification it will be necessary to bring the peasants together into tens and hundreds of organizations of all kinds, agricultural and handicraft producers' *artels* and co-operatives and consumers' co-operatives of every sort, supplying the peasantry with all the products of urban industry that they need. All these organizations will free the peasantry from commercial middlemen and enable them to exchange their products directly for the products of factory industry. All middlemen, all parasites will be swept away, and the toilers will not have to hand over to them the slightest share of what they produce.

To arrive at this complete liberation of the peasantry from all their oppressors and all the parasites who feed at their expense, the peasantry will have to wage a protracted struggle, and this not only against the foreign capitalist conquerors but also against their own sultans and shahs, against their own landlords and feudalists, against their own bourgeoisie. Today in many Eastern countries, in Turkey, Persia and India, the peasantry is marching arm in arm with its own bourgeoisie in the fight to win independence for their countries from the foreign imperialist enslavers. This path is the right one. At present, all the efforts of the Eastern peasantry must be directed to throwing off the yoke of the foreign imperialists which weighs upon them, freeing their countries from the yoke of the West-European bourgeoisie, the capitalists of Britain and France.

But the peasantry of the Eastern countries must remember that their task will not be finished when this liberation has been gained, that if they stop there, if they rest content with expelling the foreign oppressors, they will not be liberated at all. Political independence with retention of the capitalist system will not in the least guarantee liberation for the peasantry. If the government of Mustafa Kemal in Turkey, or liberal-national governments in Persia and India, were to expel the British and then make peace with Britain on the basis of political independence of the Eastern countries, but with retention of the capitalist system in these countries, all the politically-independent Eastern countries would remain dependent economically. Political independence would not save them from penetration by industrial capital, and, with this penetration, or with the formation of native industrial capital and the development of native industry on the basis of private ownership of the means of production, the peasantry would be obliged to undergo an agonizing period of primitive capitalist accumulation, in which they would be finally ruined, driven from their land, and all turned into wage-labourers with no holdings of their own. And this peasantry transformed into workers would be driven by the bourgeoisie, either native or foreign, into its plantations, factories and mines and made to work there, at miserable wages, for the enrichment of the capitalists — they would find themselves in even worse enslavement to capital than they are today.

The peasantry of the Eastern countries must firmly keep in mind the fact that liberation merely from the yoke of the foreign conquerors will not bring them real freedom. They need to liberate themselves also from their own oppressors, their own despotic rulers, their own landlords, and their own bourgeoisie, and, after setting up their own peasants' Soviet power, in alliance with the Soviet republics of Europe, they need to fight against the bourgeoisie of the whole world, fight for the overthrow of capitalism in all countries, both East and West. So long as somewhere the capitalist system has escaped destruction, so long as the entire world has not been transformed into a great federation of free workers' and peasants' Soviet republics, in which there will be no place for any exploitation or oppression, so long will the peasantry of the East be unable to attain real liberation and so long will they not have ensured for themselves a free, human existence.

Only with the final victory of the social revolution, only with the final establishment of the Communist order throughout the world, will the peasantry of the Eastern countries secure genuine freedom, both political and economic, becoming able to work for themselves on their own land, enjoying all the produce of their own labour and giving nothing to any oppressors and exploiters.

Therefore, there is no road for the peasantry of the East but to go forward together with the revolutionary workers of the West, in close alliance with the Soviet republics the latter have created, into struggle against both the foreign capitalist conquerors and their own despots, landlords, bourgeois and other oppressors, waging this fight to the end, not retreating until the complete victory of the social revolution, the establishment of the Communist order, which alone can bring real liberation to all the peoples of both West and East and alone can destroy all forms of oppression of one people by another and all forms of exploitation of man by man. [*Applause.*]

Comrades, all that I have said is summed up in the brief theses which the Congress Presidium has adopted. They explain how our Congress sees the situation of the peasants in the East, and the roads to their liberation which it advocates.

Theses on the agrarian question

1.   The peasantry of the countries of the East, being the sole productive class and sustaining by their labour not only the landlords but also the entire bourgeoisie and bureaucracy, are crushed beneath a burden of survivals of feudalism, relations of bondage, landlords' extortions and state taxes, and find themselves in an absolutely unbearable situation of utter ruin, chronic hunger, endless indebtedness and work for landlords, tribute-collectors and usurers.

The oppression and exploitation of the peasants of the Eastern countries by the ruling authority, by foreign capitalists and by their own landlords have reached such limits that not only development but even more human existence has become impossible for the peasants, and have degraded them to the position of downtrodden and perpetually hungry beasts of burden.

2.   The sources of the oppression and exploitation of the peasants are:
a) the retention of feudal relations, which place the peasants in both personal and economic dependence upon the landlords;
b) the seizure of the land by the landlords, which enables them, owing to the inadequate availability of free land, to reduce the

peasants to bondage and turn them, though legally free, into *de facto* serfs;

c) the seizure of the land by the ruling authority, which leases out considerable tracts to the privileged classes and the capitalists, thus giving the latter a monopoly of landownership and obliging the peasants to become sub-tenants and labourers, under very burdensome conditions;

d) the unbearable burden of taxes and the predatory way these are levied, by the irresponsible bureaucratic organs of the despotic ruling power;

e) the lack of personal security, anarchy, and systematic brigandage by half-savage nomad tribes, which are backed by the ruling authority in their attacks on the peasants;

f) the extreme ruin of the peasants caused by all these conditions, resulting in their complete impoverishment, and the monstrous indebtedness of the cultivators, arising from this ruin, so that they fall into a state of absolute economic dependence on usurers and the object of their work becomes the unending repayment of loans and the interest on loans to various banks, landlords, kulaks and usurers;

g) the peasants' complete lack, as a result of their ruin, of means and instruments of production — money, agricultural machinery, draught animals, seed-corn, etc. — which means that it becomes impossible for the peasants to work for themselves on their own land, even when free and accessible land is available to them.

3. In order to bring about liberation from the unbearable burden of oppression, exploitation and ruin and to create the conditions necessary for them to work for themselves so as to satisfy all their needs and make further development possible, the peasants of the Eastern countries must:

a) remove the prime source of all their oppression and exploitation, the power of the foreign capitalist conquerors and of their own despotic tyrants, the sultans, shahs, khans and beys, with their entire parasitic train of bureaucrats and spongers, and take power, with all its administrative, economic and financial functions into their own hands, by forming local and central peasants' Soviets and setting up peasant Soviet republics of the East, linked in one indissoluble federation with the Soviet republics of the countries of the West;

b) refuse to fulfil any obligations towards the feudal landlords, over-throw their power, abolish all personal and economic dependence upon them, abolish large-scale landownership, under whatever legal form it may be concealed, take the land from the landlords without any purchase-price or compensation, and divide it among the peasants, tenants and labourers who till it, along with the land, take the herds of animals belonging to the landlords and divide them, in the first place among the labourers who possess no ani-mals at all, and then among the tenants and poor peasant cul-tivators; turn over the implements found on the landlords' estates to collective ownership by the peasants who have occupied the land — the peasants should unite in groups, concentrating the imple-ments made available to them for use in collective cultivation of the land, which ensures the best results and the most rapid develop-ment of the peasants' economy and of their prosperity;

c) take over all lands belonging to the state and to its various insitiu-tions, both secular and spiritual (including *waqf* lands) and divide them among the peasants and tenants, subtenants and labourers who work these lands, with complete abolition of all the rights of the big tenant-farmers who act as intermediaries between the state and the peasants, and confiscation for the benefit of the peasants of all the animals and implements belonging to these tenant-farmers;

d) cancel all existing land legislation and all restrictions on the right to use the land and to make changes on the surface of the holdings; proclaim that all land, regardless of its origin and independently of the rights of any owners or occupiers, belongs to the state and that it can be utilized free of charge by anyone who works it with his own labour; establish by means of a single land law the rule that 'whoever works a plot of land with his own labour is the possessor of that land and the owner of its produce,' and at the same time declare that the small-scale holdings of peasants who do not use others' labour are inviolable, and nobody has the right to encroach upon them for any purpose whatsoever;

e) regulate the utilization of local irrigation water-supplies and irri-gated land, this to be the responsibility of the peasant soviets, both local and central;

f) secure the interests of the nomadic tribes, assigning for their use areas of pasture-land sufficient to meet their needs, and at the same time take all measures required to ease the transition of the nomads to a settled way of life;

g) cancel all existing taxes, including the tithe, replacing them with a single assessed levy of a proportion of all the peasants' produce, this being necessary for the maintenance of the urban workers and of the army; the amount of this levy, its assessment and also the actual process of collection to be determined and implemented by the peasant Soviets, and everything taken from the peasants by means of this levy to be compensated by an assessed payment to the peasants of all the goods produced by urban industry which they need;

h) cancel all peasants' debts of every kind, to the state and to its various secular and spiritual institutions, to banks, landlords, and traders, and recognize as invalid all manner of peasants' debt liabilities;

i) undertake, after organizing peasant soviets and peasant soviet republics in the East, with the help and support of the Soviet republics of the industrial West, the supplying to the peasants, on an extensive scale, of agricultural machinery, tools, draught animals and other means of production needed for carrying on agriculture, arranging for joint use of these means of production by all the peasants; undertake the organizing of agronomic aid to the peasants and collective working of the land, without any compulsion of individual cultivators to participate in this; undertake the organizing of peasant producers' co-operatives, both for agriculture and for handicrafts, with extensive state support and gradual statization; undertake the organizing among the peasants of consumers' co-operatives with extensive state support and gradual statization, arranging through these co-operatives the supply to the peasants of all the products of urban industry needed by them;

j) organize on free, uncultivated land, in step with the supplying of the peasants with all the means of production needed for agriculture, Communist soviet farms, to be run, under state supervision, by agricultural workers organized in production associations; endeavour to develop these Communist soviet farms on as wide a scale as possible, with a view to using their surplus produce for exchange for needed urban-industrial goods which are produced by the industrial countries of Europe.

The mere establishment of the political independence of the Eastern countries, such as Turkey, Persia, Afghanistan, etc., as also the proclamation of the merely political independence of the colonial countries — India, Egypt, Mesopotamia, Arabia, etc. — cannot liberate the peasants of the East from oppression, exploitation and ruin. If the capitalist system is retained in Europe and Asia, the countries of the East which win freedom from political dependence upon the imperialist countries of the West, being more backward industrially, inevitably remain in complete economic dependence upon the latter, and, as before, serve as areas for the application of the finance-capital of the European industrial countries, which is associated with capitalist exploitation of the peasants and workers. If the capitalist system is retained, then, even in the event of the conquest of complete political independence by the countries and colonies of the East, the peasants of these countries must inevitably pass through an agonizing period of primitive capitalist accumulation, associated with their final ruin, eviction from the land, proletarianization and transformation into wage-earning factory hands or agricultural labourers, deprived of their own holdings and compelled to sell their labour-power. The peasantry of the East, now marching arm in arm with their own democratic bourgeoisie to win independence for their countries from the West-European imperialist powers, must remember that they have their own special tasks to perform, that their liberation will not be achieved merely by the winning of political independence, and that therefore they cannot halt and rest content when this is won. The peasantry of the East must go forward, continuing to fight even after the independence of their countries has been won — they must continue the fight against their dependence on their own landlords and their own bourgeoisie, who will certainly try, after the achievement of independence, to replace exploitation of the peasants by the West-European capitalists by exploitation of these peasants by themselves, the local landlords and bourgeoisie.

For complete and real liberation of the peasantry of the East from all forms of oppression, dependence and exploitation, what is further required is overthrow of the rule of their own landlords and bourgeoisie and the establishment in the countries of the East of the Soviet power of the workers and peasants. Only the complete abolition of the capitalist system, in West and East alike, will enable the peasants of the East not to lose but to retain and develop their holdings, and, avoiding the necessity of passing through an agonising phase of primitive capitalist accumulation, to advance, with the help of the working class of the more advanced countries, through a certain stage of development, to the Communist order, which will ensure for every peasant full freedom and full use of all the products of his labour.

Only the complete triumph of the social revolution and the establishment of a world-wide Communist economy can free the peasantry of the Eastern countries from ruin, want, poverty, famine, oppression and exploitation. And so for the peasants of the East, in their struggle for emancipation, there is no other road than that of struggle, together with the advanced revolutionary workers of the West, in close alliance with the Soviet republics these have formed, both against foreign capitalist conquerors and against their own despots — landlords, bourgeois and other oppressors: carrying on this struggle without retreating until complete victory has been won over the world bourgeoisie, until the complete victory of the social revolution, until the final establishment of the Communist order, which alone' can bring true liberation to all the peoples of West and East alike, abolishing all oppression of one people by another and every kind of exploitation of man by man. [*Translation.*]

Chairman: I request the comrades to come over here so that we can take the vote. Comrades, we are going to vote on the resolution on Comrade Skachko's report. You have heard his report and his clear theses, which have been approved by the Presidium.

All in favour of the theses, please raise your hands. Anyone against? No-one. Adopted unanimously. [*Tumultuous applause. Shouts of* 'Bravo'.]

Please give me your attention. Tomorrow at 10 a meeting of the non-Party fraction will be held here. I request the non-Party delegates to be present in as large numbers as possible. Comrade Zinoviev will also be present.

Secretary: Comrades, the Communist fraction will meet tomorrow at 9 a.m. in the Red Army Club. Everyone is to attend. Important questions will be decided.

Chairman: Comrades, tomorrow at 5 p.m. we shall hold the last session of our Congress. It is understood that absolutely every delegate must be present at this last session.

The session ended at 9.28 p.m.

Seventh Session
September 7

The session opened at 7.30 p.m. Comrade Zinoviev took the chair.
Before the session began, the band played the Internationale.

Chairman: I declare the Seventh Session of the Congress of the Peoples of the East open. Today we have to deal with one of the most important, perhaps *the* most important matter for our Congress, namely, the setting-up of a permanent executive organ of the Congress of the Peoples of the East. We want to leave behind, after the Congress has dispersed, an organ that can continue the work so splendidly begun by our historic Congress.

We are sure that this Congress will not be the last but only the first of its kind, that we shall convene Congresses of the Peoples of the East not less frequently than once a year, and in order that the work of revolutionary propaganda, agitation and struggle for the liberation of the East may go on in the intervals between Congresses, we propose that the First Congress of the Peoples of the East set up a permanent Council for Propaganda and Action of the Peoples of the East. Both of the fractions and the Presidium have discussed this question, and we propose that the following resolution be adopted: The First Congress of the Peoples of the East resolves to form, under the aegis of the Executive Committee of the Communist International, a permanent organ uniting the peoples of the East to be called 'the Council for Propaganda of the Peoples of the East'. The council will be made up as follows (the secretary will read the list of members separately); that means that 47 persons will be elected to it. Eastern peoples not represented at the First Congress are entitled to send delegates to the Council in addition to these.

The Council for Propaganda and Action will organize propaganda

145

throughout the East, publish a journal, to be called *Narody Vostoka*
(*The Peoples of the East*) in three languages, organizing the publication
of pamphlets, leaflets, etc., support and unify the liberation movement throughout the East, organize a university of the social sciences
for activists in the East, and so on.[98] The Council for Propaganda and
Action of the Peoples of the East will be centred at Baku until the next
Congress of the Peoples of the East, which will be held not later than
one year from now.

Plenary (full) meetings of the Council for Propaganda and Action,
to deal with all matters arising, will be held not less often than every
three months, in Baku.

Between plenary meetings of the Council for Propaganda and
Action all questions will be dealt with by a presidium of seven, to be
elected by the Council.

The Council will organize branches in Tashkent and in other places
where these may be needed.

All the Council's work will be carried on under the guidance and
supervision of the Executive Committee of the Communist International, which will appoint two of the seven members of the Council's
Presidium, and these representatives will have the right of veto.

Particular groups may not have been given adequate representation
in this list, and, as always happens at large congresses, there are a few
minor complaints and claims that small groups have not been represented or that not all those nominated have been chosen.

This is inevitable at a large congress, but altogether we have spent
more than one session working on this list, and both fractions are
convinced that the maximum possible fairness has been achieved, and
that with a composition like this we can form an organ capable of
carrying out the task entrusted to it.

We are giving the Council a colossal task to perform, and I am sure
that the organization we are about to set up will have a great future
before it. Today it is still an insufficiently centralized organization,
but tomorrow, and the day after tomorrow, and every day in the
course of the development of the liberation movement in the East, the
Council for Propaganda and Action which we are forming today will
become a real 'great power' of the peoples of the East.

[*The Internationale.*] [*Translation.*]

Chairman: Comrades, we shall read the list a little later, so that some
few changes which are now needed can be made. I request the

Congress to confirm the proposal to set up a Council for Propaganda and Action in the form which has been explained. Who is in favour of this proposal? Anyone against? Adopted.

Comrades, during these last two days, in which our Congress has been meeting, events of major importance have taken place in Bukhara, and two Bukharan comrades will now be called upon to give the Congress of the Peoples of the East a brief account of these events. First, Comrade Rodzhabov.

Rodzhabov [speaking in Turkic]: Comrades, very important events have taken place in Bukhara. 'Bukhara the Magnificent', that well-spring of learning which a few centuries ago was named the Magnificent and regarded as a centre of learning, has for some years now been transformed into a mere wretched *kishlak*.[99] This has happened because a despotic form of government has existed in Bukhara. The Emir of Bukhara has ruled in such a way that out of the 25 million inhabitants only five million have in recent times been left under his yoke. The remaining 20 million have been split up and conquered by the imperialists and the Russian Imperial Government. Imperialism has seized purely Bukharan dominions. Until now the Bukharans have not led a human existence, they have been oppressed, they wept day and night and were unable to live like people in other countries.

Now things have changed. After the October Revolution the Emir of Bukhara sought his happiness under the wing of the British imperialists, sent presents to British officers and so on, but nevertheless the people continued to be oppressed. The workers made their preparations, and now they have done what needed to be done, and we see the revolution already on the march in Bukhara. Bukhara, Karshi, Chardzhui, Khatyrchi and Kerki have been captured by the Red troops. The red flag is flying from the towers of these five towns — hoisted there by the Soviet and workers' forces.

Comrades, the workers and peasants of the Red Army greet you on this day! The peoples of Bukhara have been freed at last — and the other peoples will very soon be freed as well! [*The Internationale*]

Chairman: The other representative of Bukhara, Comrade Dzhabar-Zade, will now speak.

[Dzhabar-Zade speaks in Uzbek.]

Kizi-Zade [interpreter]: I will just say that Comrade Dzhabar-Zade confined himself to greeting us. The rest of his speech was concerned only with the events which are now happening in Bukhara and which we know about from what the previous speaker said, and so I think there is no need for a translation.

Chairman: The Presidium has decided also to call upon a representative of the women, Comrade Nadzhiya. [*Applause.*]

[*Nadzhiya speaks in Turkish. Her speech is interrupted by applause.*]

Chairman: I call upon Comrade Shabanova.

Shabanova: Comrades, Comrade Nadzhiya said: The women's movement beginning in the East must not be looked at from the standpoint of those frivolous feminists who are content to see woman's place in social life as that of a delicate plant or an elegant doll. This movement must be seen as a serious and necessary consequence of the revolutionary movement which is taking place throughout the world. The women of the East are not merely fighting for the right to walk in the street without wearing the *chadra*, as many people suppose. For the women of the East, with their high moral ideals, the question of the *chadra*, it can be said, is of the least importance. If the women who form half of every community are opposed to the men and do not have the same rights as they have, then it is obviously impossible for society to progress: the backwardness of Eastern societies is irrefutable proof of this.

Comrades, you can be sure that all our efforts and labours to realize new forms of social life, however sincere and however vigorous our endeavours may be, will remain without result if you do not summon the women to become real helpers in your work.

Owing to the conditions caused by the war, in Turkey women have been obliged to quit the home and the household and take on the performance of a variety of social duties. The fact that women have had to take over the responsibilities of the men who have been called up for military service, and especially the fact that women in the roadless localities of Anatolia which are inaccessible even to pack-animals have been themselves dragging artillery equipment and munitions to where the troops need them cannot, of course, be called a step forward in the conquest of equal rights for women: people who see the fact that women are making up with their labour for the shortage of beasts of burden as contributing to the cause of equal rights for women are unworthy of our attention. We do not deny that at the beginning of the 1908 revolution some measures were introduced for women's benefit. In view, however, of the ineffectiveness and inadequacy of these measures we do not regard them as highly significant.

The opening of one or two lower and higher schools for women in the capital and in the provinces, and even the opening of a university for women, does not accomplish one thousandth part of what still needs to be done. From the Turkish Government, whose actions are based on the oppression and exploitation of the weaker by the stronger, one cannot, of course, expect more fundamental or serious measures on behalf of women held in bondage.

But we know, too, that the position of our sisters in Persia, Bukhara, Khiva, Turkestan, India and other Moslem countries is even worse. However, the injustice done to us and to our sisters has not remained unpunished. Proof of this is to be seen in the backwardness and decline of all the countries of the East. Comrades, you must know that the evil done to women has never passed and will never pass without retribution.

Because the session of the Congress of the Peoples of the East is drawing to its close we are obliged through lack of time to refrain from discussing the position of women in the various countries of the East. But let the comrade delegates who are entrusted with the great mission of taking back to their homelands the great principles of the revolution not forget that all the efforts they devote to winning happiness for the peoples will remain fruitless unless there is real help from the women. The Communists consider it necessary, in order to get rid of all misfortunes, to create a classless society, and to this end they declare relentless war against all the bourgeois and privileged elements. The women Communists of the East have an even harder battle to wage because, in addition, they have to fight against the despotism of their menfolk. If you, men of the East, continue now, as in the past, to be indifferent to the fate of women, you can be sure that our countries will perish, and you and us together with them: the alternative is for us to begin, together with all the oppressed, a bloody life-and-death struggle to win our rights by force. I will briefly set forth the women's demands. If you want to bring about your own emancipation, listen to our demands and render us real help and co-operation.

1) Complete equality of rights.

2) Ensuring for women unconditional opportunity to make use of the educational and vocational-training institutions established for men.

3) Equality of rights of both parties to marriage. Unconditional abolition of polygamy.

4) Unconditional admission of women to employment in legislative and administrative institutions.

5) Everywhere, in cities, towns and villages, committees for the rights and protection of women to be established.

Undoubtedly we can ask for all of this. The Communists, recognizing that we have equal rights, have reached out their hand to us, and we women will prove their most loyal comrades. True, we may be stumbling in pathless darkness, we may be standing on the brink of yawning chasms, but we are not afraid, because we know that in order to see the dawn one has to pass through the dark night.

Chairman: Comrades, Comrade Bibinur will also speak, on behalf of the women of Turkestan. [*Tumultuous applause.*]

Bibinur [*In Turkic*]: I bring you greetings, dear comrades, from the working women, both Russian and Moslem, of the town of Aulie-Ata.[100]

Dear comrades, you have gathered here in this Congress of the Peoples of the East to take decisions about the tremendous tasks that confront you. You represent the very best forces of the toiling and oppressed masses. All the oppressed nationalities of the East who have been ruthlessly exploited by Tsarism and imperialism for hundreds of years look to you, their deputies, with hope.

We, the women of the East, are exploited ten times worse than the men, and the ugly sides of the life led by those recluses, the Moslem women of the East, affect us more closely.

But now, dear comrades, a bright sun has reached us, warming and comforting us like little children in their cradles. It is the first we have known, it is the power of the Soviets of workers', peasants' and *dekkhans'* deputies. The Soviet power is our mother and we are its children. The soul of this Soviet power, the liberator and vanguard of the working people of the whole world, is the Russian Communist Party and the valiant Red Army, which has won justice for the oppressed with the blood of its fraternal workers. We too must fight tirelessly, working for the emancipation of all the oppressed peoples of the East. We women have awakened from our nightmare of oppression, and every day are strengthening your ranks with our best forces. We look forward to your fruitful work.

Long live the Congress of Peoples of the Red East!

Long live all the oppressed peoples of the East!

Long live the Third International!

Long live the women's section of the town of Aulie-Ata and of all Turkestan!

Chairman: We shall now proceed to establish the list of members of the Council of Propaganda and Action of the Peoples of the East. I call on Comrade Ostrovsky.

Ostrovosky: Here is the list of members of the Council for Action and Propaganda in the East. I shall read first the members of the Communist fraction, and then those of the non-Party members.

1) Ismail Hakki and 2) Suleiman Nuri, both from Turkey.

3) Haidar Khan and 4) Sultan-Zade, both from Persia.

5) Aga-Zade (Afghanistan).

6) Narimanov and 7) Guseinov, both from Azerbaidzhan.

8) Rakhmanov (Khiva).

9) Abdur-Rashidov (Uzbek, from Ferghana region).

10) Dzhurabayev (Tadzhik, from Samarkand region).

11) Ryskulov (Kirghiz, from Syr-Darya and Semirechiye regions).

12) Karpov (Turkmen, from Transcaspian region).

13) Acharya (India).

14) Makharadze (Georgia).

15) Avis (Armenia).

16) Dzhabar-Zade (Bukhara).

17) Krimazov and 18) Gobiyev, both from Daghestan.

19) Mansurov (Daghestan).

20) Khamzatov (Chechnia).

21) Cherkas (Kuban).

22) Amru-Sanan (Kalmuck Republic).

23) Genikoy (Tatar Republic).

24) Ibragimov (Bashkiria).

25) Dzhanuzakov (Kara-Kirghizia).

26) Ostrovsky (Oriental Jews).

27) The Kirghiz Republic.

28) Mamedov (Crimea).

29) Shabanova (Moslem women).

30) Pavlovich

31) Kirov

32) Ordzhonikdze

33) Stasova ⎬ (Communist International)

34) Yeleyeva[101]

35) Skachko

From the non-Party fraction:
  36) Baka-Shakir (Turkey).
  37) Narbutabekov and 38) Makhmudov, both from Turkestan.
  39) Musayev and 40) Yelchiyev, both from Azerbaidzhan.
  41) Kara-Tadzhiyev (Afghanistan).
  42) Abdulayev (Khiva).
  43) Nazir Sidiq (India).
  44) Abas-Hadzhi (Bukhara).
  45) Khenzatov (Terek).
  46) Wang (China).
  47) Khadzhan-Kuliyev (Turkmen).
  48) Kubse-Osman (Kighizia).

Chairman: Please be so good as to hand in to the Presidium any amendments necessary. I will take a vote on the list as a whole. All in favour of the list as a whole? Anyone against?

[*Voices from above:* 'In the case of Persia it is irregular.']

Chairman: Please stop all this noise immediately at this moment when the Congress of the Peoples of the East is electing its first Council. Comrades, in an assembly of two thousand people there will always be two or three to shout: 'Irregular!' The Council has been properly elected. Long live the Council for Propaganda and Action! [*Applause. The Internationale.*] Comrades, it has been proposed that we send greetings to the Red Army. I call upon Comrade Tadzhiyev.

Tadzhiyev [*in Turkic*]: The First Congress of the Peoples of the East sends greetings to the valiant Red Army of the Russian Socialist Federal Soviet Republic. The peoples of the East, who have been tormented for so long by the armies of the European powers, greet the Red Army as their deliverer. The Congress asks every Red warrior, on whatever front he is fighting, to remember that millions of people in the East are following his struggle with bated breath, looking forward to the moment when the military situation will permit the Red Army to turn its weapons to the task of liberating the peoples of the East. The Red Army of the workers and peasants is today the only bulwark of these peoples against international imperialism and it is the first priority and responsibility of all the peoples of the East to strengthen this bulwark.

Honour and glory to every Red soldier and every Red commander! The sons of the East, oppressed, but thirsting for freedom, await you!

Béla Kun: Long live the Red Army!

[*Shouts of* 'Hurrah'. *Applause.*]

Tadzhiyev: If this gathering approves the text of the telegram, the Presidium intends to send it to the Red Army. [*Voices:* 'Please do that', 'Hurrah'.]

Chairman: Allow me to consider the telegram as adopted.

Voice: 'Send greetings to Comrade Lenin.'

Voice: 'Send greetings to the leader of the Red Army, Comrade Trotsky.'

Chairman: Allow me to consider that proposal as adopted. I now call on Comrade Yegorov to make an unscheduled statement on behalf of the Baku Soviet of Workers' and Red Army Men's Deputies.

Yegorov: Dear comrades, a short time ago, at the beginning of this historic session, you took a decision in which it was explicitly stated that, as the location for the Council for Action and Propaganda in the East which you had elected, you chose the city of Baku. Allow me, comrades, to express to you, on behalf of the Baku Soviet, our profound Communist gratitude for the confidence in the proletariat of Baku which you have shown by taking this decision. [*Applause.*]

We, comrades, the Baku workers, are proud that the First Congress of the Peoples of the East has met in our Red capital, that it was here, in our Red Baku, that the foundation was laid for the future liberation of the entire oppressed East. [*Applause.*] We are proud that for the location of your Council, the place from which it will carry on its revolutionary struggle, the residence of the general staff of this struggle, you have chosen — Baku.

The Baku proletariat has made no few sacrifices and efforts for the cause of its own emancipation, for the emancipation of the Azerbaidzhanian and Turkish people. And now it will contribute no few sacrifices and efforts for the emancipation of the East from the yoke of the capitalists.

The sacred banner of bloody war which has been handed over to them here at the Congress will be taken up by the Baku workers as a call summoning them to this holy war. I am confident that I can assure you, comrades, that this banner will not fall from the grasp of the Baku workers, who have already proved by their revolutionary struggle in the past how firmly they uphold this banner.

Dear comrades, to commemorate this historic moment I propose on behalf of the Baku Executive Committee that the building we are now in, and where we have planned our joint actions against the common enemy, be named 'the Palace of the Peoples of the East'. [*Applause.*]

Previously, comrades, the bourgeoisie delighted their ears in this place, listening to all sorts of love-songs, but now we shall meet here to learn how to overthrow the bourgeoisie, how to free ourselves from their rule, how to build palaces like this where at present our comrades are rotting in shanties, where they are unable not merely to confer together as we are doing today but even to live like human beings.

In addition, I propose to name the building facing the boulevard, the best building in Baku, Isa-Bek Gadzhinsky's house, where formerly lived the biggest exploiter in Baku, and which he though he would enjoy for life — this building I propose be named: 'the House of the Peoples of the East'. This house will be the place where your general staff will establish itself, to which you can flock to obtain advice and instructions. [*Applause.*]

Furthermore, Comrades, Stanislavsky Street, where previously national and chauvinist passions reigned, and Armenians and Moslems could not look upon each other calmly, I propose should be renamed: 'Street of the Peoples of the East'. Today we are showing the workers of Baku that there are no more barriers between nations, but only one house of free working people, for whose liberation we are now fighting and whom we summon to combined struggle on behalf of all the oppressed masses of the East. Comrades, long live the East, which, though today enslaved, is already awakening to the bloody struggle! Long live the Council of Action and Propaganda which has been formed here! Long live the proletariat of Baku!

Chairman: I call upon Comrade Narimanov.

Narimanov: Comrades, I addressed you in a cheerful spirit at the opening of the Congress, but now I have to speak to you about something which is a matter of sadness for all of us, namely, the funeral of 26 of our dear comrades. In 1918, when Soviet power prevailed here for a few months, the Dashnak and Menshevik traitors handed over power, or at least contributed to surrendering Soviet power in Baku into the hands of the British. Until September 14 our dear comrades proudly, bravely and honourably remained at their posts down to the last moment, and then, when the Turks drew near, the Menshevik and Dashnak traitors allowed them to leave for Astrakhan. While they were on their way, these same traitors arrested them and changed their ship's course to Krasnovodsk. Our comrades fell into the hands of the British scoundrels and were shot by them over there, between Ashkhabad and Kizyl-Arvat. When Soviet power was restored in Turkestan, their bodies were removed to Astrakhan. And now the Azerbaidzhanian Soviet Republic has brought the bodies of these dear comrades to Baku, and they will be buried here tomorrow. The Azerbaidzhanian Republic considers that the presence here of the tombs of these dear comrades will have educational significance for the young generations. Our children, seeing the monument to these dear comrades, will know how the Soviet power in Azerbaidzhan, and the Soviet power generally, values honourable and brave comrades. [103]

We invite you to come tomorrow to the parapet, until 10 o'clock, and then to Petrovsky Square, to commit, along with us, with sorrow in our hearts, the bodies of our dear comrades to the ground.

Chairman: I propose that the Congress honour the memory of the fallen comrades by standing. [*All stand. The band plays the Revolutionary Funeral March.*]

Narbutabekov: Comrades, the work of the Congress is concluded. The Chairman of the First Congress of the Peoples of the East, Comrade Zinoviev, will make a concluding speech before our Congress is closed. [*Tumultuous applause. The 'Internationale'.*]

Chairman: And so, Comrades, the Congress of the Peoples of the East, convened by the Executive Committee of the Communist International, has not only been held but has successfully concluded its work, and crowned it by setting up a permanent centre for the revolutionary struggle of the Peoples of the East. [*Applause.*]

Comrades, in my many years of revolutionary activity it has been my lot to take part in more than one big congress, but I must in all conscience say that a more significant congress, fraught with greater revolutionary consequences than this one, a congress as gigantically important as this one — for it has been dealing with something quite new and unprecedented — I have never had to organize or to take part in. Such is the congress we have just been holding. It went down in the history of mankind from the moment when it began and when the enslaved oppressed, exploited peoples of the East assembled here.

The first tinkle of the chairman's bell on this platform was the funeral knell of the world bourgeoisie.

Comrades, we have not always had the time to appreciate in what a great historical event we are taking part. Just think what has happened, what has gone on in this hall. Peoples who until now have been looked upon by the whole bourgeois world as draught animals whose task was to draw water for them, as peoples of inferior blood, as peoples whose special destiny it was, so to speak, to draw water for the bourgeoisie, peoples about whom the bourgeoisie always felt tranquil (no danger of fire there, they said) — these peoples are now rising in revolt. The bourgeoisie has been afraid in the last few years that the workers in the West would revolt, but as regards the peoples of the East, it has been quite tranquil until very recently; and then, just when it was sleeping sweetly on a soft pillow, when it was sure that there was no danger to be expected from that quarter, at that very moment a congress of the oppressed peoples of the East assembles, gets organized and goes into the attack with unprecedented, amazing, heart-lifting unanimity. [*Tumultuous applause.*] That is the most important aspect of our congress.

Just think. Peoples who for decades were at daggers drawn with each other, who did not associate with each other, who baited each other — delegates from these peoples have felt from the first moment like members of one family, despite their not understanding each other's languages. A fraternal unanimity has arisen at once, so that it has seemed that we were one family, a fraternal, friendly family. This is the greatness of our Congress.

This is a simple, elementary fact, but it is precisely for that reason that it is great. And we have the right to say that such a congress as the one which the walls of this building in Baku have witnessed, at the beginning of September 1920, is without precedent in the world. This congress means that the old, bourgeois, oppressors' world has come to its end; it means that the main reserves of toiling mankind have awakened, to create a completely new order, a wholly unprecedented way of life on earth.

Comrades, our congress has been heterogeneous, motley, in its composition. Represented at it have been peoples who have already won Soviet power for themselves, who are sister-republics of our Russian Soviet Republic, while, on the other hand, also represented here have been peoples among whom the struggle is still on the boil, where it is still only just flaring up. This heterogeneity has resulted in some misunderstandings. When we discussed the question of our executive organ, some comrades felt they were at a Congress of Soviets of the Peoples of the East. That does not yet exist. We look at India, which has only a handful of representatives here — a huge country oppressed by British capital, where there is still no Soviet republic, where the struggle has only begun to blaze up. We have countries like Turkey, where an overt civil war is in progress, where several governments are in conflict and the struggle between them has not yet ceased. We see a similar scene in Persia, where there are two governments and where the struggle is burning more fiercely with every passing day.[104] And here too we have bourgeois-democratic republics like Armenia.

We have frequently spoken about Armenia here. There is not one Armenia: there is, on the one hand, workers' and peasants' Armenia, to which we extend a fraternal hand, and, on the other, the accursed, bourgeois Armenia of the Dashnak hangmen. [*Tumultuous applause.*]

And the same situation exists in Georgia. Today the Georgian workers and the Georgian peasants are oppressed as nowhere else. Because Social-Democrats are in power there, the best veteran fighters of Georgia have been put in prison. And the present leaders of Georgia, such as Zhordania, have descended to such a level of shamelessness that their own old teacher, an old revolutionary like Comrade Mikha Tshakaya, is being held in prison by these gentry.[105] There is not one Georgia; there is the Georgia of Messrs. Chkheidze, Gegechkori and Co., who scurry around in the ante-rooms of bourgeois ministers in Europe, and there is the Georgia of the honest workers and peasants, our brothers, with whom we march arm in arm and shoulder to shoulder. [*Applause.*]

It is all the more remarkable that a congress so mixed in composition should have been united on all fundamental questions.

Comrades, I want to touch upon one question which is a rather painful one for the Soviet republics, and in the first place for Turkestan and so on. These republics are our sisters. The struggle there was very hard, the workers and peasants there achieved the Soviet form of government only with great difficulty, and they are loyal to their fraternal alliance with Soviet Russia. There, alongside gigantic work to establish workers' and peasants' rule, along with tremendous changes and overturns, a phenomenon has been observed which we have to admit is extremely undesirable and regrettable, and about which we make a point of speaking in this very great, triumphant and historic assembly. Yes, the Soviet power in Russia, the Council of People's Commissars and the Communist International know that in Turkestan and in the other fraternal Soviet republics in the East, certain elements which have attached themselves to the Communist Party act in such a way as to bring shame on the title of Communist, inciting one section of the population against another, offending the native peasantry, taking their land from them. Certain scions of the old bourgeois Russia who have settled there and have wormed their way into our ranks, carry on the accursed tradition of the bourgeoisie and of Tsardom, continuing to look upon the local population as an inferior race. And this gives rise to the most legitimate and justified indignation. We address ourselves in this assembly to the Russian Communist comrades, to the Red Army men, to all the activists whose task it is to carry out the line of the Soviet power in the East — we turn to them and say: remember that you are at a post of threefold responsibility — every mistake you make, even a very small one (not to speak of straightforward abuses) will cost us dear. We address ourselves to the activists from Russia who are called upon to work in Turkestan and other Soviet republics of the East, to point out that our Party and the Communist International require of them to remain firmly at the height of the honoured title of Communist, so that they never forget that the native working population are our brothers, so that they break once and for all with the accursed old heritage left to use by the bourgeoisie and Tsardom, so that they do not dare to insult the toilers, the local inhabitants, so that they would rather cut off their hand than commit an injustice. [*Tumultuous applause.*]

There was a period, a dark, sad period, when Russian officers and a Russian army of serfs led by these officers were sent by the Tsar to suppress popular revolts and destroy the best section of the Polish people of those days. And at that time one of Russia's best writers, A. I. Herzen, exclaimed: 'When I see what my kinsmen are doing, what the Russian army and Russian officers are doing, I am ashamed to be a Russian.' So spoke A. I. Herzen. We do not live in such a time as that, none of us need be ashamed to be Russian, for Russia has been the first country to raise the red flag and the first to help other peoples to emancipate themselves. But it is a matter for shame that persons who have wormed their way into our ranks, through misunderstanding or self-interest, are behaving in our sister-republics in a way that compels us to blush and to remember the harsh words of A.I. Herzen.

Comrades, at this assembly we give a solemn undertaking to those

present that our Party and the Communist International are doing
everything in their power to clear the weeds right out of our garden
[*Tumultuous applause*], to purge our ranks, and to ensure that every
one of us who is called upon to carry out Soviet policy in the awakening East understands that this is a holy place, that this work needs to
be approached with clean hands and a clear head.

The distrust which decades of experience have implanted in the
peoples of the East, their justified distrust of Europeans, who have
always merely deceived and swindled them, only mocked them — this
distrust is sometimes involuntarily, semi-consciously transferred
today to the new, workers' Europe, and, in the first place to our Soviet
power, to Soviet Russia. As people of labour, as serious
revolutionaries, we have to understand where the roots of this distrust
lie, and we have by our work and our fraternal support in these years
— the most difficult years — to create the feeling that we are one
fraternal family, all members of which look with the same horror on
the old, accursed past, and all as one fight against those who divide us.
I hope, I am sure, that this congress and the fact that we have heard
here what you have told us at this congress, will bring us so close
together and bind our fraternal family so firmly that no mistakes made
by individuals, or even crimes committed by particular groups, will
divide us from you, henceforth and forever. We are one single,
fraternal family, with the same enemies and wanting the same friends,
and knowing only the same ideas. [*Tumultuous applause.*]

Comrades, the revolution of 1905 in Russia which was essentially
only a dress-rehearsal for that great revolution which we are
experiencing today, that revolution, though it was soon crushed,
nevertheless, as you remember, spread at once to the East, evoking
echoes in Turkey, in Persia and in other Eastern countries. Just as the
1905 revolution was, in comparison with the great revolution of
October 1917, mere child's play, so the response with which our
revolution is meeting in the East today is a million times greater than
in 1905.

Yes, comrades, across thousands of *versts*, despite the distance and
the differences of language, a great revolution in a great country will
inevitably kindle the hearts of the toilers of other countries. And the
greatest pride for a Russian revolutionary must be the knowledge that
the sparks of our revolution have spread to the powder-magazine of
the East, and that the effect of this is being borne back to us here in
explosion after explosion. In this lies the great significance of our

revolution. It has not only set fire to the West, but the East too is in conflagration before our eyes. Our congress has stepped forward in the role of the greatest organizer and collective incendiary of the East, for it is kindling the greatest revolt on earth — against the bourgeoisie, against the serfowners and capitalists. [*Applause.*]

We have discussed only a few questions, but we have discussed them very seriously and have adopted completely unanimous resolutions. Comrades, we have had to translate everything said into various languages, but it has not been necessary to translate the word 'Soviets', for this is known throughout the world, in West and East alike. The East will be Soviet! [*Applause.*]

Comrades, we have set up a Council of Action. At the moment this is still a young organization, only just born, but no-one sitting in this hall will say that I am a great optimist if I express the view that this Council of Action is already stronger in the East than the bourgeois cabinet in Britain, or than any other cabinet. [*Applause.*] The cabinets of Britain and France will decline in power, will wane with every passing day, will perish before the eyes of mankind — they are living out their last days like dogs. But the peoples of the East are the rising star. We and you, comrades, will become a greater power with every day that passes. Paraphrasing Marx's words we can say that all the British and French imperialists are unable now to take a single step without first thinking: but how will the peoples of the East react? Won't they do something against us, against the imperialists?

We have not disputed here as to whether Soviets are necessary or not — that is clear to us. We have not disputed as to whether we need to be united — that also is clear. But look at how united the bourgeoisie are. They say, in all languages: 'Entente, Entente.' What does this word mean? An entente is a cordial agreement. But we say that in this agreeement it is not so much the heart as the purse that is operative. [*Applause.*] Look and see how this Entente is breaking up before our eyes. It cannot decide a single question, the partners are tripping each other up, they are quarrelling, they are travelling around all the spas of Europe discussing the 'Russian question'. They discuss the Russian question more than any other. It is a hard nut for them, which they cannot crack and never will. [*Tumultuous applause.*]

Comrades, after our Congress we are perfectly justified in saying that the brigands, the British and French imperialists, will never solve the so-called Russian question which is such a curse to them — but we and you and the Communist International will within a few years completely solve the European question. [*Tumultuous applause.*] Comrades, the first two days of our congress were spent in discussing what our attitude should be towards the Entente, towards imperialism. And for us that moment after the first report, when the assembled representatives of the peoples of the East swore to begin a holy war, that moment will be preserved in our hearts as a sacred experience. That was the basis for everything else, that is what unites us all. *Yes, a holy war against the plunderers and capitalists!* And all of you will, as practical people, translate that oath into the language of facts. When you return home you will tell the peasants, both men and women, you will tell all the working people, what we have decided, the oath that we took, the line we marked out. And we shall feel with every hour how our unity is growing, our forces strengthening, we shall climb still higher, drawing near to the last barrier, and this last barrier we shall take: we shall end the civil war, stretch out a fraternal hand to the West — to Europe and America — and unite in one family, so as, together, to build a new life! [*Applause.*]

Karl Marx, the teacher of us all, issued 70 years ago the call: 'Workers of all lands, unite!' We, Karl Marx's pupils, the continuators of his work, can expand this formulation, supplementing and broadening it, and say: 'Workers of all lands *and oppressed peoples of the whole world, unite!*' [*Tumultuous applause. The 'Internationale'.*]

Comrades, we cannot bring to the Communist International and to the workers of the whole world any more joyful news than that, after the uniting of the workers of the West and of America, the toilers of the whole East have united. Let us remember only what unites us. Let us tear out of our hearts whatever can disunite us. Let us remember that we have one enemy — British and French imperialism. Let each of us devote his life — even dozens of lives, if we had them — to the cause of liberating the peoples of the East and of the whole world! [*Tumultuous applause. The 'Internationale'.*]

Comrades, the Presidium congratulates you on the successful conclusion of the Congress and declares the First Congress of the Peoples of the East closed.

Long live the Third International!

[*Tumultuous applause. Shouts of 'Hurrah'. The 'Internationale'.*]

The session ended at 10.40 p.m.

Manifesto of the Congress to the Peoples of the East

On September 1, 1920, in the city of Baku, the capital of Azerbaidzhan, a congress of representatives of the peoples of the East was held. Our congress was attended by 1,891 delegates from the following countries: Turkey, Persia, Egypt, India, Afghanistan, Baluchistan, Kashgar,[106] China, Japan, Korea, Arabia, Syria, Palestine, Bukhara, Khiva, Daghestan, Northern Caucasia, Azerbaidzhan, Armenia, Georgia, Turkestan, Ferghana, the Kalmuck Autonomous Region, the Tatar Republic, and the Far Eastern District.

The Congress of the Peoples of the East was convened by the Communist International. Every peasant, every toiler, needs to know what the Communist International is. It is a union of workers and peasants, of the Communists of the whole world, which has set itself the aim of smashing the power of the rich and bringing about the complete equality of all. At the Second World Congress of the Communist International, held in Moscow in August 1920, the following countries were represented: America, Britain, France, Austria, Italy, Spain, Poland, Bohemia,[107] Yugoslavia, Hungary, Switzerland, Belgium, Holland, Denmark, Sweden, Norway, Finland, Estonia, Latvia, Lithuania, Romania, Bulgaria, Turkey, Persia, India, China, Japan, Korea, Indochina, Georgia, Azerbaidzhan, Armenia, Khiva, Bukhara, Afghanistan, Argentina, Russia, the Ukraine.

The Communist International wants to put an end not only to the power of the rich over the poor but also to the power of some peoples over others. For this purpose the workers of Europe and America must unite with the peasants and other working elements of the peoples of the East.

163

The Congress of representatives of the Peoples of the East calls on these peoples to realize such unity, which is needed for the liberation of all the oppressed and all the exploited.[108]

Peoples of the East! Six years ago there broke out in Europe a colossal, monstrous slaughter, a world war in which 35 million human beings were killed, in which hundreds of big towns and thousands of other centres of population were devastated, a war which ruined all the countries of Europe and subjected all its peoples to the torment of unheard-of want and unprecedented starvation.

This colossal conflict has hitherto been carried on mainly in Europe, affecting Asia and Africa only partially. The war was fought between European peoples, with the peoples of the East participating in it only to a relatively small extent. Some hundreds of thousands of Turkish peasants, deceived by their rulers, who acted for the benefit of the German imperialists: two or three million Indians and Negroes, bought like slaves by the British and French capitalists and, like slaves, hurled to their deaths on the fields of France, far-distant and strange to them, in the service of the interests, alien and unintelligible to them, of the British and French bankers and industrialists.

But although the countries of the East remained aloof from this gigantic conflict and the Eastern peoples played only an insignificant part in it, nevertheless this war was fought not only for the countries of Europe, not only for the countries and peoples of the West, but also for the countries and peoples of the East. It was fought for the partition of the world, and chiefly for the partition of Asia, of the East. It was fought to decide who was to rule over the countries of Asia and whose slaves the peoples of the East should be. It was fought to decide whether the British or the German capitalists should skin the peasants and workers of Turkey, Persia and Egypt.

The monstrous four-year carnage ended in victory for France and Britain. The German capitalists were crushed, and along with them the German people were crushed, destroyed and doomed to starvation. Victorious France, almost all of whose adult population had been wiped out by the war and all of whose industrial areas had been devastated, was bled white by the struggle and left quite powerless after its victory. As a result of the colossal, barbarous slaughter, imperialist Britain emerged as the sole and omnipotent master of Europe and Asia. Britain alone in all Europe was still able to muster sufficient strength, for it had waged the war with other peoples' hands, those of the enslaved peoples, the Indians and Negroes, it had waged the war at the expense of the colonies it oppressed.

Being left the victor and the omnipotent master of half the world, the British Government proceeded to carry out the objectives for which it had waged the war — to consolidate its hold on all the countries of Asia and to enslave, fully and finally, all the peoples of the East.

With no-one to hinder them, and fearing no-one, the handful of greedy banker-capitalists who are at the head of the British state, casting aside all shame, set about openly and brazenly reducing to slavery the peasants and workers of the Eastern countries.

Peoples of the East! You know what Britain has done in India, you know how it has turned the many-millioned masses of the Indian peasants and workers into dumb beasts of burden without any rights.

The Indian peasant has to hand over to the British Government a proportion of his crop so large that what remains is not enough to sustain him for even a few months. The Indian worker has to work in the British capitalist's factory for such a miserable pittance that he cannot even buy the daily handful of rice he needs for subsistence. Every year millions of Indians die of hunger and millions perish in the jungles and swamps where they are engaged in heavy labour undertaken by the British capitalists for their own enrichment.

Millions of Indians, unable to find a crust of bread in their own very rich and fertile homeland, are obliged to join the British armed forces, to leave their homeland and spend their whole lives enduring the hard lot of the soldier, fighting endless wars in all corners of the world, against all the peoples of the world, upholding everywhere the ruthless dominion of Britain. While paying with their lives and their blood for the unceasing expansion of the wealth of the British capitalists, securing monstrous profits for them, the Indians themselves enjoy no human rights: the British officers who rule over them, insolent sons of the British bourgeoisie which has grown fat on Indian corpses, do not regard them as human.

An Indian dares not sit at the same table with a Britisher, use the same quarters, enter the same railway carriage, attend the same school. In the eyes of the British bourgeois every Indian is a pariah, a slave, a beast of burden, an animal which dare not have any human feelings or put forward any demands. Every demand, every expression of anger by the Indian peasants and workers when driven to extremities is met by ruthless mass shootings. Hundreds of corpses of those shot cover the streets of revolted Indian villages, and British officers force the survivors to crawl on their bellies, to amuse them, and to lick the boots of their enslavers.

Peoples of the East! You know what Britain has done in Turkey. Britain offered Turkey a peace by which three-quarters of Asia Minor, inhabited exclusively by Ottoman Turks, with all the country's industrial cities, was to pass into the possession of Britain, France, Italy and Greece, while what remained of Turkish territory was to be burdened with such payments that the Ottomans would become permanent undischarged debtors of Britain.

When the Turkish people refused to accept such a peace, which would have destroyed them, the British occupied Constantinople, a holy place to Moslems, dispersed the Turkish Parliament, arrested all the popular leaders, shot the best of them, and exiled hundreds of others to the island of Malta, where they were imprisoned in the dark and damp dungeons of an ancient fortress. Now the British rule the roost in Constantinople: they have taken from the Turks everything that could be taken. They have taken banks, money, factories, railways, ships, they have closed all the approaches to Asia Minor, thereby depriving the Turks, who are without factories of their own, of the possibility of receiving any goods from Europe. There is now in the whole of Asia Minor not one piece of material, not one fragment of metal. The Turkish peasant is obliged to go about without a shirt and to plough the soil with a wooden plough.

The British used the Greek army to occupy the vilayet of Smyrna, the French to take Adana and colonial troops to take Brussa and Izmid. They have beleaguered the Turks on all sides, and are steadily pushing into Turkish territory, trying to reduce to complete exhaustion the Turkish people who have already been as tormented and ruined as they can be by decades of continuous war.

In those parts of Turkey which the British have already occupied, they scoff and jeer intolerably at the Turkish people, in their usual way. In Constantinople the British have taken all the schools and universities for use as barracks, stopped all Turkish educational activity, closed down all Turkish newspapers, broken up all workers' organizations, filled the prisons with Turkish patriots and placed the entire population under the uncontrolled authority of British police who consider themselves authorized, in broad daylight in the streets of Constantinople, and without any excuse, to hit over the head any persons wearing a fez. As the British see it, if a man wears the fez, if he is a Turk, then he is a creature of an inferior species, a pariah, a slave, a beast of burden, who can be treated like a dog.

In the places they have occupied in Turkey the British treat the Turks like dogs, subjecting them to forced labour and punishing them with blows, and endeavouring by means of all sorts of tricks, base methods and violence to turn Turkey into a conquered country, so that all the Turks may by blows be made beasts of burden to work for the enrichment of the British.

Peoples of the East! What has Britain done to Persia? After crushing a peasants' revolt against the Shah and the landlords, shooting or hanging thousands of Persian peasants, the British capitalists have restored the overthrown rule of the Shah and the landlords, taken from the peasants the landlords' land they had seized and thrust the peasants back into serfdom, making them once again *rayats*, slaves without rights of the *mulkadars*.

Then, having bribed the Shah's venal government, the British capitalists have by means of a base, traitorous treaty acquired all Persia and the entire Persian people as their absolute property. They have laid hands on all the wealth of Persia, they have installed in all the cities of Persia their garrisons of deceived Indian sepoys, bought into slavery, and have begun to behave in Persia as though in a conquered country, treating the nominally independent Persian people as a people who have become slaves.

Peoples of the East! What has Britain done to Mesopotamia and Arabia? It has, without any ado, proclaimed these independent Moslem countries to be its colonies, driven from the land the Arabs who have owned it for centuries, taken from them the best, most fertile valleys of the Tigris and the Euphrates, taken the best pasture-land, which the people need in order to survive, taken the very rich oilfields of Mosul and Basra [*sic*], and, stripping the Arabs of all means of livelihood, is trying to force them through hunger to become its slaves and its workers.

What has Britain done to Palestine? There, at first, acting for the benefit of Anglo-Jewish capitalists, it drove Arabs from the land in order to give the latter to Jewish settlers; then, trying to appease the discontent of the Arabs, it incited them against these same Jewish settlers, sowing discord, enmity and hatred between all the communities, weakening both [*sic*] in order that it may itself rule and command.

What has Britain done to Egypt? There the entire native population has for eight decades groaned beneath the heavy yoke of the British capitalists, a yoke even heavier and more ruinous for the people than was that of the Egyptian Pharaohs who built their huge pyramids with slave labour.

What has Britain done to China? That enormous country, Britain, together with its partner, imperialist Japan, turned into a colony and, exploiting and oppressing its 300 million people and poisoning them with opium, it is with its own and Japanese troops putting down with unheard-of cruelty the revolutionary ferment which has begun there. Restoring the old despots whom the people had overthrown, it strives with all its strength to prevent the many-millioned Chinese people from winning their freedom, and keeps them as before under its yoke of despotism, oppression and poverty, so as the better to be able to exploit them.

What has Britain done to Korea, to that flourishing land with a thousand-years-old culture? It has handed over Korea to the Japanese imperialists for them to tear to pieces, and they are now with fire and sword making the Korean people submit to the British and Japanese capitalists.

What is Britain doing to Afghanistan? By bribing the Emir's government it has kept the people in maximum subjection, in the greatest poverty and ignorance, trying to reduce this country to a desert, in order that this desert may guard India, which Britain oppresses, from any incursion from without.

What is Britain doing with Armenia and Georgia? There by means of its gold it keeps the peasant and worker masses under the yoke of the hated Dashnak and Menshevik governments it has bought, which terrorize and oppress their own peoples and drive them to fight against the peoples of Azerbaidzhan and Russia who have freed themselves from the bourgeois yoke.

Imperialist Britain penetrates even into Turkestan, Khiva, Bukhara, Azerbaidzhan, Daghestan and Northern Caucasia, its agents dart about everywhere, generously scattering, as bribes, British gold which has been extorted from the blood and sweat of the oppressed peoples. Everywhere these agents seek to uphold the tyrants and despots, the khans and landlords, to combat the incipient revolutionary movements, to keep all the peoples, at any cost, in a state of oppression and ruin, in want and ignorance.

Oppression and ruin, want and ignorance among the Eastern peoples serve as sources of enrichment for imperialist Britain.

Peoples of the East! To you belong the richest, most fertile, most extensive lands in the whole world; these lands, which were once the cradle of all mankind, could feed not only their inhabitants but the entire population of the world, and yet now, every year, ten million Turkish, Persian and Indian peasants and workers are unable to find a crust of bread or any employment in their wide and fertile homelands, and are obliged to go abroad and seek a livelihood in alien lands.

They have to do this because in their homelands everything — land, money, banks, factories, workshops — belongs to British capitalists. They are not masters in their own homelands, they dare not give orders there — on the contrary they themselves are ordered about by foreigners, the British capitalists.

This is how it has been up to now, this is how it was also before the war, when imperialist Britain still had rivals in the shape of the German, French and Russian imperialist predators, when it still hesitated to stretch out its paw over all the countries of the East, for fear of receiving a blow on this paw from some rival beast of prey. But now, when imperialist Britain has beaten and rendered powerless all of its rivals, when it has become the omnipotent master of Europe and Asia, now the capitalists who rule Britain are giving free rein to their wolfish appetites and without restraint or shame are sinking voracious teeth and claws into the bleeding body of the peoples of the East.

British capital feels cramped in Europe, it has grown, and cannot find places for investment: besides, the European workers, enlightened by revolutionary consciousness, have become bad slaves: they are not willing to work for nothing, they want good wages. In order that capital may have elbow-room, in order that it may bring in a good profit, in order that the European workers may be thrown a sop so as to hold back the growth of their revolutionary mood, in order that it may be possible to bribe the leading strata of the worker masses, British capital needs fresh land, fresh workers — rightless and unenfranchised slaves.

And the British capitalists think they have found these fresh lands in the Eastern countries, and these rightless and voiceless slave-workers in the peoples of the East.

The British capitalists are trying to grab Turkey and Persia, Mesopotamia and Arabia, Afghanistan and Egypt, so as to drive all the peasants from the land, after buying from these ruined and indebted peasants, for trivial sums, all their holdings, which they want to merge into huge estates and plantations, on to which will then be driven to work as slave-labourers the Eastern peasants reduced to landlessness. They want, in Turkey, Persia and Mesopotamia, using the cheap labour of the hungry Turkish, Persian and Arab labourers, to build factories, lay out railways and work mines. They want, by means of the cheap goods produced by factory industry, to destroy the handicrafts and the millions of local craftsmen with whom the cities of the East are filled, to throw them into the street, unemployed. They want, by setting up huge trading firms, to ruin the petty local merchants, throwing them too into the street, into the ranks of the proletariat which has only its labour-power to sell.

The British capitalists want to proletarianize completely the peoples of the East, to ruin the economic activity of all the peasants, craftsmen and merchants and to force them all to work as hungry slaves on their plantations and in their factories and mines. And when they have so forced them, they intend to ruin their health with unbearable labour and starve them to death on wretched pay, squeezing sweat and blood out of the enslaved peoples of the East. And this sweat of the workers, this blood of the peasants, they mean to turn into surplus value, into profit, into pure, ringing gold! This is the future which imperialist Britain is preparing for the peoples of the East.

Britain, which is a country of barely forty million people, only one-fortieth of whom constitute the group of oppressors and exploiters, while the remaining 39 million are oppressed and exploited workers and farmers, wants to rule over half the world and to hold in slavery the 800 millions of the peoples of the East. One British bourgeois capitalist, having already forced 39 British workers to work for him, wants to force to work for him, in addition, 2,000 workers and peasants in Persia, Turkey, Mesopotamia and Egypt. Thus, 2,040 hungry and tortured people, enjoying none of the good things of life, are to work all their lives long for one idle parasite, a British capitalist. One million such exploiters, British bankers and industrialists, want to reduce 800 millions of the peoples of the East to slavery. And it must be said that they know how to achieve their aim — they have neither shame, nor conscience, nor fear; they have nothing but savage greed and unlimited thirst for gain. The ruin, hunger, blood, suffering and groans of 800 million people mean nothing to them. All that matters is profit, all that counts is gain! And in pursuit of this profit and gain the British imperialists have taken a tenacious grip on the throat of the peoples of the East, and are preparing a dark future for them. A future of utter ruin, permanent slavery, rightlessness, oppression and unlimited exploitation — this is what is in store for the peoples of the East if the present government remains in power in Britain, if imperialist Britain keeps its strength and stabilizes its rule over the Eastern countries. A miserable handful of British bankers devour hundreds of millions of peasants and workers in the East.

But this shall not be!

In face of the British capitalists, the rulers of imperialist Britain, there is rising up the organized might of the peasants and workers of the East, united under the red banner of the Communist International, under the red banner of the union of revolutionary workers, who have made it their aim to liberate the whole world and all mankind from every form of exploitation and oppression.

The First Congress of representatives of the Peoples of the East loudly proclaims to the whole world, to the capitalist rulers of Britain: This shall not be! You dogs shall not devour the peoples of the East, you wretched handful of oppressors shall not reduce to everlasting serfdom hundreds of millions of Eastern workers and peasants. You have bitten off too big a piece, more than you can chew, and it will choke you!

The peoples of the East have long stagnated in the darkness of ignorance under the despotic yoke of their own tyrant rulers, and under that of foreign capitalist conquerors. But the roar of the world-wide conflict, and the thunder of the Russian workers' revolution, which has released the *Eastern* people of Russia[109] from the century-old chains of capitalist slavery, has awakened them, and now aroused from their sleep of centuries, they are rising to their feet.

They are waking up and are hearing the call to a holy war, to a *ghazavat*: this is our call! It is the call of the First Congress of representatives of the Peoples of the East, united with the revolutionary proletariat of the West under the banner of the Communist International. Thus we — representatives of the toiling masses of all the peoples of the East: India, Turkey, Persia, Egypt, Afghanistan, Baluchistan, Kashgar, China, Indochina, Japan, Korea, Georgia, Armenia, Azerbaidzhan, Daghestan, Northern Caucasia, Arabia, Mesopotamia, Syria, Palestine, Khiva, Bukhara, Turkestan, Ferghana, Tataria, Bashkiria, Kirghizia, etc., united in unbreakable union among ourselves and with the revolutionary workers of the West — summon our peoples to a holy war. We say:

Peoples of the East! You have often heard the call to holy war, from your governments, you have marched under the green banner of the Prophet, but all those holy wars were fraudulent, serving only the interests of your self-seeking rulers, and you, the peasants and workers, remained in slavery and want after these wars. You conquered the good things of life for others, but yourselves never enjoyed any of them.

Now we summon you to the first real holy war, under the red banner of the Communist International. We summon you to a holy war for your own well-being, for your own freedom, for your own life!

Britain, the last powerful imperialist predator left in Europe, has spread its dark wings over the Eastern Moslem countries, and is trying to turn the peoples of the East into its slaves, into its booty. Slavery! Frightful slavery, ruin, oppression and exploitation is being brought by Britain to the peoples of the East. Save yourselves, peoples of the East!

Arise and fight against this beast of prey! Go forward as one man into a *holy war* against the British conquerors! Stand up, Indian exhausted by hunger and unbearable slave labour! Stand up, Anatolian peasant crushed by taxes and usury! Stand up, Persian *rayat* strangled by the *mulkadars*! Stand up, Armenian toiler driven out into the barren hills! Stand up, Arabs and Afghans, lost in sandy deserts and cut off by the British from all the rest of the world! Stand up and fight against the common enemy, imperialist Britain!

High waves the banner of the holy war ... This is a holy war for the liberation of the Peoples of the East, for the ending of the division of mankind into oppressor peoples and oppressed peoples, for complete equality of all peoples and races, whatever language they may speak, whatever the colour of their skin and whatever the religion they profess.

Into the holy war to end the division of countries into advanced and backward, dependent and independent, metropolitan and colonial!

Into the holy war for the liberation of all mankind from the yoke of capitalist and imperialist slavery, for the ending of all forms of oppression of one people by another and of all forms of exploitation of man by man!

Into the holy war against the last citadel of capitalism and imperialism in Europe, against the nest of pirates and bandits by sea and land, against the age-old oppressor of all the peoples of the East, against imperialist Britain!

Into the holy war for freedom, independence and happiness for all the peoples of the East, all the East's millions of peasants and workers enslaved by Britain!

Peoples of the East! In this holy war all the revolutionary workers and all the oppressed peasants of the East will be with you. They will help you, they will fight and die along with you.

It is the First Congress of representatives of the Peoples of the East that tells you this. Long live the unity of all the peasants and workers of the East and of the West, the unity of all the toilers, all the oppressed and exploited. Long live the battle headquarters of this united movement — the Communist International! May the holy war of the peoples of the East and of the toilers of the whole world against imperialist Britain burn with unquenchable fire!

Honorary members of the Presidium
Radek (Russia), *Béla Kun* (Hungary), *Rosmer* (France), *Quelch* (Britain), *Reed* (America), *Steinhardt-Gruber* (Austria), *Jansen* (Holland), *Shablin* (Balkan Federation), *Yoshiharo* (Japan).

Zinoviev, Chairman of the Congress

Members of the Presidium
Ryskulov, Abdurashidov, Karriyev (Turkestan); *Mustafa Sub'hi* (Turkey; *Wang* (China); *Karid* (India); *Mulabekdzhan, Radhmanov* (Khiva); *Mukhamedov* (Bukhara); *Korkmasov* (Daghestan); *Digurov* (Terek Region); *Aliyev* (Northern Caucasia); *Kostanyan* (Armenia); *Narimanov* (Azerbaidzhan); *Yenikeyev* (Tatar Republic); *Amur-Sanan* (Kalmuck Republic); *Makharadze* (Georgia); *Haidar Khan* (Persia); *Aga-Zade* (Afghanistan); *Narbutabekov* (Tashkent); *Makhmudov* (Ferghana); *Takhsim-Baari, Kaavis-Mahomed* (Anatolia); *Kuleyev* (Transcaspia); *Niyas Kuli* (Turkmenia); *Kari Tadzhi* (Samarkand); *Nazyr-Sedyki* (India); *Sidadzheddin, Kardash-Ogly* (Daghestan); *Yelchiev, Musayev* (Azerbaidzhan); *Azim* (Afghanistan); *Abdulayev* (Khiva).[110]

Ostrovsky, Secretary to the Congress.

(*Kommunistichesky Internatsional*, no. 15, December 20, 1920)

Appeal from the
Congress

Appeal of the Congress of the Peoples of the East to the Workers of Europe, America and Japan:

Workers of Britain, America, France, Italy, Japan, Germany and other countries! Hear the representatives of millions of toilers of the East! Listen to the sorrowful voice that speaks to you from the enslaved countries of Asia and Africa, from Turkey, Persia, China, Egypt, Afghanistan, Bukhara and Khiva! We have been silent for many years, for many decades. You have not heard our voice and no-one had told you of us, how we live, how we suffer under the rule of those who were also your masters. Your masters, the European and American factory owners, merchants, generals and officials, broke into our peaceful villages and towns, plundered us for centuries, took from us what our labour had created and sent all this off to Europe, so as to embellish their lives, embellish their homes, with the work of our hands, of our ancient culture. They made slaves of us.

While we had previously had to pay tribute to our own rich men, to the landlords, slaveowners, sultans, emirs, khans and maharajas, now the whip of the European slaveowners was also laid across our backs. We were forced to labour on the plantations of the European capitalists. Our sweat was poured out so that they might obtain at a cheap rate the rice, tea, sugar, tobacco and rubber they wanted. Our children were born and died in bondage. If it suited the interests of your bosses and ours, they parted child from mother, wife from husband, and drove them from one country to another. They told you that they were spreading European knowledge and science in our countries, but in fact what they spread was opium and vodka, so that the Asian and African slave, when sorrow welled up in his heart, might more easily forget his intolerable life, and would not dare to lift his chained hands against his enslaver.

174

Your bosses, the European capitalists, supported our own enslavers and made them their guard dogs to watch over us. But when the whip of the local ruler was not enough, they sent in guns and destroyed the independence of our countries, subjecting us to their laws and their governors, making slaves of us in the full sense of the word. They said that the aim of their colonial rule was to train us for future independence, but they fought against nothing so hard as against the spread of knowledge among us toilers of the East. They had prisons and barracks enough for us, but they did not build schools in which the children of Asia might learn what the white men had discovered that was great and good. They looked upon us as inferior races, they forbade us to sit in the same railway carriage that white men travelled in, they forbade us to live in the same quarters as white people, or to eat at the same table with them.

You have not seen our wounds, you have not heard our songs of sorrow and complaint, you believed your own oppressors when they said we were not people but cattle. You, who were dogs to the capitalists, saw us as your own dogs. You protested in America when Chinese and Japanese peasants, evicted by your capitalists from their villages, came to your country in search of a crust of bread. Instead of approaching them in a fraternal way in order to teach them how to fight along with you for the common cause of emancipation, you denounced us for our ignorance, you shut us out of your lives, you did not let us join your unions. We heard that you had founded Socialist parties, that you had formed an international workers' association, but these parties and this International had only words for us: we did not see its representatives come amongst us when the British shot us down in the streets of Indian cities, when the united forces of the European capitalists shot at us in Peking, when in the Philippines our demand for bread was answered by the American capitalists with lead. And those of us whose hearts were athirst for the unity of the working people of the whole world stood on the threshold of your International and looked through the grille, and saw that although in words you accepted us as equals, in fact we were for you people of inferior race.

Six years ago the great slaughter began. The capitalists of the whole world quarrelled amongst themselves as to which of them should have most slaves, which of them should grab most land in Asia and Africa. You, the workers of Europe and America, saw this robbers' war as your own war, a war for the independence of your countries, although you owned no part of these countries, although the land which you soaked in your sweat belonged not to you but to your exploiters, your bosses. You helped your factory-owners and bankers to force us to take part in this war, which was a war against you and against us. The bayonets of European soldiers forced Moroccan and Algerian peasants to die on the battlefields of Flanders, Normandy and Champagne, from bullets, cold and disease, they forced the peasants of India to die in the sands of Mesopotamia and Arabia, and the fellahin to carry out hard labour in the wilderness for the British expeditionary force fighting against the Turks. They make Indian peasants act as pack-camels carrying shells on their backs for the white soldiers in Mesopotamia. For the gold of the European capitalists Chinese and Annamite workers were sold to Russia and France, to dig trenches under a hurricane of fire, the trenches in which you died, and to toil to the point of exhaustion in arms factories, making shells that killed you.[111]

Our blood and sweat merged in a single stream with yours, but even on the field of battle, dying in the dead of night, yearning for his homeland, the coloured man was not seen as your brother, but regarded as a savage slave, whose death caused no-one to sigh or shed a tear. But in our homes, beyond the rivers, seas and mountains, the wives of our fallen husbands and the children of our fallen fathers, the breadwinners, wept for those they had lost.

The war is over and now your masters and ours, who waged this war under the banner of justice and democracy, the banner of emancipation for the oppressed peoples, have thrown off the mask. In the cities of India the bayonet, the sabre and the machine-gun rule. In Amritsar your General Dyer was able to shoot down peaceful Indian citizens with machine-guns, and order them to crawl on their bellies. But in the British Parliament not one workers' M.P. got up to demand that this murderer be sent to the gallows.

In Mesopotamia the British capitalists keep 8,000 Indian soldiers, brothers of the victims of Amritsar, and force them to subdue the Arabs, so that the Arab people may be deprived of their only wealth, the petroleum of Mosul. In Smyrna Greek soldiers who have been hired by the British capitalists run berserk, massacring Turks. In Southern Anatolia the French bayonet rules. In Syria the jackboot of a French general has kicked over the newly-erected edifice of Syrian independence. For two million pounds sterling the British Government has bought the freedom of Persia from a handful of Persian traitors, so as to make that country a stronghold of British capital against the Persian and Russian working people. In Algeria, Tripoli[112] and Annam the absolute power of French generals prevails, just as before the war. In Northern China and in Korea Japanese gendarmes and officers are in charge, shooting and hanging anybody who dares so much as think of freedom. Out of the blood of the Asian and African workers and peasants shed in this war has grown not a tree of liberty but gallows for those who fight for liberty.

But through the creaking of the gallows, through the groans of those suffering under the whip, we hear new cries, we hear the voice of the workers who have risen arms in hand against their enslavers, we hear the roar of the cannon of the Russian workers' and peasants' Red Army, created by the workers and peasants of Russia who have risen in revolt. We hear that they have overcome the Russian capitalists and landlords, and in our hearts grows a great joy, a feeling of certainty that the humiliated and insulted working people are able to find sufficient strength in their breasts to put an end to the rule of bondage and establish the reign of labour and freedom.

We hear, through the roar of the guns in this just war which is being waged by the Russian workers and peasants, your voice, the voice of the workers of Germany, Austria and Hungary. We hear that you too have taken up arms, that you too have raised your hands against your enslavers. And although we know that your enemies have as yet been victorious over you, we are confident that the ultimate victory will be yours. We hear from the cities of Italy the voice of hundreds of thousands of workers who are confronting the bayonets of the Italian capitalist bandits.

We hear the voices of the French workers from behind the bars of the prisons into which they have been thrown by the government of the French rich, who fear their great wrath and tremble at the flame burning in their hearts. Our ears have been reached by the sound of the waves of the rising sea of the British workers, beating against the cliffs on which stands the stronghold of British capitalism, that strangler of the peoples, that world-robber, that destroyer of peaceful lives! With profound joy, with profound inspiration we listen to these sounds, and there grows within us the belief that the day will soon come when our torments will cease, when our struggle will be united with yours. We believe that you will not fight for your own victory, your own liberation, alone. We believe that you will not cast off the chains from your own hands and feet while leaving them on ours. We believe that you will discard, like a dirty shirt, all that contempt with which our masters filled you towards the toilers of the East, striving to set the white workers against the coloured ones in order to be able the better to oppress both. Only a common victory of the workers of Europe and America and the toiling masses of Asia and Africa will bring liberation to all who have been hitherto working to make life better for a handful of rich men. If you were to free yourselves alone, leaving us in slavery and bondage, you yourselves would fall the next day into that same slavery and bondage, for, in order to keep us in chains and in prison, you would have to form, in the East and in the South, forces of prison warders and packs of bloodhounds to guard us, you would have to raise armies to keep us under an iron heel, you would have to give power over us to your generals and governors, and they, having tasted the sweetness of life without work, at the expense of our labour, and having learnt how to hold generations of coloured toilers in bondage, would soon turn their bayonets against you, and the wealth accumulated in Asia and Africa would be used to thrust you back into your previous slavery. If you were to forget us now you would have to pay for that mistake, you would have cause to remember our chains when you felt chains on your own hands. You cannot free yourselves without helping us in our struggle for liberation. The wealth of our countries is, in the hands of the capitalists, a means of enslaving you. So long as the British capitalist can freely exploit Indian, Egyptian and Turkish peasants, so long as he can rob them, so long as he can force them to serve in the British army, he will always have wealth enough, and executioners enough, to subdue the British workers. Without our revolt there can be no victory for the world proletariat over world capital. And just as you cannot wrest power from the hands of the capitalists without unity with us, so we are not in a position to hold this power in our hands unless we have unity with you. The capitalist countries of Europe do not produce enough corn and raw materials to provide food, clothing and footwear for their workers. Our countries, the countries of the East and of Africa, are rich in corn and in raw materials. This corn and these raw materials, without which the workers would die of starvation after their victory, they will be able to obtain if they are united with the toilers of Africa and Asia, if, by helping the toiling masses of Africa and Asia, they inspire the latter with confidence and love.

Unity between ourselves and you will signify invincible strength. We shall be able to feed and clothe each other, we shall be able to help each other with armies of warriors fired with the single idea of common liberation.

To this common struggle we have been summoned by the Third, Communist International, which has broken with the rotten past of the Second International — that International stained with our blood and yours, disgraced by its servility to imperialism, its betrayal of the interests of the toiling masses of the whole world. The Communist International has not only given us the slogan of a common holy war against the capitalists, but also summoned us to a congress in Baku, where workers from Russia, Turkey and Persia, and Tatar workers, worked for many decades for the capitalists while at the same time learning how to struggle together against their oppressors. Here in Baku, on the borders of Europe and Asia, we representatives of tens of millions of peasants and workers of Asia and Africa in revolt showed the world our wounds, showed the world the marks of the whip on our backs, the traces left by the chains on our feet and hands. And we raised our daggers, revolvers and swords and swore before the world that we would use these weapons not to fight each other but to fight the capitalists. Believing profoundly that you, the workers of Europe and Asia, will unite with us under the banner of the Communist International for common struggle, for a common victory, for a new life in common, based on fraternal aid between all toilers, we have formed here a Council for Propaganda and Agitation [sic], which, under the guidance of the Communist International, that union of our elder brothers in revolutionary struggle, will rouse the working masses of all colours, organize them and lead them to the attack on the fortress of slavery.

Workers of Britain, America, France, Italy, Japan, Germany and other countries! Listen to the voice of the representatives of the millions of the peoples of the East in revolt, who are telling you of their oath to rise up and help you in your fight, and who look for fraternal aid from you in our fight. Notwithstanding the centuries of bondage and enslavement, we turn to you with the faith in your fraternal feelings, with confidence that your victory will mean the liberation of mankind, without distinction of colour, religion or nationality. Repay this confidence of ours in you with confidence that our struggle is not a struggle of darkness and obscurantism, but a struggle for a new and better life, for the development of the peoples of the East on the same foundations of labour and fraternity on which you want to build your life. May your ears be reached by the thunder with which tens and hundreds of millions of working people in Asia and Africa are responding to our oath, and may this thunder meet with response in the thunderclaps of our fight for the common liberation of all the toilers.

Long live the unity of the workers of all countries with the labouring masses of Asia and Africa! Long live the world revolution of all the oppressed!

Long live victory over the world of oppression, exploitation and violence! Long live the Communist International!

Chairman of the Congress: *G. Zinoviev*
Secretary: *Ostrovsky*

(*Kommunistichesky Internatsional*, no. 15, December 20, 1920.)

APPENDICES AND NOTES

Appeal from the Netherlands

Appeal of the Communist Party of the Netherlands to the Peoples of the East represented in Baku:[113]

Comrades of the East! I greet you in the name of the Communist Party of Holland, and also on behalf of the Communists of the Dutch East Indies, who are fighting out there in the Far East, along with us, the Communists of the West, for the destruction of Dutch capitalism. And I know that thousands of Indonesians whom *Sarekat Islam*[114] has united for the common struggle against the Dutch oppressors will join with me to send you their greetings.

Comrades of the East! The Dutch Communists and their supporters in the Dutch East Indies feel unspeakable joy this day: for the first time in the world's history the representatives of the proletariat which is exploited by the capitalists of the West are meeting here in Baku, at this Congress of the Third International, with the representatives of the peoples of the East who are also oppressed by the Western capitalists.

We Communists of the West greet with enthusiasm this Congress of the Third International at which, together with you, we have taken the decision to fight against capitalism until it is completely destroyed.

Comrades of the East! I represent the revolutionary proletariat of Holland. Our country is not large: it has only six million inhabitants. But our masters, the capitalists, are rich and powerful.

They have been exploiting the Dutch proletariat for over 300 years, and for the same length of time they have also been oppressing all the peoples of the East Indian Archipelago, the population of which exceeds 50 millions.

For over 300 years the white Dutch proletarians have by their labour been making their masters and bosses ever richer and richer, and for over 300 years these same Dutch capitalists have been oppressing millions of inhabitants of Asia, robbing and ravaging the Dutch East Indies and drawing countless riches from them.

The Dutch capitalists, exploiters and masters of white serfs in Holland, are at the same time exploiters of the native population of the East Indian Archipelago.

183

Comrades of the East! Our capitalists, by exploiting the proletarian masses of their own country and squeezing their colonies in the East Indies, have acquired riches not inferior to those of the biggest capitalists of Great Britain, although the latter is a much stronger country.

The Dutch oil kings, who have drawn their wealth from the soil of the Indies, have formed, along with their British colleagues, an oil trust in which they hold a big share and which intends to monopolise the entire oil industry everywhere in the world.[115]

The British government, behind which the big Dutch capitalists hide themselves, is aiming at the conquest of Persia, and these capitalists hope, with the help of the Anglo-Dutch oil trust, to extract fresh profits from the oil-wells of Persia.

The Dutch proletariat, striving to bring about the downfall of its own capitalists, is happy and proud to salute its Persian brothers, who are driving the British imperialists out of their country.

Comrades of the East! The Great War, in which Holland did not take part, gave Dutch capitalism such an impetus that victorious Entente capitalism treats it as an equal. The League of Nations has formally proposed to the Dutch government that it undertake a protectorate over Armenia.

This means that the imperialist great powers which have emerged victorious from the Great War, and which today have divided the surface of the globe amongst themselves, want to hand Armenia to the Dutch capitalists for exploitation.

Comrades of the East! The Dutch Communists are fighting to prevent these aims from being realized. The revolutionary proletariat of Holland will learn with joy that its brothers in Armenia are opposing with all their strength the acquisition of new wealth by Dutch capitalism through exploiting and despoiling Armenia.

Peoples of the East! The revolutionary Dutch proletariat will rejoice to learn that each one of you, in your respective countries, is working to prevent the big Dutch capitalists from investing their capital profitably and so adding to their riches.

Comrades of the East! The Great War has brought all the capitalist countries to bankruptcy, and today capitalism has been considerably weakened.

Our Russian brothers have smashed capitalism in Russia and established there the power of the workers' Soviets.

In Central Europe, as in Western Europe, the peoples are rising, or are preparing to revolt, against the capitalists and the powers that be, who are also your masters and oppressors.

The proletarians of all the countries of Central and Western Europe are ready to join with their brothers, the Russian workers, in striking capitalism down for good and all. This is why the strength of capitalism is today so much weakened.

European capitalism has become so weak that it has only one resource left for meeting the harsh consequences of the war, namely, the colonies, or, in other words, exploitation and oppression of the colonial peoples.

This is why, at this moment when capitalism is showing so many weak sides, the time has come for you to strike your blow. If you all unite for this struggle with the heroic, victorious proletariat of Russia, which is holding at bay, single-handed, all the capitalist powers, and if you all unite for this purpose with the proletariat of Europe, which is rising against its oppressors, then capitalism's days are numbered.

Comrades of the East! The Dutch Communist Party ardently desires the end and the collapse of Dutch capitalism: it knows that it is from the Indies that the Dutch capitalists draw all their strength and their wealth, which has increased immeasurably since the War.

During the last eighteen years, our oil kings have pocketed more than 1,600 million florins profit, and the sugar-cane harvest, reaped in May of this year, brought the Dutch capitalists 500 million florins, whereas before the war these profits never exceeded 900 million florins.

The Dutch Communists know that the strength of their oppressors is rooted in the wealth they get from exploiting the East Indies. This is why they fight against the economic policy that the Dutch capitalists are pursuing so rapaciously in the Indies, just as they also fight against the oppression of their brothers out there. 'Hands off Indonesia' is their slogan.

At this Congress of the Third International, assembled in Baku, we address our appeal to you and we hope that it will reach the remotest corners of the Dutch East Indies.

Enslaved peoples of the Dutch East Indies! The struggle you are waging against your oppressors is the same as that which the Dutch proletariat is waging against its oppressors: the Dutch capitalists are our common foe.

This is why we must wage our struggle in a united way. Indonesian brothers! Do not rest content with the miserable wage-increases which you try to wrest from your exploiters by means of strikes. Indonesian brothers! Do not let yourselves be seduced by the insignificant political rights which the Government of the Dutch East Indies has granted to some of you. Beware of this fraud: it is only a sort of dole they have thrown to you with the sole aim of sowing discord in your ranks.

Indonesian brothers! Drive out your oppressors, the Dutch barbarians, from your islands, which are distinguished by a very ancient and lofty culture.

Drive out the Dutch slaveowners, their police and their soldiers — throw them into the sea!

Indonesian brothers! The revolutionary Dutch proletariat will hail the day when you rise up against your masters, who are also ours.

The Dutch proletariat is striving to smash the domination of the capitalists in its own country. If you rebel, the Dutch proletariat will do everything possible to prevent its Government from sending troops to put your movement down.

In a joint effort, we in Holland and you in the Indies will crush Dutch capitalism.

Indonesian brothers! Rise up against Dutch capitalism.

Indonesian brothers! Join with your oppressed brothers of the East who are also rebelling, against the British capitalists, the allies of your oppressors, the Dutch capitalists!

Peoples of Asia! The Third International calls on you to come together under the standard of the great Russian revolt which is gradually spreading all over the world.

Come together for a universal insurrection of all the slaves of the earth, without distinction of race or colour, against capitalist domination and tyranny.

This is what the Congress of the Third International calls upon you to do.

Enslaved peoples of all parts of the world! Unite to destroy the tyranny of capitalism, attack it without delay, take advantage of its weakness, do not wait for it to recover from the blows it suffered in the Great War. Smash it! And, with the same effort, build the new society of the workers and peasants, on the basis of Soviet power.

The Communist Party of the Netherlands

APPENDIX II

Composition of the Congress
by Nationalities
From the stenographic report

1.	Turks	235	19.	Sarts	10
2.	Persians		20.	Adzhars	10
	and Farsis	192	21.	Kabardians	9
3.	Armenians	157	22.	Chinese	8
4.	Russians	104	23.	Kurds	8
5.	Georgians	100	24.	Avars	7
6.	Chechens	82	25.	Poles	5
7.	Tadzhiks	61	26.	Hungarians	3
8.	Kirghizes	47	27.	Germans	3
9.	Jews	41	28.	Kalmucks	3
10.	Turkmens	35	29.	Koreans	3
11.	Kumyks	33	30.	Arabs	3
12.	Lesghians	25	31.	Tekintsi	2
13.	Ossetians	17	32.	Abkhazians	2
14.	Uzbeks	15	33.	Bashkirs	1
15.	Indians	14	34.	Ukrainians	1
16.	Ingushes	13	35.	Croats	1
17.	Jamshidis	12	36.	Czechs	1
18.	Hazaras	11	37.	Letts	1

Total   1275

Total number attending the Congress	1891
of whom, Communists	1273
No nationality stated	266
Did not complete above questionnaire	100
Total number of women delegates	55

Editor's Note

It will be noticed that the figures in the above register do not add up: the French report says that *more than* 100 delegates failed to complete the questionnaire.

In a book on the Congress published in Russian in 1961, G.N. Sorkin says it was originally planned to have 3,280 delegates, and that the list of delegates he found in the archives gives 2,050 names. They may not all have attended the first session.

The same archive source, according to Sorkin, gives a breakdown of 1,926 of the delegates in terms of party membership. The figures given are: Communists, 1,071; Communist Party sympathisers, 334; Young Communists, 31; non-party, 467; Socialist-Revolutionaries, 1; Left Socialist-Revolutionaries, 1; Anarchists, 1; Communist Bundists, 11; 'Persian revolutionaries', 9.

A social breakdown of all 2,050 delegates gives: workers, 576; peasants, 495; intellectuals, 437; no occupation stated, 542.

A breakdown of the delegates by country of origin gives: Azerbaidzhan, 469; Caucasian Highlands, 461; Turkestan, 322; Persia, 202; Georgia, 137; Armenia, 131; Turkey, 105; Kirghizia, 85; Afghanistan, 40; Tataria, 20; India, 14; Bukhara, 14; Khiva, 14; Bashkiria, 13; Crimea, 8; Kalmuck Republic, 8; China, 7.

As regards national composition of the delegates, Sorkin's source gives: Azerbaidzhanis, 336; Turks, 273; Lesghians (probably including *all* the Daghestan nationalities, i.e., th Kumyks and Avars at least), 218; Persians, 204; Armenians, 160; Georgians, 110; Russians, 109; Uzbeks, 90; Chechens, 85; Kirghizes, 77; Tatars, 70; Indians, 14; Chinese, 7; Arabs, 6. There were 291 other delegates of different nationalities, and the figure given for women delegates is 53.

Azerbaidzhanis. They do not appear in the register given here from the report of the Congress, for reasons which are unclear. (The term Azerbaidzhanis refers to the Azeri people, speaking a form of Turkic and Moslem by religion, sometimes loosely called 'Tatars' by the Russians at this time. This nationality, though a majority in Azerbaidzhan itself, was a minority in the city of Baku.)

Persians and Farsis. This category in the Congress report is unclear. It is possibly meant to include both Persians and other Farsi (Persian language) speakers.

Chechens and Ingushes. Two Caucasian Highland peoples of Moslem faith. Their joint republic was liquidated by Stalin in the 1940s, but has since been restored. The *Ossetians*, a mainly Christian people, have a republic, Northern Ossetia, on the northern slopes of the Caucasus, and an autonomous region, Southern Ossetia, within Georgia, on the southern slopes. The *Kumyks*, *Lesghians* and *Avars* are three of the nationalities of Daghestan ('Land of Mountains'), the only one of the Russian autonomous republics not to bear the name of a particular nationality. The *Kabardians* live to the west of the Northern Ossetians, sharing a republic with the Balkars.

Southern Caucasus (Transcaucasia). Nationalities represented at the Congress included the *Adzhars*, from the Batum area of Georgia, *Kurds*, mainly from Armenia and Nakhichevan, and *Abkhazians* from the north-west corner of Georgia.

Other Soviet nationalities present were the *Kalmucks* and *Bashkirs*, from the European part of Soviet territory, and from the Asian part, the *Kirghizes*, *Tadzhiks*, *Uzbeks*, *Sarts* (the term then used for Turkic-speaking town-dwellers of Central Asia) and *Tekintsi* (one of the largest Turkmenian tribes).

Non-Soviet Eastern peoples included the *Jamshidis* and *Hazaras*, two of the peoples of Afghanistan.

It is not clear who the *Jews* referred to were, though there may have been delegates from the Caucasian community of the Mountain Jews, and also from the Jewish community in Bukhara.

Explanatory Notes

[1] This was the original 'appeal' for the holding of the Congress, published on July 20, 1920. There seems to have been some confusion about the date for the opening of the Congress — August 15, mentioned at the beginning, was altered to September 1, but in the editing of the appeal the original date was left unchanged when first mentioned.

[2] The Kajars, or Qajars, were the dynasty then ruling over Persia. Reza Khan seized power in 1921, reduced the Shah to puppet status, and in 1925 proclaimed himself Shah — the first of a new dynasty, the Pahlevis.

[3] The coal-mines of Heraclea (Eregli), on the Black Sea coast, supplied Constantinople.

[4] A reference to the pilgrimage to Mecca.

[5] Delegates to the Second Congress of the Communist International. Their biographies are included in the two-volume edition of the proceedings of the Congress published by New Park Publications, 1977.

[6] The Azerbaidzhan Trade Union Congress had opened in Baku on August 29, 1920, so that delegates to that congress were available to attend.
   The French report of the Congress proceedings describes this as a ceremonial meeting of the Baku Soviet and of all the local soviets of the various districts of the city.

[7] It will be noted that there were translations into both 'Turkish' and 'Turkic'. The former is the language of what is now the Republic of Turkey, the latter is the name of a large group of languages related to Turkish which are spoken in the Caucasus (including Azerbaidzhani and Kumyk) and in Central Asia (including Uzbek and Turkmen). The translations 'into Turkic' were probably made into either the language of Azerbaidzhan or into Chagatay, the so-called standard Turkic of Central Asia.

[8] Shaumyan and Dzhaparidze were the leaders of the Baku Commissars — see note 103 below.

[9] In Zinoviev's remarks about the Russo-Polish war, the French report of the Congress gives a different sentence following this one: 'But, comrades, not two weeks have passed since then, and our armies, which have recovered themselves, are standing firm under the walls of Brest-Litovsk.' A few lines further down, in place of 'its red hand', the French report gives: 'its mighty hand'. In fact, in October 1920 an armistice was

189

signed with Poland; and Brest-Litovsk was ceded to Poland in the peace treaty signed in March 1921.

[10] The French report of the Congress inserts after this sentence and at the beginning of the next the words: 'At this precise moment when the guns of the Red Army are about to roar once again before Warsaw . . .' Actually, the Red Army never recovered the initiative in the Russo-Polish war after August 15.

[11] Why Béla Kun should associate the Regent of Hungary particularly with *American* capitalism is not clear. The French report has him speaking of 'Admiral Horthy, the man of straw of the American businessmen'.

[12] Petrov is presumably the man of that name who was in Britain not long before. Known as Peter Petroff, he was a member of the British Socialist Party. An emigré from Russia, he returned there after the Revolution.

[13] V.M.Pavlovich (Veltman) was the leading Soviet Orientalist until his death in 1927.

[14] In May 1920. The strike was defeated — a serious setback for the French working class.

[15] As Rosmer mentions in *Lenin's Moscow*, John Reed travelled to Baku with Rosmer, Kun and Quelch. He died soon after his return to Moscow (October 17, 1920). According to Angelica Balabanova (*My Life as a Rebel*, p. 318), 'Jack spoke bitterly of the demagogy and display which had characterized the Baku Congress and the manner in which the native population and the Far [*sic*] Eastern delegates had been treated.' Another prominent foreign Communist who criticized the Baku Congress even before it took place, calling it 'Zinoviev's circus', and refusing to attend, was M.N. Roy (*Memoirs*, p. 391).

[16] Karl Steinhardt, also known as Gruber (1875-1963), was one of the founders of the Austrian CP and a member of the original ECCI.

[17] Trotsky was engaged at the time of the Congress in directing the civil war operations of the Red Army as People's Commissar, and did not attend. The French report gives the reference to him in Steinhardt's speech (as translated by Zinoviev) as: 'Comrade Trotsky is the leader of the armed vanguard of the revolution.'

[18] The Kariyev mentioned here *may* be the same person as the one mentioned as 'Karayev' and other similar variants elsewhere in the report.

[19] Mustafa Sup'hi (the name is also sometimes given as Subhi) was the founder of the Turkish Communist Party. He was murdered by the Kemalists in January 1921.

[20] 'Acharya' is an interpretation of the report's 'Agariya'. Perhaps it was meant to be M.P.T. Acharya, an early Indian Communist — though there seems to be no evidence of his attendance at the congress. 'Naazir Sedyki' (below) is another Indian delegate whose identity is unclear. He may perhaps have been the Indian Communist Mohammed Shafiq Siddiqi who was active at about this time. (See note 55 below for more information on the Indian delegation to the Congress.)

[21] 'Haidar Khan' is a rendering of the report's 'Gaidarman': there was a prominent Persian Communist of that name. He appears later as 'Gaidarkhanov'.

22 Called in the report 'Yants' but identified as 'Jansen' on the basis of Rosmer's statement in *Lenin's Moscow* that Holland was represented in Baku by a man of that name. Jansen was elected, along with Wijnkoop, to represent Holland on the Executive Committee of the Communist International following the Second World Congress.

23 'Hodo-Yoshiharo' is a guess for the report's 'Khodo-Io-Shikro'. According to Beckmann and Genji, *The Japanese Communist Party*, the Japanese who attended the Baku Congress was named Yoshiwaro Gentaro.

24 As a demonstration of support for Menshevik Georgia, after the strong attacks made at the Baku Congress, some of the top personalities of the Second International — Vandervelde, MacDonald, Renaudel, Kautsky, etc. — visited that country later in September 1920.

25 Instead of: 'The bourgeoisie has brought black troops into Germany and into other countries as well,' the French report of the Congress has: 'The French bourgeoisie has sent black troops into Germany.' The use of black troops in the Rhineland was much commented on by the pro-German left in the 1920s: see for example E.D. Morel's pamphlet *The Horror on the Rhine*.

26 At this time, Kemal's line was that the Sultan was 'under constraint', so that it was not he who was guilty of the measures taken in his name. Later Kemal abolished the Sultanate and the Caliphate as well — though much of the support his movement had enjoyed in the Moslem world (notably the *Khilafat* movement in India) had been based on the idea that he was defending the Caliphate against the infidels.

27 Presumably the reference to the 'Jewish' rich here was made in relation to the Zionist activity then under way in Palestine.

28 'Musavatism' refers to the *Musavat* (Equality) party which had ruled in Azerbaidzhan under Turkish protection, and had a Pan-Turanian, Pan-Islamic ideology.

29 This refers to the Amritsar shooting of April 1919. Here and elsewhere Zinoviev calls it the 'Dvair' affair — the general who ordered the shooting was called Dyer, and the Lieutenant-Governor of the Punjab at the time was Sir Michael O'Dwyer. What happened was that a large crowd assembled to hear nationalist speakers, in defiance of an order prohibiting meetings. Dyer had his soldiers fire into the crowd and keep on firing. Afterwards he ordered that any Indian using a certain street in which a female missionary had been attacked must do so crawling on all fours, and posted a picket to see to this.

30 Sir Edward Grey at the time of which Radek speaks. He was made a peer in 1916.

31 The battle of Marash, in February 1920, was the first major battle of the Turkish War of Independence, and their victory gave a big boost to the morale of the Kemalists. The French had with them a small force of the Armenian Legion which had fought alongside the Allied armies in Palestine and Syria. The Armenian troops apparently committed atrocities against the Turkish population of this region (Cilicia and neighbouring districts) where there had previously been a larger Armenian population that had been decimated by the Turks, and which figured in Armenian nationalist claims for 'Greater Armenia' extending to the Mediterranean. The French, who were secretly negotiating for a separate peace with Kemal (leaving Britain in the lurch), withdrew

abruptly from Marash under cover of darkness, leaving the Armenian soldiers and civilians to bear the brunt.

Feisal, whom the British rather than the French had put on the throne of Damascus, hindered French military activity during the Cilician campaign by refusing to let French reinforcements use the Beirut-Aleppo railway, so they had to go by sea. He was driven from Damascus by the French in July 1920 — and as a consolation prize, the British made him King of Iraq.

[32] This is the article to which Radek refers, from the *Manchester Guardian*, May 12, 1920, entitled: 'The Crisis of Armenia', by A Correspondent:

'The Prime Minister has remarked in regard to Armenia that "we cannot rule the world". True, and it would be relevant to the case if the British government were proposing to take on no further responsibilities whatever in Asia or Africa beyond those we were burdened with already before the war. But the facts are very different. A few days ago, at San Remo, our government undertook to police the oilfields of Mosul. If you could isolate the question of Mesopotamia from those of our military and financial resources, and of the priority of other claims, that decision might be defensible. But, confronted with the Government's attitude towards Armenia, it threatens to cover Great Britain with shame.

'At Mosul we are to have a "mandate". But have not mandates been devised in order to set backward or broken peoples on their feet? No doubt mandates properly administered, as we trust that we shall succeed in administering them, would be a benefit to every country and people in the Ottoman Empire. But if there has to be an economy of mandates because there is a narrow limit to the capacity of the Powers for taking them up, who will venture to argue that Mesopotamia has a priority over Armenia? On the showing of the 1915 atrocities alone Armenia ought to be secured a mandate, even if all our other aims in Turkey have to be given up.'

(Radek says the Allies are letting their friends in Armenia down because Armenia has no natural resources to attract their greed. Contrast Reed on the alleged reason for American interest in Armenia, p.83.)

[33] Radek's quotation from *Le Temps* has been corrected by reference to the original. The book by Lord Curzon which he mentions is *Persia and the Persian Question*, published in 1892.

[34] The book which Radek describes as 'a sort of Koran for British imperialism' is *The Expansion of England*, by J.R. Seeley, published in 1883. The author, who was Professor of Modern History at Cambridge, was made a KCMG on Lord Rosebery's recommendation on account of this book. The passage to which Radek refers appears to be the one on pp. 233-234 where Seeley discusses the view that because there is great poverty in India there will be a revolution there one day. He notes: 'I do not find in history that revolutions are caused in this way. I find great populations cowering in abject misery for centuries together, but they do not rise in rebellion; no, if they cannot live, they die, and if they can only just live, then they just live, their sensibilities dulled and their very wishes crushed out by want. A population that rebels is a population that is looking up, that has begun to hope and to feel its strength.'

[35] Despite this claim, parts of the Soviet state were to suffer from famine in 1921 and had to call for relief from other countries.

[36] The French report of the Congress has 'Korkmasov' in place of 'Artmasov'.

[37] What the speaker presumably meant was that France agreed to allow Italy a free hand to grab Tripoli in exchange for being allowed a free hand in Morocco, and that Britain endorsed this arrangement.

[38] 'Comrade Gaidarkhanov' is presumably the Persian Communist Haidar Khan.

[39] No meeting of the Congress was held on September 3. This was a Friday, the Moslem Sabbath.

Sorkin mentions that a film of the military parade and workers' demonstration in Baku on September 3 has survived. Apparently Lloyd George, Millerand and Woodrow Wilson were burned in effigy during the proceedings.

[40] Narbutabekov's figure of 53 languages and dialects 'for the East' appears to refer only to that part of the East which was formerly included in the Russian Empire and was then in 1920 in the process of being Sovietized.

[41] A reference to the failure of the 'international general strike' on July 21, 1919, which the Comintern had called for as a measure of support for Soviet Russia and Soviet Hungary. It appears to have met with a mass response only in some Italian cities.

[42] The Russian Imperial territory of Turkestan was made up of the regions of Syr-Darya, Samarkand, Transcaspia, Semirechie and Ferghana. Embedded in it (or surrounded by it) were the 'native states' of Khiva and Bukhara. Khiva had been occupied by the Red Army shortly before the Baku Congress opened, and Bukhara was occupied during the Congress. Khiva and Bukhara became Soviet *People's* Republics (as against Soviet *Socialist* Republics). In 1924-1925 a new delimitation of territories took place in Central Asia, as a result of which Turkestan, Khiva and Bukhara disappeared, being replaced by the Uzbek and Turkmen Soviet Socialist Republics, together with the Tadzhik Autonomous Soviet Socialist Republic and the Kirghiz Autonomous Regions, both of which have since become Union Republics.

Soviet Turkestan went through a very difficult period when it was cut off from the rest of Soviet Russia, by the White Cossacks of General Dutov, at Orenburg, and the 'Transcaspian Government' at Ashkhabad, which was backed by British forces coming in from Persia.

The abuses of which Narbutabekov complains are discussed in R. Vaidyanath, *The Formation of the Soviet Central Asian Republics*, New Delhi, 1967.

On October 12, 1920 the Politburo of the Russian Communist Party held a discussion with 27 Baku Congress delegates, and it was decided to initiate a strict investigation of alleged abuses by local Russians against natives in the Soviet East. (*Leninsky Sbornik*, Vol. 36, pp. 133-134.)

[43] The Highlanders to whom Korkmasov refers are the various peoples inhabiting the Caucasus mountains, in and to the west of Daghestan. The volunteers he mentions are the men of the White 'Volunteer Army', commanded by General Denikin, which was based in Northern Caucasia, in the Kuban and Terek regions.

[44] The usual English practice of writing *ulemas* has been followed, although *ulema* is already a plural word — the plural of *alim*.

[45] General Bicherakov commanded the Russian forces which had occupied the Caspian coast of Persia, as a security measure, during the world war. In 1918, when Baku was threatened by the Turks, Bicherakov was invited to come over to Azerbaidzhan and help defend the city. This he did, but proved unsuccessful (some say he deliberately

'opened the front' so as to give the Turks the opportunity to teach 'Red Baku' a lesson). He then withdrew northward into Daghestan, where he linked up with Denikin.

[46] Korkmasov refers to Shamil, the political, military and religious leader of the Moslem peoples of Northern Caucasia (then usually known in the West as 'Circassia', from the Cherkesses who inhabited part of it), whose struggles against the Russians were applauded by Marx.

[47] 'Not Imam but Ivan' implies that Najmuddin Gotsinsky was acting as a stooge for Russian, infidel interests, and so was not a true Imam. In fact one of the main reasons for the failure of the counter-revolution in Northern Caucasia was that it consisted of two incompatible camps — the Whites, based mainly on the Kuban and Terek Cossacks, whose slogan was 'Russia One and Indivisible', and who treated the Moslem peoples with contempt; and the reactionary elements among the Moslems themselves, who cultivated an ideology of hostility to everything Russian and Christian.

[48] Korkmasov's 'Chervomayev' is presumably Chermoyev, a Chechen oil millionaire (this is the country of the Grozny and Maikop oilfields), and his Kotsov is the Kabardian horse-breeder of that name.

[49] A reference to the Shamkhal of Tarki, the principal feudal chieftain among the Kumyks. The fighting between the Red Army and counter-revolutionary bands in Daghestan went on well into 1921.

[50] The chairman's remarks in reply to the 'Voice' are far from clear. The incident reflects the confusion surrounding the arrangements for translation of speeches at the Congress.

[51] See p. 85 for the speech of the American representative, John Reed, which is inlcuded in the Russian report of the Congress. Apart from this and the Dutch Communists' report (see Appendix), which was included as an appendix to the French report, it is not known whether any other contributions from among those listed by Zinoviev were published.

[52] 'Azerbaidzhani-Turkish' presumably means the form of Turkic spoken in Azerbaidzhan.

[53] British-Indian troops were at the time entering Transcaspia from Persia. The military intelligence agents Macartney, Etherton, Blacker and Bailey were active all over Russian Central Asia in this period, helping the anti-Bolshevik elements.

[54] According to the French report, Rosmer adds, after 'and other Moslem countries?' the following: 'And why is France now carrying on a war in Cilicia and Syria in order to enlarge her empire by adding a piece of Asia?'

[55] The language he used was probably the classical Persian (Farsi) known to some educated Indians.
'Fazli Kadyr' is probably the Abdul Kadir referred to in the main source of information on the identities of the Indian delegation, an India Office document classified as 'secret' and dated February 9, 1921. Entitled *Information concerning the Baku Conference*, it is an account of the Congress provided by a member of Baku University who had recently arrived in England. A note on the report says: 'He was present throughout the proceedings of the Conference and appears to be thoroughly reliable.'

This agent for the British records:'Amongst the Indian delegates, Abdul Kadir wore . . . the Peshawari turban . . . Most of the Indian delegates were dressed almost in the same fashion, while one of them, Abdul Fazal, wore a sword. The latter speaks the Russian language fairly well . . . All the rest speak Urdu and Persian fluently . . . Abdul Kadir is an Attar [Indian chemist] by profession, and all the rest are Bisatis [petty merchants of miscellaneous goods]. All are residents of Peshawar. They spoke to me very highly of Professor Barkat Ullah and two others, I think, if I remember rightly, Messrs. Shankar Ally and Mohamed Ally.'

'Seven Indians came from Tashkent as representatives of India, among whom were Abdul Kadir . . . He spoke Persian excellently . . . and was a leader of the delegates . . . Abdul Kadir is the only man who apparently had any education; the rest could scarcely read or write. They all came from Peshawar and are general merchants.'

Other Indians named as present in Baku are Abdul Fariq, Maqbul Hussein, and Misri Khan.

Abani Mukherji (Mukerjee) was in Baku, but not as a delegate to the Congress. He had come from Moscow on a special mission 'in order to centralize the work of propaganda by the Indian Revolutionary Party'. He was also occupied with getting, from Tiflis, some special type needed for the printing of the newspaper *Azad Hindustan*, published in Baku in Urdu. There was some friction between Mukherji and members of the Indian delegation: he 'tried to take all the Indians away to Tashkent, but Sardar Misri Khan refused to go back then with his followers, because these had some disagreements with Abdul Rabb, the President of the Revolutionary Committee at Tashkent . . .' (eventually, however, they did all go to Tashkent.)

Abdul Kadir was presumably the Abdul Qadir Sehrai who had left India for Tashkent in 1920 as an agent of the Central Intelligence Bureau of the Government of India, and who betrayed to the British authorities those Indian Communists who later returned to India, figuring in the Peshawar Conspiracy Case of 1923. See on this Sukhir Choudhury, *The Peasants' and Workers' Movement in India, 1905-1929*, New Delhi, 1971, pp. 131-132.

[56] N. Shablin, whose real name was Nedelkov, was an old Tesnyak. He was killed by the Bulgarian police in 1925.

[57] Enver Pasha (1881-1922) was a hero of the Young Turk Revolution of 1908 in the Ottoman Empire and one of three men who ruled it from 1913 to 1918. He supported Turkey's entry into the war in 1914 on the side of Germany. Minister of War in 1914, he dreamed of a pan-Islamic state in Central Asia to include parts of the Tsarist Empire. After Turkey's defeat and the 1918 Armistice he went to Germany, where he got to know Radek. Visited Moscow in August 1920, at the time of the Second Congress of the Comintern. He went to Baku determined to cut a figure, and when refused permission to speak to the Congress, owing to the hostility of many delegates, he insisted on positioning himself on horseback during the September 3 parade through Baku, where he could be hailed by his admirers. After Baku he returned to Western Europe, making further contacts with exiled Moslem revolutionaries, culminating in a 'congress' of the 'Union of Islamic Revolutionary Societies' in February 1921. He again visited Moscow, urging the Soviets to send him to Anatolia as leader of a 'People's Soviet Party'. In July 1921 he went to Batum in a bid to cross the frontier and take over from Kemal, who was receiving setbacks on the Greek front. His hopes were dashed by Kemal's defeat of the Greeks on the Sakarya. In October 1921 he secretly left Batum for Bukhara, and joined the Basmachi, an undisciplined mixture of bandits and partisan cavalry then fighting against the Red Army. Enver hoped to be accepted as leader of the Basmachi but was treated with some suspicion. He was killed in a clash with Red forces.

[58] The expression 'refuge-seeking life' is unclear, and may be an unfortunate translation of some Turkish expression meaning 'trying to avoid trouble'.

[59] The people of Tripolitania and Cyrenaica (Libya) had succeeded during the World War, with German and Turkish help, in forcing the Italians to withdraw to the principal seaports. Starting in 1921, however, the Italians began a reconquest of the country, which remained under Italian rule until the Second World War.

[60] Enver had evidently heard of 'defeatism' (the Bolshevik position of being in favour of the defeat of one's own bourgeoisie in war), since he claims that Turkey, by acting as Germany's ally in the war, had contributed to the defeat of Tsarist Russia, and *therefore* had contributed to bringing about the Russian Revolution!

[61] See note 57. The 'union of revolutionary organizations of Morocco' etc no doubt existed largely in Enver's imagination.

[62] Probably Mehmet Emin (who was himself a Turk) was in fact reading out Enver's original Turkish text.

[63] Nothing appears to be known of Sheikh-Radjeb or Sheikh Eshref, or of Yuzgada, though this may be a corrupt form of Durrizade, then the 'Sheikh-ul-Islam', the highest eccesiastical dignitary in Turkey. The Chaban-Oglu family were *derebeileri* — something like feudal chieftains — in an area of Central Anatolia. Anzavur Pasha was a bandit with pretensions to being a fervent warrior for Islam.

[64] Cleveland H. Dodge, a director of the National City Bank, was president of the board of trustees of Robert College, Constantinople, and treasurer of the American Committee for Near East Relief. He died in 1926. His son Bayard Dodge wrote the introduction to Stanley H. Kerr's book, *The Lions of Marash* (1973).

[65] Cf. note 32.

[66] Clemenceau fell from power in January 1920.

[67] Pavlovich refers here to the action of Petlyura, after his expulsion from the Ukraine, in forming an alliance with Pilsudski and trying to help the White Poles in their war with Soviet Russia in 1920.

[68] 'The Zaporozhian Camp' — i.e., the *Syech*, the Cossack headquarters on the Dnieper, from which struggles were waged in the 16th and 17th centuries against the Poles, and against the Crimean Tatars and their Turkish backers.

[69] Bogdan Khmelnitsky was the leader of a great Ukrainian peasants' revolt in the 1650s, led by the Zaporozhian Cossacks, which inflicted severe damage on Poland. Cromwell is said to have sent Bogdan a message of congratulation on his fight against the great Catholic power of Eastern Europe.

[70] M.S. Hrushevsky was a Ukrainian nationalist historian who at first supported Petlyura, but emigrated to Vienna in 1919. He returned to the USSR in 1924. V.K. Vinnichenko, another Ukrainian writer of nationalist outlook, also emigrated in 1919, but returned in 1920. However, he re-emigrated soon after, and for the rest of his career opposed the Soviet Government.

[71] An *aul* is a village of Moslem peasants in Turkey or Caucasia.

[72] The attempt on Venizelos's life took place in Paris in August 1920. The assailant was a Greek Monarchist.

[73] The book by Charles Dumas was presumably *Libérez les indigènes ou renoncez aux colonies*, published in Paris in 1914.

[74] Joseph Lagrosillière was the socialist deputy for Martinique in the French Parliament at this time. He wrote a pamphlet on the socialist movement in the French West Indies.

[75] *Mirza* is a Persian word for a man 'of good birth', often used for any educated man who is not an ecclesiastic; it corresponds to *agha* in Turkey and *effendi* in the Arab lands.

[76] *Mulk* means 'property' in Persian; *molkadar* is a man of property, and landowner.

[77] The Chinese revolution took place in 1911, so Pavlovich's dates ought to have been 1908-1911.

[78] Alexandropol, in Armenia, is now called Leninakan.

[79] The activities of Tukhareli in Abkhazia and the treatment of Southern Ossetia by the Georgian Mensheviks are mentioned in Trotsky's *Social Democracy and the Wars of Intervention (Between Red and White)*, New Park Publications 1975, pp. 42-43.

[80] The 'secret letter' of General Dro has not been identified. (The French report gives '1918' instead of '1920', but this is almost certainly a misprint.) Dro was the Dashnak Commander-in-Chief. Between June and August 1920 the Dashnak Armenians were fighting the Bolshevik Azerbaidzhanis for control of Zangezur and Karabagh, territories in the borderland between them, and on August 10 the Armenians surrendered these territories to their opponents.

[81] This means something like 'Long live the emancipation of the women of the East!'

[82] The party usually known in the West as the Young Turks, who made the revolution of 1908, called themselves the 'Committee of Union and Progress'.

[83] *Ambali* are apparently porters and general labourers, doing very heavy work — e.g. on the docks — for very little money. The poorest section of the workers in Baku seem to have been the immigrants from Persia.

[84] In Lermontov's poem he imagines a conversation between Elbruz and Kazbek, the two highest peaks in the Caucasus. Elbruz warns Kazbek to 'beware of the East', and Mutushev here quotes Kazbek's answer.

[85] *Voyenmor* means a sailor in the fighting navy, and was probably the name of a sailors' paper.
  S.M. Gorodetsky's poem has been 'improved' for the occasion. In the original the white slave-driver is a Dutchman (the scene is set in Java), but here, in accordance with the general opposition to British imperialism expressed at the Congress, he becomes a

Britisher. (Care should be taken with Stalinist editions of Gorodetsky's works. In one 1960s version the call to 'Blow up Europe!' is changed to'Down with violence!')

[86] T.R. Ryskulov, a Kazakh Communist active in Turkestan, later became a victim of Stalin's purges. He opposed the so-called 'national re-delimitation' in Central Asia, seeing this as an artificial splitting up of what was basically a single national entity. He seems to have been liquidated in 1938.

[87] 'Gadzhiyeva' (Hadjieva?) was presumably an Uzbek woman delegate.

[88] For developments in Poale Zion in the early 1920s, see Degras, *Documents of the Communist International*, Volume I, pp. 365-6.

[89] The Mountain Jews are also referred to as the 'Daghestan Jews'.

[90] 'The Moslems of South-Western Caucasia' may be the Adzhars of the Batum area.

[91] Kun's remarks about Feisal had already been contradicted by Radek (pp. 40-41).

[92] When Kun refers to 'the Bashkir-Kirghiz republic' he probably means 'the Tatar-Bashkir republic'. There *was* a project to form such a republic, but eventually it was divided into separate Tatar and Bashkir republics. (At that time the name 'Kirghiz' was often incorrectly used for the Kazakhs, and their western borders approach the eastern borders of the Bashkirs, which may explain Kun's mistake.

[93] *Waqf* lands are lands in Moslem countries set aside for religious purposes, to provide revenue to support various charitable activities — something like an Islamic equivalent to monastic endowments.

[94] The *shariat* is the canon law of Islam.

[95] *Rayat* means 'ox', 'beast of burden', and was the term used for the tax-and-tribute-paying peasantry.

[96] *Maraba* means a shepherd's assistant.

[97] A *mujtahid* is a Shi'ite divine, similar in status to a Sunni *mufti*. In Persia the Shi'ite form of Islam is the state religion.

[98] Only one issue of *Narody Vostoka* appears to have been published. The Council for Action and Propaganda appears to have existed for about a year. Two important results of Baku, however, were the formation of the Institute of Oriental Studies and the Communist University of the Peoples of the East (KUTV).

[99] The city of Bukhara was known in its great days as *Bukhara-i-Sherif*, 'Noble Bukhara'; cf. Russia's 'Novgorod the Great'. The town named here as 'Khatyrchi' has not been identified. A *kishlak* is a Moslem village in Central Asia, cf. *aul* in Turkey and Caucasia.

[100] Aulie-Ata is now called Dzhambul.

[101] 'Yeleyeva' may be the Georgian Communist Sh. Z. Eliava.

¹⁰² The dissenting voice said *Ot Persii nepravilno. Nepravilno* can mean 'wrong', 'irregular', 'unfair', etc.

¹⁰³ At the end of July 1918, when the Turks were advancing on Baku, the opponents of the Bolsheviks gained control of the local Soviet and sent an invitation to the British General Dunsterville, who was on the Persian shore of the Caspian, to move into the city with his troops. They arrived on August 4. On August 10 the Baku Bolshevik leaders — the '26 Commissars' — fled in a ship bound for Astrakhan. They were intercepted, brought back to Baku, and imprisoned. On September 14 the British withdrew from Baku and the Turks entered. The 26 escaped from prison and fled once more, but the ship's officers were hostile and diverted the vessel to Krasnovodsk, in Transcaspia, where a counter-revolutionary government supported by British troops was in power. The Baku Commissars were all shot on September 20, 1918, in circumstances which have never been completely clarified.

¹⁰⁴ In 1920 there was a revolt in Ghilan province of Persia, on the Caspian shore, which spread to neighbouring areas of Northern Persia. It was led by Kuchik Khan, and raised nationalist, anti-British slogans directed against the government of Vossughed-Dowleh, in Teheran, which had signed the August 1919 treaty with Britain. When the Red Army entered Baku in April 1920 the White forces crossed the Caspian to the Persian port of Enzeli, where they encamped under British protection. A Red naval force led by Raskolnikov followed them and bombarded their camp in May. The British withdrew to the interior and the Red forces landed and occupied Enzeli (now called Pahlevi). They linked up with Kuchik Khan, but when Reza Khan (father of the present Shah) seized power in Teheran in February 1921 the Soviet Government opened negotiations with him. After the signing of a treaty and the withdrawal of Soviet troops from the Caspian coast, Reza's forces marched in and took over, and Kuchik Khan's head was sent to Reza in Teheran.

According to Sepehr Zabih's book, *The Communist Movement in Iran*, the leading Persian delegates at the Baku Congress were 'Haydar Khan, Alioff, Sultan Zadeh, Javad Zadeh, Lahuti, Zarreh and Ehsanollah Khan'.

¹⁰⁵ Mikha Tskhakaya, an old Georgian revolutionary, active since the 1880s (one of his pseudonyms was 'Gurgen'), was kept in prison by the Georgian Mensheviks in 1919-1920.

¹⁰⁶ Kashgar is in Sinkiang, then only very loosely attached to China.

¹⁰⁷ Chekhia has been rendered here as 'Bohemia' since that is what it means in Russian; evidently the composers of this document did not wish to accord recognition to 'Czechoslovakia'. Slovakia had in the previous year been fought for between Communist Hungary and the bourgeois Czech government. The Comintern manifesto of March 1919 saw both Czechoslovakia and Yugoslavia as artificial constructions, 'established by armed force' (Degras, *op.cit.*, p. 33).

¹⁰⁸ The introductory paragraphs, down to *'Peoples of the East!'* are taken from the version of the manifesto printed in *Narody Vostoka* and reproduced by Sorkin; they were not included in the *Kommunistichesky Internatsional* version.

¹⁰⁹ Here the manifesto, specifically and with emphasis, refers to the Russian people as an *Eastern* people.

¹¹⁰ 'Karid (India)' may be a misprint for Kadir.

[111] The Chinese workers sold to Russia were the gangs of Chinese labourers brought into Russia from Manchuria during the World War, to perform various forms of war work. Many of them joined the Bolsheviks when the Revolution came and provided the factual basis for the legend that the Soviet Government's power was based on 'Chinese troops'.

[112] 'Tripoli' is evidently a mistake for 'Tunisia'.

[113] This Dutch Communist document is printed as an appendix to the French report of the Congress and is translated here *from the French*.

[114] *Sarekat Islam* was a popular mass organization of Indonesian Moslems, with a Pan-Islamist ideology, in which the Indonesian Communists then worked. There was a big dispute at the Fourth Comintern Congress (1922) about how far Communists could work in or with such organizations, in which Tan Malaka figured prominently. Attacks in Comintern publications on 'the reactionary ideology of Pan-Islamism' were used by anti-Communists in Indonesia to embarrass the local Communists.

[115] The oil trust referred to here is Royal Dutch Shell.

Index